Inside Eritrea – A Volunteer in East Africa

Kevin Morley

For my family

Inside Eritrea – A Volunteer in East Africa

Introduction

Year 1 – 2005/6

1. September – Induction Eritrea
2. October – Acclimatisation
3. November – Villagers and Teachers

Introduction

The seed was planted – or germinated? – on the back seat of a bus taking school kids to Anglesey for a camping holiday. One lad had brought along a college rag his older brother had given him. Full of schoolboy humour, we were splitting our sides laughing. Then the next joke was about starving children in Africa. A story about the war and famine in Nigeria had caught my eye in the papers that morning, don't really know why as I usually only read the football pages. I stood apart from the explosion of laughter that erupted when the punch line was delivered. The feeling wasn't anything clearly defined, miles away from anything I could put into words as a coherent protest but it was there inside. You just don't laugh about starving kids.

Years later a now dormant seed was nourished by the publicity surrounding *Live Aid*. This time I did something. There was no grand plan, no strategy to be performance-managed, just a vague idea that maybe sometime in the future I could try and help children in desperate circumstances – maybe with their education. I started to take evening classes and resat my GCE in maths. I'd managed to get a reasonable grade in school but didn't know why. This time I got a reasonable grade and did know why.

A-levels, a couple of Open University credits and a two-year sabbatical at Sheffield Hallam led to a degree and qualified teacher status. Throughout this time I was working full-time for Royal Mail. No way was I going to pack that in and walk away. We had three children to bring up, they came first and they would have a 'provided for' childhood. Royal Mail was proving to be a fairly solid employer in the turbulent Thatcher-years and regular, reliable income was needed to put food on the table.

Following the graduation nothing changed much. Stayed with Royal Mail – family still dependent – and acquired teaching experience a couple of evenings a week at the local college. At that point the 'help kids in Africa' idea was still far from defined – maybe I'd do nothing and the good intention would be forgotten. Then, after 27 years of marriage, my wife walked out. The children were now even more dependent but, of course, years passed and one by one they became independent. What do I do now? I know, I'll apply to VSO for a teaching post overseas.

Passed the interview, tests, medical. Question from VSO – 'What country do you want to teach in?' Answer – 'Somewhere in Africa.' Response from VSO – 'We'll send you to Eritrea for a couple of years.'

Later I learned that this was how most of the volunteers working in Eritrea found themselves in Eritrea. Didn't meet anybody who'd actually specified the placement – we were the 'don't knows.' Fair enough, it'll do, I'll do a spot of research. Trouble is, Eritrea being Eritrea, there's not much written about the place to research so it didn't take long. Anyway, managed to find out a few bits and pieces.

Eritrea is a small country in East Africa. It has been at war for more than thirty of the years between 1961 and 2000. Since the turn of the century there has been a No War, No Peace policy in place which sees 150,000 Eritrean and Ethiopian soldiers facing each other across the southern border with no UN peacekeepers between them.

No War, No Peace has the effect of stagnating Eritrea. Nobody travels without a permit, nobody chooses where they want to live, nobody decides on a career path. Families, communities and church groups are deliberately split to discourage nucleus opposition groups forming. There is no operational university in Eritrea – it was closed down following a minor student protest. The perpetrators were imprisoned.

All young people go to military camps like Sawa to be trained for an indefinite period of time. Food production and water availability are at the mercy of a harsh climate. No rain in August means you fear for your family.

People disappear.

It is estimated that 25% of the population has fled over the past 20 years even though the government classifies emigrants as traitors and border guards are ordered to shoot on sight the people trying to escape.

Eritrea is one of the most repressive nations on Earth. Many thousands of imprisoned journalists, former government officials, religious leaders – anyone raising an opposing voice – are held indefinitely without charge.

Human Rights Watch said that 'Eritrea's government is turning the state into a giant prison.'

And, to supplement my library and internet investigations, I had a chance meeting in Sheffield with an Eritrean taxi driver called Yemane.

Yemane told me he was sleeping on the floor of a friend's house in Burngreave, Sheffield along with five other Eritreans. This was seen as a step up from sleeping on the floor of the church in Pitsmoor where they were getting a lot of abuse from the locals.

Yemane had been on military training in Sawa when he and a friend had decided they'd had enough. Like all other young people leaving school in his country he had become a conscript being trained to fight the Ethiopian enemy should war break out again. There was no end-date to the military service, the training was severe and brutal punishment was regularly administered to transgressors.

One night Yemane and his friend escaped the camp and made for the border with Sudan. After many miles stumbling through the darkness constantly on the lookout for armed guards they spotted the checkpoint. Dawn was breaking so they hid in a thorn bush the whole day in searing heat without food and water. The soldiers on guard were playing football and several times the ball rolled to within yards of where Yemane was hiding.

Night fell and they had got through the day without being spotted. If they had been seen they would have been shot or imprisoned in a shipping container. Over the border and they were running free. During the next few weeks they made their way to one of the many refugee camps dotted along the Sudan-Eritrean border. Thousands live here and many have done so for years. Children have been raised here knowing no other life and their situation is as precarious as any on earth. The Eritreans in these camps are now pariahs, unwanted by any country on earth including their own. You're out of the clutches of a severe military dictatorship but what now? And don't forget, you have left behind a family and friends who are now the subject of suspicion with the certainty of facing interrogation and the likelihood of persecution.

Like many Eritreans in their position Yemane and his friend decided to head for the UK – there is a chance of work even if it is illegal, benefits, housing and a population that is relatively tolerant of foreigners. First stop Libya – a few thousand miles across the biggest desert in the world. Yemane said they considered heading for Israel instead but that would have meant crossing the Sinai Peninsula and the trade in Eritrean internal organs was very lucrative for the nomadic tribes who lived there. Nobody is going to stick up for a wandering Eritrean and nobody is going to press charges against his or her murderer. The only interest shown is by those who want to buy his or her heart, lungs and liver.

After months Yemane made it to Libya – many don't get that far. From then on it's a search for a boat to get over the Mediterranean. By now the Eritreans have been joined by thousands from Central and West Africa all seeking to escape the oppression of their own countries, all seeking to make their fortune in Europe.

The boats are overloaded with three, four times the number of people they were built to carry and, so, many sink. Thousands of Eritrean bodies have been washed up on Italian shores. Official estimates suggest that for every body found there are at least two more that are not. Yemane got on his boat and it didn't sink. Through Italy and France he managed to secure a place in the squalor of a camp in Calais. Then, of course, it's time to get on the back of a lorry heading across the Channel. Broadcasts covering this activity are about the only time the word 'Eritrean' appears on British TV.

After numerous attempts Yemane made it and was picked up by the police walking at the side of the motorway heading towards London. A short trip to the Dispersal Centre in Ashford led to him being placed in Sheffield and the church floor in Pitsmoor. When I pushed him he summarised his reason for risking everything to leave Eritrea in four words, 'I needed to breathe.'

Now, for anyone to undertake a journey as outrageous as that, Eritrea must be a fearsome place mustn't it? This book is about the two years I spent living and working there.

Got a first powerful message about my destination when I stupidly tried to change currency - British pounds into Eritrean nakfa – in Barclays Bank. The clerk said 'What's Eritrea?'

September 2005 – Induction Eritrea

No rules. 'If you tell them you're flying out to East Africa to teach kids for a charity they let you off the excess baggage charge.' Charlie's advice was offered to our steadily increasing group of volunteers who were gathering in a café at Heathrow. Morven and myself were the early birds soon to be joined by Sandy, Phil, Mel, Rachel and Charlie. As our numbers increased there were greetings all round as we recognised faces from the training at Harborne Hall in Birmingham. The training was over, this was it, we were going. Big deal for me, the son of a steelworker born in a pit village in north east Derbyshire.

I was pleased to have a window seat. Was joined by Kim, a friendly Canadian bloke. His wife Barbara and their three children Mary, Louis and Sam, aged between nine and thirteenish, were across the aisle. On the short trip to Frankfurt Kim told me about the few days they had spent in London. Was able to hold up my end of the conversation as I knew a bit about London having worked for Nat West in Blackheath in the Seventies and since then had taken my three children – now grown up – on many a day trip. Assumed that Kim and his family were tourists. Think I hid my shock pretty well when it dawned somewhere over the North Sea that Kim and Barbara were VSO volunteers flying out to teach in Eritrea just like me.

Now just a minute. In the Derbyshire mining community I grew up in during the Sixties you got born, went to school, had a week's holiday in Skegness every year, followed your Dad down the pit or to the steelworks, married a girl you'd known since you were five, put your name down for a council house, had two or three children and repeated the pattern your parents had set. Solid stuff – you and everybody else knew where you stood. Okay I'd bucked the trend going to live in London after leaving school. Nobody knew what to do with a kid who'd amassed a 'staggering' six average GCEs – 'too clever for t' pit.' Even so you definitely didn't get on a plane with a bunch of pre-teenage kids and head off to an African village for a couple of years. And yet Kim and Barbara are decent folks with a family they are rightly proud of. First instalment of the attack on my 'rules are rules' mentality. Different doesn't mean wrong.

After changing planes in Frankfurt we boarded the Lufthansa flight bound for Eritrea. At that time four airlines flew to Eritrea – Yemen, Egyptian, Eritrean and – the most expensive – Lufthansa. Many empty seats and was able to estimate that our group of volunteers numbered about twenty spread around the plane. There were also a few Eritreans – men in suits, ladies in traditional white dress – and a small group of Americans next to me. All the other passengers looked like Saudi Arabians. Night fell somewhere over the Mediterranean which made the view approaching Jeddah pretty stunning. Jeddah has a lot of light bulbs and they clearly don't worry about the meter. Didn't get off the plane – just refuelling – but all the Saudi Arabians did.

Felt like we had the 200-seater plane to ourselves and this added to the anticipation, trepidation, bonding. What did the folks getting off at Jeddah know that we didn't? Over Eritrea it went dark. Not a single light pierced through the blackness. Our group was getting on well – lively spirits. The American said, 'You're going to be busy keeping your lot in check.' For the first time I realised I was a bit older than most of the other volunteers and this had led to the misunderstanding that I was in charge. I wasn't here to keep anybody in check.

Not that they were all younger than me. Donard was in his seventies and had lived and worked in many countries around the world. Margaret was the other 'pensioner'– what a way to spend your retirement – and was a bit of a character. Not sure how old she was but she had a wrinkle or two. Spent the next year with us telling tales of her three other VSO volunteering experiences in Guinea Bissau, Vietnam and Laos. All, apparently, were much friendlier, better resourced and far more professional than Eritrea. She had some epic arguments with some of the younger volunteers – shouting, tears, the works – all over nothing much. Bit of a livewire was Margaret – great fun, quite often on the lookout for a man.

Our group never made me feel anything other than 'one of them' and I'm sure that Donard and Margaret would agree. After an hour or two of blackness the lights of Asmara shone down below – we were landing.

The soldiers took the laptops from the volunteers who had brought them. Yohannes – VSO Director who had come to the airport to welcome us to Eritrea – protested mildly but to no avail. After a bit of milling around waiting for bags we jumped into the cars outside and within ten minutes we were in the lobby of the Lion Hotel. Getting lateish that Saturday night so we made our way to our rooms. I shared with Donard Britten – cousin of Benjamin. All part of the slightly unreal scenario for me. I'd only heard reference to Benjamin Britten on *University Challenge*. Donard had taught in half a dozen countries across Africa as well as Romania. Public school-educated, we were from different worlds. The coal mining village I came from had a 'share one book between three kids' school. You didn't need much formal education when you were going down the pit.

Donard and me got on well. He had an easy, relaxed humour that came into its own in uneasy situations. One evening in the hotel Charlie, Rachel, Sandy and myself were discussing kidnappings by extremist groups. Over the course of half an hour the conversation became increasingly serious with Charlie's graphic stories of beheadings and torture. 'Well I hear they look after you, show you a good time,' chipped in Donard in his off-hand laconic tone. Tension punctured.

The Lion Hotel is pretty decent and has a few nice features. The kites nesting in the tree next to the rooftop bar were spectacular. They're a common sight soaring overhead in Eritrea. The rooftop bar/restaurant is worth a mention in its own right. It's all painted white and relaxed with plenty of sun or sunshade whichever you prefer. Noticed several unused large solar panels rotting in a corner which gave an indication of the kind of problems worthy projects have to overcome if they are going to be beneficial. Witnessed this kind of thing several times during my years in Eritrea. Successful aid donation is more complex than just giving and walking away.

Wouldn't describe it as a nice feature but certainly different; a tank graveyard is not a common view from the top of most hotels. Round the back was a large expanse of level ground. Centre stage was a huge pile of rusting turrets, gun barrels, caterpillar tracks and tank armour. Legacy of over thirty years' warfare since the Sixties.

First Sunday in the hotel was quiet but important in that we got to know each other a bit. A fairly major event did happen for me that day although I wasn't aware of its significance at the time. Donard showed me how to use email – a first for me. Without my Yahoo account my time in the country would have been very different.

We spent two weeks in the hotel. Truth is I was ready to leave and get on with the job I had come to do after a few days. That's not to say that what we learned during our time there wasn't important. 'Find it yourself,' had been the response when we asked where the VSO office was. We were quite rightly being pushed to stand on our own two feet. If we couldn't get our bearings in the capital we would struggle in a village situated, in some cases, hundreds of miles from Asmara. We did find it ourselves. Up from Harnet Avenue it stood directly across from the Norwegian Embassy. Miriam's office was just inside, and a bigger congregating room to the right with bookshelves full of books on two walls and pigeon holes – one for each volunteer – for our mail. Upstairs a meeting room and a couple of offices and upstairs again to the rooftop. Breath taking view over the city. St Mary's Catholic Church in the foreground, St Mary's Orthodox Church over to the right, palm trees lining the main roads, expansive dusty plains beyond the city, craggy mountainous horizon and blue sky. Always blue sky.

Miriam was Accounts Manager and there were four Programme Managers who were each allocated a number of volunteers to support. My Programme Manager was Bereket, an elegant looking man, very thin with scars cut into his temples which had been there since he had been marked as a child. Traditional practice.

Kicked off every day with Tigrinya language training in the Lion Hotel. I picked up a few phrases and numbers up to a hundred.

Selam – hi/peace be with you

Kemay Welka/ Hadeerka – good morning/afternoon

Dhando? – how are you?

Sidrebet Kemay Alo? – how's the family?

Segi Bere – I've eaten enough

Segam Yelen – no problem

Grp – little, little. (used to describe how much Tigrinya I knew)

Kebiroo! – how much! (used in the market when being overcharged)

With these plus a few numbers reckoned I would get by. I concluded that some part of the brain has to be developed to get languages and I didn't have that part. Then again, perhaps I was just lazy. In reality I was totally focused on why I had come to Eritrea and gave little time to gathering what I thought was superfluous knowledge. I was here for one primary reason – to teach maths using the English language. As a teacher I believed/believe that education is the key and for my part that was what I was going to be involved in. Didn't want to be distracted which I thought was highly likely in a foreign country with all kinds of influences and behaviours I'd never encountered before. Mistake of course. I needed the essential tools such as language and local knowledge and could do little without them. At what point does 'focused' become 'blinkered?'

In the afternoons met with VSO staff, found our way around Asmara, had briefings on how to be a villager and played football on some spare ground with a team of local kids. They won. The VSO staff had put a lot of work into the induction training and to their credit they minimised the talk and chalk sessions and maximised the get stuck in and learn by doing and experiencing activities. We learned where not to take photographs and ride bikes in the city. In certain sensitive areas such as the Presidential Palace these could have – and did in some cases – lead to imprisonment.

The staff showed us Himbol where we could change pounds into nakfa legally. The volunteers who had done a year already showed us where we could change pounds into nakfa illegally. Half a mile from the VSO office was a clothes shop. 'Pick up an item, walk into the changing room at the back and a guy will come and give you the black market rate.' Foolishly (?) I was the only volunteer (only person in Eritrea?) who used Himbol. It was a lonely place but I kept the nice man in the suit and tie who worked there in a job and never had to queue.

The 'old' volunteers – those who had already been in Eritrea a year or even longer were a decent bunch of folks. Expected a superior attitude from them due to their acquired knowledge and our ignorance of Eritrea but that wasn't apparent at all. There was a genuine enthusiasm – really keen to meet us, find out about us, tell us their Eristories. Thought, 'I need to be like this with new folks who come here in the future.'

Claire and Tony had whizzed by us on their bikes as we strolled through the city centre. 'See you at the American Bar in ten minutes,' Claire shouted. Exhausted, I sat with a cup of coffee on one of the pavement chairs talking with them. It was all energy, smiles and a hundred-mile-an-hour Irish craic. 'Where are your placements?' 'Have you met Elsa?' 'Don't miss the beach at Massawa.' I tried to take in the fragments of local knowledge thinking this would be valuable but after a while it clicked. The real lesson here was of the heart. The need for drive, passion, resilience, enthusiasm, optimism, eagerness, openness, willingness and friendliness were the messages. Positive, positive, positive.

A few more of the 2004 intake joined us. I asked Dave how to find somewhere-or-other in Asmara. 'Haven't a clue mate. I've been in Nakfa for a year (town in the north of the country after which the currency is named). You know more about Asmara than I do.'

Jane looked a bit different to the others – sophisticated, aloof, the kind that might rub shoulders with politicians and dignitaries in city bars. Tony told us that was, in fact, what she did. In Asmara, apparently, she was on first name terms with Isaias military dictator, hater of the West, victorious leader of the struggle for independence, a regular in bars and cafes in Asmara. This accessibility was a frequent boast of Isaias and he was regularly seen out and about in the city and across the whole of Eritrea. Not so much these days though. The evidence of the years of warfare is apparent not just in tank graveyards and with the Kalashnikov-carrying soldiers on street corners. There are also the numbers of one-legged and/or one-armed men and the noticeably young age profile of the population. Youngsters predominate – very striking when you arrive from a country with an ageing population like the UK. Gives the place a buzz – even if that buzz is strictly confined and often forcibly suppressed as we came to know during our time in Eritrea.

On the back of a five nakfa note is a picture of the Big Tree in Segenetti – I climbed it.

As part of the in-country training new volunteers like me were sent to visit volunteers who had already been in the country a year or two. Deng – young, bright, tiny girl from the Philippines - and I went to visit Hannah and Eddie in Segenetti. We were very fortunate to be able to spend this time with the couple. Their experience and, equally importantly, their desire to share that experience was invaluable. The realisation that this basic human quality of willingness to help and pass on knowledge was a vital attribute that was being reinforced again and again.

Heading south out of Asmara the road forks. The south-west fork goes to Mendefera and then down to the border. The south-east fork goes to Dekamhare and then down to the border. Just beyond Dekamhare is Segenetti. The bus was not too full. All the seats were taken and a few stood but that counts as not too full in Eritrea. Out of the window every hill seemed to have a church on top. All had their own characteristic design. Would think students of architecture would have a field day.

Dekamhare was considered a big town but didn't have a town 'feel' – more overgrown village with lots of the small white block houses. I learned later that this was the centre of the Eri-Italian grape cultivation region during colonisation. Fertile – but didn't see too many crops being grown now.

Hannah and Eddie were waiting for us at Segenetti bus station. We followed them to their home which was on the outskirts of town. They had been in Eritrea a while and both had spent that time teaching in secondary schools. Eddie was continuing in that vein but Hannah had gone into teacher-training. This was the path I had already decided I would like to take. It made sense to actually get into the classroom first and experience the challenges before attempting to train others.

Their wedding photo on the shelf was not all it seemed to be but had been taken to satisfy the locals' sense of decency. Hannah and Eddie had become a couple before flying out to Eritrea and wanted to spend their time in the country working together. They had learned that living in the same house as boyfriend and girlfriend would not be 'acceptable' in an Eritrean village so they had the photo taken during their summer break in Brighton. Hannah was in wedding veil and all, Eddie in a chavvy suit and tie.

After a drink of tchai we set off for the Big Tree. Segen – as in Segenetti – means ostrich. Didn't see any of those but did see camels chewing on beles cactus fruit. We were out of town now treading a sandy path. We passed big tree after big tree each one seemingly bigger than the one before. One of them was circled by stone seats used by village elders to discuss village matters. There was no mistaking THE BIG TREE. It was about seventy feet tall but the impressive aspect of its size was its spread which must have been around fifty yards. Underneath the massive branches it was cool and shady. Had a moment as I noticed the swallows circling it catching flies on the wing. We'd both flown south for the winter.

Actually, this was just me romanticising as most of these swallows were probably resident or had flown in from other countries besides England. However, in my mind at least, they were the same ones I had seen the previous summer flying over Walton Dam.

I'd seen the Major Oak in England which is equally impressive as a tree. Totally different setting though. The Major Oak's branches are supported by enormous props and you can't get near it – all cordoned off with wires. Predictable tourist shops full of plastic Robin Hood stuff, cafes and car parks all around in what's left of Sherwood Forest. Great contrast here. Not a soul in sight so the Big Tree is open to any activity. Eddie and me climbed to the lower branches as Hannah and Deng rolled their eyes – 'kids eh.' Hard to believe that this national treasure was so accessible. Even harder to believe that dozens of carvings had been hacked into its trunk and branches, not fancy artistic ones but the kind made by schoolchildren of the 'Abel was here 1997' variety.

Bit special this tree. So special I got up early the next morning while everyone was still sleeping and went to see it again all on my own.

Another day and another day trip. The VSO staff really were determined not to be labelled as talk and chalkers and our induction continued along the lines of the 'get out and have a look for yourselves' variety. Up at six we were all loaded on the bus to Massawa – Eritrea's seaside town. Heading east out of Asmara we soon hit the winding sixty-mile downhill road to the Red Sea, and does it wind! The bus driver didn't bother with the brakes much but he was definitely an expert with the horn. At every bend in the corkscrew road an elongated beeeeeep was sounded so Donard and a few others had some difficulty trying to nap and recover from their early start.

The scenery was dominated by hills which had been terraced to support cultivation. This was conscript work – every July and August the youth of Eritrea are employed on this kind of task which looked endless. Stopped at Ginda for a tchai – very green area – and caught glimpses along the way of the one train track in the country. Italian-built, it was narrow gauge due to the incline. No train running though as this only ferried passengers to Massawa if specially commissioned. The steam engine in question was housed in its shed in Asmara where half a dozen men tinkered and polished all day. Never got the bug myself but I knew train spotters back in England who would probably have given their right arm to see this and spend a day chatting with the engineers.

Around the last bend and we could see the sea. This place was hot and we were told to forget Massawa in June, July and August because of extreme temperatures but we were not told that September was only a degree or two less and we were being baked alive. Never mind – cool off in the sea. Swimwear on, everybody ran across the sand and we immediately burned the soles of our feet. Dashing into the water to ease the blistering skin was not much relief – the water was steaming. After kicking a ball about in the waves for half an hour everyone headed for shade and found a large tent outside a restaurant overlooking the sea. Lunch was fine and we considered the merits of Massawa as a tourist spot. There was no real development here but the potential was obvious. If, as we were told many times, the temperatures eased to something reasonable from October to March this could be a great venue. The sea was clean and the islands looked beautiful. The cats kept interrupting our train of thought. About twenty of them were meandering around the tables. Courtenay – already in Eritrea one year – had warned Charlie about the cats before we had set off. The story was that she had been bitten by one and had dashed straight to hospital believing she might succumb to rabies. After Charlie had relayed the tale the cats didn't get stroked much.

And then everyone dozed off – the early start and increasingly savage heat were taking their toll. After a while Yohannes herded us back on the bus for a tour of the port. Only one ship was docked which, given the strategically advantageous position on one of the worlds busiest stretches of water, looked criminal. On the bus driving back uphill to Asmara I made a mental note that Yohannes' idea of cycling down to Massawa and catching a bus back sometime was a good one. Sixty miles downhill with only the odd goat or two in the road sounded okay and bus drivers were quite happy for bikes to be thrown on top for the return journey along with the baggage and animals. Maybe, when the temperatures eased a bit later in the year.

Bereket showed me his crooked forearm which had been broken when stamped on by a soldier's boot. He had been part of a student protest in 2001. It was crushed. Many of his friends who had led the protest had disappeared. He suspected they had been taken to the desert where they were being held in buried shipping containers. More likely, he conceded, they were dead. I had been surprised to find only one university in Eritrea when I had been researching the country prior to departure. Went on my own to have a look round. Nice enough building but not operational in any sense. Dictators who rule by the gun have always been scared of the masses acquiring knowledge and developing an enquiring mind.

The pointer to the future was set when we met the Directors and officials of the Education Offices and schools from where we were to be placed. I was introduced to Mr Meles, Director of Mai Nefhi High School. He was short and wiry and wore a flat cap (which tickled me being from up north). His face was serious and hard but he was friendly enough and he talked at some length about the school and he seemed supportive and forthcoming. He had authority. Over the coming year I was to learn that he, like others in supervisory roles, were not there due to their prowess in that field but due to the level of trust afforded them by the government. They were 'party' men and women (usually men). They were ex-fighters which is a term heard all the time in Eritrea. They had killed people on the battlefield.

So I knew where I was going and had met the man I would be working with. Over the last couple of days in the Lion Hotel we busied ourselves getting the necessary documentation together. Trooping around the city – looking very obvious – we visited various government offices to get residence permits, work permits and travel permits. We were given some money and told to go to the market and buy what we wanted for our village homes. I bought some pots and pans but was most proud of my table. Scruffy old thing but it was to be the work base in my home. Nice little drawer in it for my bits and pieces. Lovely. Walked all the way from the market to VSO office carrying it on my back. This sight, predictably, caught the eye and it was referred to several times in later months when I made acquaintances in Asmara. 'You're the guy who carried the table up the High Street.'

Went to the British Embassy (not with the table) and, briefly, met Mike the ambassador. Big picture of the Queen in the entrance hall. Met Brian – Head of the British Council and had a look at the library there. All very interesting but I was ready to go. Fish, the VSO driver, had already started ferrying volunteers and their bits and pieces out to their placements. After two weeks my turn came and we loaded my stuff on the back of the pick-up truck and were off to my new home in my village – Abarda. It was fifteen miles south of Asmara and didn't take long. Fish helped me unload and he was gone. I was on my own. Now – standing alone – that's a moment.

Got on my bike to ride to Mai Nefhi High School for the first day of term. Was inwardly quite proud of the 'High School' tag as all the others in my group had been allocated to Elementary and Middle schools. The school was about two miles down a straight, smooth, usually traffic-free tarmac road that had been constructed by the Chinese with an army of Eritrean labourers. The basic idea was to provide a transport link to Himbirti – the biggest of the villages in that area. Great ride all slightly downhill to the school. Clear blue sky, mountains rising from the scorched plain, an occasional shouted 'Selam' or 'Kemay' from a passer-by – bright, hopeful day.

The school is in a walled compound enclosing an area equivalent to four football pitches. Large metal gate securing the entrance next to which was a tiny canteen which would prove to be an oasis of replenishment over the coming year for teachers and students alike. Tchai one nakfa a glass. Hot tea with no milk – of course–and three spoons of sugar. Usually accompanied by a bit of barney – bread – to dip and a chat with between one and a dozen or so teachers and sometimes students. Got into the habit of five visits a day to this place.

There were nine shoebox-shaped classrooms arranged as the three sides of a rectangle with metal grilles at every window and a metal door. Inside was a large chalkboard and around twenty five desks. That was it. The large parade-ground area overlooked by the classrooms was the usual patch of rough dusty ground dotted with the occasional tree. Two big cows and a few scraggy sheep scoured the dust for bits of growth to chew. The flagpole complete with flapping Eri-flag stood at the top of the compound.

Didn't know what I would find that morning. Got off the bike and pushed open the gate. Went into one of the shoeboxes that looked a bit bigger than the rest. Guessed rightly that this was the staff room. Welcomed by the only two people in the place – Meles, the Director who I had met at the Lion Hotel and Kasi, a smartly dressed Indian teacher. Friendly natter about school-type stuff. Difficult to pin down basic facts and didn't want to push too hard at a first meeting. Felt a bit uneasy when Meles responded to the question about the maths syllabus by tossing me a forty-year-old textbook and said 'teach that'.

On this first day no students turned up.

Left Meles and walked back to Abarda with Kasi helpfully pushing my bike. Kasi explained that Meles lived in the school from Monday to Friday and slept on the floor of the staffroom. The students would drift in and numbers would grow to a full complement over the next three to four weeks. By the end of October they should all be in.

Parents would be paid a visit by soldiers if their offspring were not in school by then. It was sort of accepted that the need to work on the land took precedence at this time of year. And that is what happened. For the next few weeks I rode down to the school arriving at 7.45 on the dot every morning. Meles, Kasi, Fasi, Curvilla and me stared up the road to Abarda and down the road to Himbirti and counted no students in and no students out. By 9.30 after a glass of tchai at the canteen we were walking back home.

So the days and weeks went by and as Kasi had said students did start to trickle in and individuals grew to groups and groups into crowds. Initially no classes were taught. Most teachers were there to take names and feed numbers to Meles so that he could decide when actual teaching would start. Around mid-October that decision was made.

It was good to see green-jumpered groups in the distance heading for Mai Nefhi. A large number were from Leeban on the other side of the mountains about fifteen miles away. Thankfully they were transferred to another school with only an eight-mile walk. This kind of journey was seen as acceptable and probably represented the average distance our students covered to get to school. Before or after school was not idle time either – ploughing, stock and the home needed to be taken care of.

The day started with the anthem, a jaunty number sung hand on heart facing the flag. Hundreds of students lined up in rows, surrounded by stick-wielding teachers, not singing very passionately. The crackly tannoy belted out the words and set the meter.

I had six classes a day – all forty minutes long. All were grade 9 so first year at Eri-High School. Ages mostly around 16-18 – nobody had a birth certificate, nobody celebrated a birthday. 'My mother didn't tell me the day I was born Teacher Kevin.' No textbooks for students, between forty and sixty in a classroom sitting three to a desk.

The lessons started 'okay' but I was uneasy. The initial steady honeymoon period would not last long and I was concerned that the structure, content and method wasn't right.

In an attempt to motivate class 9.5 I pointed to three students in turn. 'Habtom – work hard and you can be a lawyer, Rigat – you can be a doctor, Gebremeskel – you can be a teacher.' Abel stood up, 'Teacher Kevin – we are all going to be soldiers.' Thanks Abel. Of course he was right. All these young people, the same as all the young people in Eritrea, would leave school and go to army training camps like the dreaded Sawa for an indefinite period of time –a period of time determined by government officials.

Violence was evident every single day. Boys and girls were punched and then kicked by teachers in the stomach as they lay on the floor, others were chased across the grounds screaming until caught and beaten. I knew that by not having a stick carried with it the risk of being seen as weak, soft. It was not a conscious decision to carry or not carry a stick – I just didn't do it.

Tiredness started to overtake me during the first weeks – you don't sleep much in Eritrea. After the Muslim call to prayer, the Orthodox Christians pipe up with their chanting. Then the animals join in. Donkeys do not go 'hee-haw' in Eritrea – they screech. Sheep, goats, chickens belt out their own chorus. Oh and packs of dogs have been racing round howling all night. Kids are up bright and early not wanting to miss out on the chance of getting their voices heard. The cockerel crowing around five o'clock is a bit ironic following the night's din.

Teachers across Eritrea teach by writing out on the chalkboard a page or two from the single textbook. Students then copy this into their books. This is repeated six times a day. Simple. I went and brought the whole range of interactive pedagogy that had been fed to me in the UK. My idea was to encourage discussion and debate. Demonstrations and group-work would open up the subject matter and bring it to life. Case studies and role playing (role playing!) would blow their minds. True, they didn't know what had hit them. The problem, of course, is that in trying to encourage ownership of the material by these techniques it can lead to a loss of control and I had dived in head first.

Attendance was patchy. In addition to the gradual start to term a noted slack day was Friday. Learned fairly quickly that this was market day in Himbirti. If you were from Himbirti you were selling, if you were from outside Himbirti you were buying. Goats, cabbages, clothes, tools – you name it and students were expected by families to contribute which meant a day off school.

The syllabus was non-existent as was information about the background and academic standard of the students. I pressed Meles for a syllabus until after a few weeks he gave Andimariom the task. Eventually Andi distributed a syllabus. It was clear he had just copied the contents page from the battered textbook I had been given.

Language? I had benefited from the morning Tigrinya lessons I had attended during the first couple of weeks in the Lion Hotel but was light years away from being able to hold a conversation. Truth is I should have worked much harder on this. I kidded myself that the students and teachers would improve their English if I didn't speak much Tigrinya. This, of course, was just a cover for my laziness in this aspect and that I became too focused on the challenges of the classroom not appreciating that the language was a great 'way in' and a key tool not just in the school but in Eritrea. I did, though, really concentrate on my English softening my Derbyshire accent, speaking slowly and clearly and, importantly, maintaining volume and clarity to the end of sentences whereas I had tailed off or rushed concluding remarks previously.

After a month or so I was asked to cover Grade 10 classes not teaching maths but health education. The standard book was issued and I got stuck into malaria and AIDS. My delivery in class – in English – was to a sea of blank faces until one session Gezae stood up and said, 'Teacher Kevin – we can't understand you.' Two things dawned. Firstly, their English and my Tigrinya were not at any level that made discussion-based classes possible. I took on the Eri-teaching approach of 'I copy from the book to the board – you copy from the board to your books.' Rubbish teaching – but I got through it. Secondly – I realised that I was fortunate being a maths teacher as maths has its own universal language. Trigonometry, algebra, pi cross language boundaries whereas everyday communication hits obstacle after obstacle.

All of this – students' lack of motivation, discipline, tiredness, methodology, attendance, syllabus and language issues were all apparent from day one. Ah yes – having been in the country for two minutes – so was my total ignorance of Eritrea and its people. The writing was on the wall from the start. The sleeves would need to be rolled up.

October 2005 – Acclimatisation

You've never seen anything like Abarda transport. Chickens in boxes, sacks of lentils and spices, furniture, bikes, a few wobbly goats and a couple of children – the usual load on top of a village bus. Never saw a child fall off and only once saw a goat fall off. It was quickly retrieved, dragged back on to the roof and tied to the railings by its horns as its more sure-footed companions skipped and jumped over it.

Getting on one of these buses is an intimate experience. 'Find a rock, find a rock,' they shouted. First thing – on joining the queue – you find a rock and put it on the ground roughly where you reckon the bus will stop. The line of rocks formed indicates your position in the queue and also the number of passengers waiting to get on. Sometimes the line stretches away into the distance. Sometimes queuers are more creative making snake-like swirls. Either way, there's usually a lot of rocks. Ok so far. Then, after anything up to six hours (if it appears at all) the bus chugs into view. If there is no policeman or soldier to ensure the rock line is adhered to (and there is never a policeman or soldier at the bus stop in a village) the rocks are completely ignored and everyone charges for the bus. Sixty, seventy, eighty men, women and children jam the door. Old men use their sticks to lever advantage, squawking chickens are held aloft to avoid them being crushed. Fights break out.

The most impressive fight I ever saw was in one of the bus charges. A heavily pregnant woman carrying a two-year-old on her back in the traditional Eritrean manner was outraged at another woman who had gained some unfair advantage in the insane squeeze for the bus door. The fists flew, the crowd parted to give them space and the pregnant woman won. The expression on the face of the toddler on her back during the scuffle was a picture. 'Go on Mum – belt her!'

The slow-squeezing process through the bus doorway takes a long time. Shoulders and knees are stiffened then eased to progress a few inches and bit by bit everyone gets on. Inside, of course, is terrible – a solid block of unwashed bodies in contorted arrangement. In extreme cases it is not possible to move your head. Once I stared into the wizened face of a wrinkly old man for the entire journey with our noses almost touching. It occurred that this was probably better than getting his other end in my face. Neither of us could move an inch. He kept smiling at me. As his disgusting breath wafted up my nostrils and mine up his I think a lifelong bond was created.

On another journey I found my face up against the window. As the pressure grew the glass bowed and I prepared for the imminent shatter and the likelihood of my face being torn off. Unbelievably, despite the potholes and a dozen or so emergency stops, the glass held.

Once, on a one-off journey in the middle of the day, I did actually sit on a bus with a few spare seats. Even this trip wasn't without its drama. A man got on with a monkey – a big one. After describing it to a few volunteers the following weekend in Asmara the consensus seemed to be that it was probably a vervet monkey. Whatever variety it was it had big yellow teeth. It sat next to the window besides its owner who held the bit of rusty chain that went round its neck. It sat perfectly still admiring the view and looking for its stop. Nobody batted an eyelid of course.

Early days in Eritrea but prejudice and judgements based on nothing more than a minimal understanding were being blown out of the water with some regularity.

Never had much time for beggars, folks wanting something for nothing. Always happy to help out those who are grafting – not so those sitting down with an outstretched hand. Indoctrinated working-class ethics.

Asmara has few beggars, I was given different answers in response to my questions why this was the case.

'Soldiers don't allow it – they move the beggars on.'

'Elderly and sick are cared for by close, supportive families in their homes.'

'Eritreans are too proud to beg – we are not like Ethiopians.' (Contrast Addis Ababa with 100,000 beggars).

I only saw about five or six old and wrinkled women sitting on street corners with their hands out during my time in Eritrea. Used to walk straight past them with hardly a glance.

One particular day I was sitting drinking tchai in a pavement café on Harnet Avenue. Across the road was one of the beggar-ladies who had been motionless for an hour. A man dropped a note into her hand. Slowly she got up, I could almost hear the bones creaking, and walked the few yards to the cathedral where she posted the money in a slot for donations. Then she returned to her spot and resumed her daily vigil hand out, motionless.

The small concrete cube that was Mai Nefhi High School canteen was a water hole for teachers and students alike. Regularly visited by me – at least five times a day – it served a triple purpose by satisfying the need for refreshment, offering a break in the battle and proving to be a goldmine of the kind of informal but often essential information that is shared at many a water-cooler in England. The one nakfa for a small glass of sweet tchai was the same price as a cigarette and a piece of barney. Often I took the bread to dip in the tchai. Not a smoker but many were and the canteen did good business. Only downside is tchai turns your teeth brown or yellow or both. Many volunteers needed a spot of whitening after leaving Eritrea. The odd thing I noted was that although

Eritreans drank as much (more) tchai and coffee than the volunteers their teeth in many cases were snow white.

Anyway. Tchai. Real lift throughout the day. Inside the shop were three small tables and these were usually occupied by students. A few large rocks were strategically placed outside under a couple of sparsely foliaged trees. Weaver birds nested in these trees and they flitted in and out of their pouch-shaped nests. Most days the tchai drinking sessions were attended by lecturers from the college next door. Mostly Indian and usually speaking perfect English, we used to have regular chats about cricket. India were due to play England in early 2006 so plenty of banter about how the series was going to finish.

Most times I used to sit on the rocks with Kasi, Fasi and Curvilla. Eritrean teachers did occasionally drink at the canteen but not often as one nakfa was usually beyond them. Rats kept us company darting in and out of the rocks eagerly looking for crumbs.

One morning at assembly the students were singing the anthem or, rather, groaning along to the ear-splitting version belting out from the speaker. All were stood in their usual rows surrounded by staff. A shout went up, then another followed by a scream. From my position I could see what was happening as dozens of rats swarmed over the parade ground lemming-style. They were coming from the direction of the canteen which was behind me. The commotion was the students' reaction as the rats ran across their feet. From the other side of the massed ranks teachers couldn't see the rats and were only aware of the unthinkable – disturbance during the anthem. All singing stopped, hands removed from hearts as teachers waded in sticks held high then lashing out at any student's head unfortunate enough to be within striking distance. Panic levels rose, scream volume rose and my shouts of 'It's rats! It's rats!' just added to the chaos.

Then, quite suddenly, there was calm and everyone went off to their classes rubbing cracked heads and bruised shoulders. Welcome to another day at Mai Nefhi High School.

The stick thing was bothering me – how was I going to come to terms with this? Should I come to terms with this? All teachers in Mai Nefhi High School Eritrean or Indian, men or women, carried sticks. The sticks seemed to be an extension of ego just as they were with teachers in England during my teenage years. The variety of implements tested for effect (or variation?) seemed endless. Hard to imagine that someone who had come into the profession to educate and enlighten should spend so much time considering the impact of different sticks and footwear before honing their ability to inflict pain with them.

At Mai Nefhi there was the usual array of weaponry. Meles led the way by carrying lengths of fluorescent pink rubber pipe. Don't know where he'd salvaged that but it was visible on the other side of the compound which, of course, is what he intended. The Eritrean teachers preferred flexible, whippy branches, the Indians went for unyielding lengths of wood. Madam Latha had a metre-long broom stick. When I told her she could break bones with it she laughed.

The most disturbing aspect of this practice was not the sticks themselves or even the sticks in action but the total acceptance by the students that they should be punished in this way. It caused great anxiety that I was stick-less throughout my time at Mai Nefhi High School to the extent that students would bring me sticks to beat them with. 'Teacher Kevin, you need a stick to be a teacher.' I used to take the sticks and throw them to the side of the compound and always replied, 'You are not an animal.'

I think this upset the other teachers. I hope so.

To me the word 'pension' meant the money you got when you retired. In Eritrea, and many other countries, it's what you call small and cheap, usually low-grade, hotels. In Asmara there are dozens of them with prices ranging from thirty nakfa (one pound) to two hundred and fifty nakfa a night. At the top end of the scale was Africa Pension – looked round the place but never booked in. Italian statues in the garden, shiny bedspreads, ornaments and the like. At the bottom end are places like Stella Pension and Bristol Pension. When in Asmara all volunteers used pensions and were welcomed by the proprietors and appreciated for the income they represented.

My week was starting to take shape and the pension in Asmara was part of that. Working week in the village and school, weekend in Asmara. Good to have a break, meet the other volunteers, pick up the post and check the internet, see a bit of the city. Had started by spending weekends in the village but felt the pull of the capital and the need for contact with the outside world. Some volunteers spent weeks, even months in their placements without visiting Asmara. In some cases it was impractical due to long distances and the seriously erratic or non-existent bus services. For others it was their way of maximising their chance of integrating with the villagers. I can see this. If you disappear off to the city every weekend you run the risk of alienating yourself. On the other hand it is possible to lose perspective, become unbalanced. One young lad deliberately immersed himself in village life seven days a week. After a few months a couple of his concerned friends visited him to see if all was okay. Came back with stories of him seeming a bit 'odd'. When he finally came into Asmara I had a chat with him. He seemed alright, no permanent damage. For myself I reckoned I was involved enough in Abarda over the course of the working week and really appreciated what the city had to offer on Saturday and Sunday.

Friday evening had the sort of feel it does for most people in England – work done, time to relax. Had used the bus to get into Asmara to start with. Didn't enjoy the three-hour wait at the village bus stop. Did enjoy the atmosphere created by the young folks waiting with me. Friday night feeling. The sitting round wondering if the bus would ever come was too much though and the bike was preferred after that first excursion. Nice ride through the villages, turn left at the Asmara-Mendefera high road, through Adi Guadad, past the airport, on to Gordaif and down into the city. A steady ninety minutes. Used to arrive as the sun went down.

End point of the journey was my pension – Bristol Pension with Alga and Mama. I'd tried Stella but it was noisy. Lots of screaming, grunting and groaning in the night. Learned later it was a well-known haunt of prostitutes. Mama and Alga would have none of that. 'You cannot take anyone – man or woman – up to your room, doors locked at 10.30, no alcohol, no smoking.' And they meant it.

'Ten nakfa!'

'Ooer' (Yes)

'TEN NAKFA!'

'Ooer'

'That's it then – I'm never stopping here again.'

I heard the above interchange between Steve – American volunteer – and Alga. There was no water in the taps at Bristol Pension. Ever. Didn't bother me as I used plastic bottles of water for washing, drinking, everything. Cost a bit but the bugs weren't going to get me. Steve had asked

Alga for some water for a wash. She had popped down the street to a friend's house with a plastic bucket, filled up, walked back and now wanted paying. Steve was indignant. He'd paid his nightly rate and couldn't believe she was charging extra for the bucket. Off he went. 'Stuff your water.' For the next two years I only saw about half a dozen other folks stay in the place besides me. God knows how Alga and Mama stayed in business on the couple of quid I chipped in for the weekend.

There were sound reasons – I thought so anyway – for sticking with Bristol. The back street setting (and no other people in the place) meant it was quiet. I could recover from the cockerel-crowing, donkey-braying, dog-barking filled nights in the village with a bit of sleep. The VSO office was five minutes' walk away as were the internet café, British Council library, City Park – everything really. Asmara is not big. The cockroaches only made occasional appearances usually coming down the tap where the water should have been. Although water never came out the taps it did occasionally come out of the shower down the corridor. Freezing cold, steady trickle but it did the job. I was comfortable in Bristol Pension.

Best thing about the place was the Friday night welcome. Getting off the bike at the end of my journey (usually worn out) Mama would have a little stove burning in Bristol Pension entrance lobby and a coffee ceremony would be prepared. Small finjal (porcelain cups) of strong, sweet, black coffee boiled in a jubana (coffee pot) on the charcoal. Smoke and coffee aroma everywhere. This is the Habesha coffee ceremony famed throughout Eritrea and Ethiopia. There are all sorts of traditional stages, all kinds of rigmarole and the full-blown affair can take hours, all day if people have nothing to do.

Abol – first boiling

Kelai – second

Beroka – third

Deraja – fourth and so on

If you don't say 'Trrum' (appreciative noise corresponding to something like 'yum yum') unprompted in some houses the coffee maker smashes the pot in disgust at their own poor coffee making not because of the guest's lack of appreciation. Coffee is serious stuff for some.

Problem starts when well-meaning villagers start the coffee ceremony at ten o'clock at night. Eyes popping after six cups, sleep doesn't come naturally. Well not until about two o'clock the next afternoon. The coffee is only the setting of course, the important thing is the human contact, the conversation. No stimulus provided by television, no radio, no newspapers to speak of – there is a basic human desire to communicate and in the absence of modern media chat is king and the coffee ceremony provides a rich backdrop.

Mama was welcoming, sparky, edgy and creased. At least 80-years-old she looked like she had been drained of her bodily fluids. Hips shot, she wheeled from side to side as she walked. When she laughed her wheezy laugh, which was often, her face cracked and crinkled in all the right places. She busied herself around the pension constantly – this was her life.

Alga, Mama's daughter, was strongly-built and strong of character. In Eritrea women who shook hands in the way that men did (with an accompanying shoulder to shoulder bump) were assumed to be ex-fighters. Alga shook hands like a man. Her stories told to me over the years I stayed at her pension confirmed the assumption that she knew which way to point a Kalashnikov. As well as running Bristol Pension she also served on the Eritrean Tourist Board. Now there's a thankless task as she freely admitted. Used to chip in my thoughts over coffee. The Red Sea off the east coast was unspoilt – perfect for diving. The history of the place – colonial occupation, the struggle for independence would be of great interest to some. The architecture of Asmara's buildings is unique in Africa. To be honest though I, like she, was struggling and I didn't like to tell her that most people in the West had never even heard of Eritrea unless it was preceded by the term 'war-torn.'

If you don't get Billy Connolly's endless stream of swearing you don't get Billy Connolly. His use of swearing is endearing (to many) not offensive. This is a gift. Carlo had that gift. Day to day conversation was enhanced by his range of obscene vocabulary – every sentence. Nobody tutted, nobody even referred to his profanity. If I had asked Carlo 'why do you swear so much?' he would doubtless have sworn and laughed. If I had asked others why Carlo swore I would doubtless have got the answer 'Oh that's just Carlo.' I didn't bother asking.

Carlo was joint leader of the Asmara Hash. The other joint leader – a fantastic contrast – was Barbara, the refined and elegant wife of the German Ambassador to Eritrea. Carlo and Barbara – they made a great team.

Never heard of a Hash before Eritrea. It was described to me as either a 'drinking club for walkers' or a 'walking club for drinkers.' Apparently in cities all over the world ex-pats meet up once a week for a walk followed by food and a drink which appears out of the back of their cars. Carlo said the Asmara Hash was not, now, really a Hash. He had experience of Hashes in other countries and in Asmara a year or two earlier when it was attended by some Irish soldiers who were out here with the UN. I think his understanding of a real Hash was an excuse for getting blind drunk. If that is what a 'real' Hash is about then he was right. The Asmara version was not a drunken affair but a group of folks from numerous countries who had a simple desire to get together for social reasons, share stories about the locals, explore a bit of the country while walking a few miles and follow this with at the most a couple of bottles of Asmara beer or juice and a bite or two of imported food.

I became a regular on the Hash. Enjoyed seeing parts of Eritrea I would not otherwise have seen, appreciated the food and drink but mostly, as with anything to do with Eritrea, it was really all about the people. Having the chance to meet folks with such a range of backgrounds, occupations and nationalities made this a must for me. Three o'clock every Saturday afternoon I was usually there at Alpha supermarket near the Lion Hotel – the Asmara Hash meeting place.

Through the week Carlo had bought the food and drink and given a bit of thought to where we were going to head off to and by the middle of the afternoon most who were going were assembled – usually between twenty to thirty folks. Carlo, Brian and two or three Americans who worked at the US Embassy or with UNMEE (United Nations Mission in Ethiopia and Eritrea) came in their 4 x 4s and everyone piled in. The destination was always within seven or eight miles of the capital as Americans had to stay in touch with base at all times. This was not too restrictive as there are some eye-opening places within half an hour's dusty drive of Asmara.

Found that I and the other VSO volunteers who went on the Hash were of some interest to the rest of the group. Most of us were out in the country – we lived and worked in villages and we could offer an insight to Eritrea that the city dwellers didn't get. Because of their role or status within the organisation they worked for the security awareness was much greater than ours. I suppose volunteers like me were a bit more expendable.

It took a while before I really understood the makeup of this group. I had been told at the outset that it wasn't the done thing on a Hash to question people too much on what they were doing in the country. Bit by bit the group's constituent parts did eventually become clear. Broadly, there were the people working at embassies or with UNMEE, professionals such as Brian who was a surveyor with the Ministry of Public Works (or Doesn't Works as he told me), wives or husbands of the two former groups, a few Eritrean girls and us, the VSO volunteers. Volunteers paid twenty nakfa for the Hash, everybody else paid forty nakfa.

The wives or husbands of the dignitaries or professionals were the group that took me the longest to figure out – especially the husbands. As far as I could see, and eventually by their own admission, they did nothing in the country but while away the days looking for something to occupy themselves. Carlo's wife was a hard working teacher at the Italian School. Carlo bought the beer for the Hash and that was about it. The wives seemed a close-knit group who organised little outings and social events for themselves to fill their time in the week. Tours of the Omo washing powder factory and the Coca-Cola factory (Coca Cola was on sale for two weeks during my time in Eritrea – big talking point) were highlights as was the Happy Hour at the American Embassy bar on Thursday evenings. All felt a bit decadent to a scruffy volunteer who had just spent an exhausting week in the village. Despite this there were some amazing characters in this bunch, some decent people and I always looked forward to meeting them.

Some volunteers seemed uncomfortable with the Hash and never went. Others went once or twice then never again and a few of us went most weeks. After a week in school I found it a real pick-me-up and felt that the non-attending volunteers missed out on something a bit special.

I thought she had a beard. As I approached the tiny girl it became clear that around her mouth was a mass of crawling flies. Used to walk around Abarda in the evenings either on my way to Mai Nefhi Hotel for a bite to eat or just on a circular tour around the village. Get a feel for the place, make myself visible, accessible. On my first little walk, on a typically beautiful warm evening, I saw the girl with the 'beard'. Children seemed to fill the village playing, screaming, shouting and working. The games they played were those from my own childhood. Skipping with an old rope, hopscotch and a game with stones we used to call snobs were all popular. Older children were a bit more organised and had set up a rope between two sticks so they could play volleyball. Used to join them sometimes.

The clothes they wore were rags except when the charity clothes had been given out which, although they were in good condition, rarely seemed to fit. Didn't matter to the kids. Never seen anyone as proud in my life as six-year-old Samuel as he strutted round the village in his man-size electric blue Adidas trainers.

Wish I'd bought the little metal football game from Robbel and Abraham. Fashioned out of an old UN cooking oil tin it was one of those where you spun the players round to kick the ball (in this case a round seed) and tried to score. Only about a foot by six inches they told me their dad had made it for them. The other football-influenced game was a bunch of rags screwed into a ball and tied by a long string so that it hung from a tree trunk. This was then kicked around the tree with a swing ball technique. Kept them happy for hours. No sitting in front of the telly here – no telly.

A big crowd of wide-eyed boys ran towards me one evening as I was heading home. 'Mantilla! Mantilla!' Never proficient in Tigrinya I had no idea what they were shouting about but got the idea that it was some kind of creature, something out of the ordinary. The only word I knew that sounded anything like mantilla was Godzilla. Prepared myself for the worst. It turned out they'd caught and killed a big rabbit. No doubt one family was going to eat well that night.

Wasn't the only scare I had that involved kids and animals. Tesfai, the landlord, had been moaning at me for burning my rubbish (scribbled ideas for lesson plans) in the compound. He thought I'd set fire to the house so he pointed me in the direction of what I eventually gathered was the local rubbish tip. About two miles outside the village in the direction of the mountains in the middle of a dusty plain was the tip. Rusting bits of metal and old bits of ripped plastic were piled in between a few dead trees. Got into the routine of walking to the tip every Wednesday afternoon after school. It was a strange place, quiet and desolate, never saw a soul except for one afternoon when Solomon the goat-boy was mooching around. Had a little chat with him about his animals before heading back to the village. After I'd gone about ten yards Solomon screamed at the top of his voice, 'Hyena!' Looked around quickly – no sign of anything but Solomon was running. Seemed a good idea to do the same. I could see the little church tower next to my home in Abarda – it looked a long way. Better get up a tree sharpish. Thorns everywhere I was being scratched all over as I struggled up to the lower branches. After making it to what I thought was a reasonable height (how high can a hyena jump?) I looked down to see Solomon rolling on the floor holding his sides in fits of laughter – the fiercest creature in sight was one of his small goats. Little so-and-so. Me and my clothes were in shreds. Comforted myself with the thought that one day he just might be a student in one of my classrooms.

Although there seemed plenty of time for play it was work that dominated the children's lives and from a very early age. Two-year-olds tottering around the village with big tins picking up donkey droppings were a regular sight. The stuff burns so you don't waste it. By the time girls are four they have yellow plastic 'jerry cans' (containers) tied to their backs and are expected to fetch the water, This can be a long haul and there are a number of medical reports written detailing the harm this can cause and how it can affect growth. As a five-year- old you are big enough to contribute to the chores that are undertaken by an adult – cooking and cleaning for girls, goat-herding like Solomon for boys. Collecting fuel for the fire is a never-ending task. Gathering sticks and cow pats, which are then stuck on walls to dry in the sun, is a daily ritual.

Once a boy has developed some strength he is tied to a wooden plough which is in turn tied to one or sometimes two oxen. The ploughing has to be done. Couldn't help comparing the monumental effort required by a fourteen-year- old to take this on with kids in England getting Repetitive Strain Injury from playing computer games. Oh, and after the ploughing is done then you set off to walk mile after mile to school.

November 2005 – Villagers and Teachers

Mehari was a regular visitor to my home. About thirteen-years-old he had a sharp face and spoke with assurance like an adult which was disconcerting at first. No doubt he had had to grow up quickly. I never saw his mother or father and never asked. He lived with his grandfather who was my landlord. Mehari was very welcome, his chatter about the village helped me as I tried to construct a picture of the place and the people I had come to live with and, simply, it was good to see a friendly face.

One evening my fluorescent light tube went – pitch black now inside as well as outside. This was important and needed fixing. I stumbled outside to find Tesfai, the landlord's house in the dark. After several falls I finally made out the rectangular box where he lived. Unlike my white-painted stone cube he had a traditional hudmo – all wood and mud. He said that he would fetch Gebremeskel and bring the tube.

'How much?'

'Thirty nakfa.'

'Ok.'

After half an hour Tesfai, Gebremeskel and Mehari banged on my door and within a minute the light was fixed – old tube out, new tube in.

'Sixty nakfa,' said Gebremeskel holding his hand out.

'How much?'

'Sixty nakfa.'

It had been a long, hot day in school. Sleep had been disturbed since I had moved in by the nightly village racket going on. My relief at having the light fixed so quickly was replaced by irritation bordering on anger at being conned. The heated exchange finished with me throwing thirty nakfa at Gebremeskel and shouting 'No more – clear off you bloody thieves!' before banging the door shut in their faces.

Not a good night – worse than usual. Had I misheard Tesfai? Would they let me stay in the house? What would happen if the tube went again and a dozen or so other self-preservation type thoughts mixed up with self-critical reflections about my behaviour? By the morning I'd arrived at a single, specific conclusion. I hadn't come to Eritrea for this. Battling neighbours in the village over a quid. I knew that volunteers did move house and, sometimes, village over confrontations such as this – some of them two or three times. From what I could make out usually the friction was caused by silly misunderstandings, arguments that festered and spread making relations with villagers difficult. I had to sort this quickly. I wasn't moving anywhere.

The next evening after school I got thirty nakfa and strode round to Tesfai's hudmo. Mehari saw me first. His face was angry and I was sad that I had caused this. Mehari had been one of the first to approach me in the village and make me feel welcome. This time I had not been invited, was not expected and was definitely not welcome. 'Where's your Grand dad?' Not a word from Mehari, he just pointed inside. I walked straight in and saw Tesfai sitting comfortably drinking out of the familiar Asmara beer bottles with three old mates of his. Grabbing his wrist I put the thirty nakfa in his hand fully intending to turn round and walk straight out without speaking. That moral high ground was going to be mine.

Tesfai's face lit up with a big toothless smile. 'Cof, cof.' ('Sit, sit.') The animosity was completely gone. I had beer after beer shoved into my hand and I sat and listened (understood very little) but appreciated the warmth and generosity. Right decision Kevin, learn from it.

They looked like nice girls to me.

'Hi Guy,' they giggled as I walked past the Nice Hotel in Asmara one Friday evening. I stopped, smiled and said, 'Hi.' The three girls were strikingly dressed – low tops, short skirts, colourful. 'Kemay Weelket?' I enquired in, no doubt, a strangled north Derbyshire version of Tigrinya. They giggled again. Friendly girls. 'I'm Teacher Kevin,' I ventured and followed up with the usual stuff about how I worked in Mai Nefhi School. 'Do you know it?' Smiles all round. This was going well – thoughts along the lines of 'I can even build good relations with complete strangers' and, with totally misplaced confidence in my linguistic ability, 'this communication lark is a doddle.' Totally deluded.

Next level and out come the trusty photographs of my children and grandchildren. 'This is my family back in England.' The girls were very interested even asking for my sons' email addresses. (My sons were probably about the same age as the girls.) Didn't pass on the email addresses – seemed an odd request. Left the girls with a chorus of 'Ciaos' ringing in my ears accompanied by sweet little waves and crossed the street to where Amanuel from the VSO office and a friend of his were standing outside a shop. Should have known I'd been in 'one of those situations' by Amanuel's laughter. 'Do you always talk to prostitutes Kevin?'

I'd looked forward to seeing sunsets in Eritrea. Television programmes of African wildlife often use spectacular evening skies as a backdrop to herds of wildebeest or a lion sitting majestically on top of some crag surveying the plain for its next meal. I settled back in a chair facing the mountains with an Asmara beer at Mai Nefhi Hotel. I'd just finished my pasta and thought I'd take in the event – appreciate the beauty of the sun going down. Always thought November sunsets in England can be a sight worth seeing. Colours merging into each other across the sky, elongated cloudy strands providing relief, vibrancy increasing to a crescendo – that kind of thing.

In this country, and I watched many a sunset during my time in Eritrea, the sun sort of just went down, and fairly quickly. The three mountain peaks in the distance were as striking as ever and to see the sun inch its way behind them conveyed a strong awareness of the passage of time but no dramatic colours – orange ball followed by no orange ball – and no clouds so no cloud formations.

The big deal in Eritrea is the night sky and in particular the moon, the planets and the Milky Way. No electric light in the village to speak of so the universe comes alive. The moon's phases became a real show to look forward to marking the time as they changed through crescent, half, three-quarter, full and back again. It lifted the spirit as it waxed, there was a slight feeling of sadness as it waned. Bit weird. However, it provided a steady, reliable source of progression in strange, demanding and erratic times.

With no street lighting the sky regularly put on a spectacular show. Giant full moons with sculptured features were hypnotic. I'd seen somewhere on the internet that the moon was closer to the Earth than for hundreds of years and, so, appeared even bigger than usual. Crescent moons were tilted to a curious 'smile' orientation and the silver rays lit up the village providing illumination and, on a practical note, reduced my stumbling and falling on the stony ground.

During the run-up to Christmas in 2005 Venus – dazzlingly bright – seemed to play in the vicinity of the moon. One evening they almost seemed to touch.

Another Friday evening I'd had a guava juice at City Park after cycling from the village. Pushed the bike up the incline past Photo Walter and stood at the top of Harnet Avenue. Looking down the straightness of the long bustling highway I saw that a bright yellow full moon had positioned itself just above the end of the road beyond Barti Meskerem Square. Looked like the President had erected an enormous cardboard disc.

Absence of moon had its moments too. Walking back from Sembel where I had eaten with John and Janet late one Saturday night there was a power cut. Strange feeling. Absolute, absolute blackness yet surrounded by milling crowds occasionally brushing each other and me and all accompanied by the low hum of conversation. Nobody changed their pattern or behaved differently just because the lights had gone out. It happened.

All staffrooms are venues oozing basic animal instinct for no other reason than they are confined spaces populated by human beings who crave the comfort of an established hierarchy. Seating arrangements, mug ownership, pigeon hole position are critical indicators of status. The staffroom at Mai Nefhi High School was no different, in fact the rank structure was even more pronounced partly because half the teachers were Eritrean, almost half were Indian and one, me, was English. Now that was a great mix. Throw in the military background and training of the Eritreans, the fact that most were conscript teachers being paid 450 nakfa (£15) a month while the Indians were being paid $4,000 a month by the UN on top of their 1,200 nakfa teacher's salary and you have a ticking time bomb.

Given the potential for fireworks it is amazing that for the most part the teaching staff got on pretty well. Clear lines were drawn. Chairs were arranged in the staffroom on three sides of the square room, Eritreans occupying one side and Indians the other. I sat smack in the middle and this was the position I took when the tension was pricked by some incident and it all bubbled to the surface. Not really able to take up any other position picking up only the tone but not the detail. It was easy to spot when something was up as speaking in English was ditched – Indians resorting to Hindi (very loud Hindi) and Eritreans to low, growling Tigrinya.

Kasi was the leader of the Indians. He had tried commuting from Asmara but the journey was a nightmare on the bus and minibus so after a year he had decided to set up in Abarda and walk the couple of miles to school each day. Not only that but he had the foresight and strength of character to persuade others to do the same. By the time I came to live in Abarda there was a small established community of Indian teachers and professors (who taught at Mai Nefhi College) living in the village. Kasi, Curvilla and a college professor had made their home in a compound. Fasi lived on the other side of my house and Madam Latha and her husband lived in the same compound as me. They had all invested in the village and made their lives comfortable. The crazy commuting which could mean spending anything up to six hours a day either waiting for, or squashed on, buses was gone. All the Indians had satellite dishes and CD players, all had well-stocked larders. Sensibly they shared costs and Kasi's place had sacks of spices, lentils, tea and vegetables. Small boys used to catch fish in Mai Nefhi dam and bring them directly to the Indians for ten nakfa each – no point trying to sell them to the impoverished villagers.

Kasi sent most of his UN salary back to his wife in India. They had three daughters and the money was paying for their education and also being used to buy land in India. He wanted his daughters to be doctors or, failing that, nurses, and was always keen to discuss this with me and ask for my help with them coming to England at some point in the future.

Ruta was Kasi's maid. Before Ruta the maid had been Akberet – Ruta's older sister. Both had been students in Mai Nefhi High school, both in Kasi's Home Room class. He had selected carefully getting to know their parents in Himbirti well. The girls' mother and father were delighted that their daughters had been given this employment for two reasons. Firstly, Kasi paid well and second he seemed to have some influence over when and where the girls went for compulsory military training. He actually went to the military camp in Sawa to talk to commanders when

Akberet had been drafted in and she was allowed early release not long after.

Kasi and the other Indian teachers became a welcome support group for me during my time in the village and I will always be grateful for what they did. Kasi understood the difficulties I was having in the classroom as he had gone through something similar himself during his first year in Eritrea. Each day after our last classes – usually around 4.30 we would walk as a group back up the road to Abarda. Sometimes students walked with us, sometimes not. Kasi and Curvilla always invited me in as we got to their compound and I was given tchai and rice and biscuits while we talked. It was a nice way to end what was often an exhausting day.

Doesn't do to be cynical sometimes. Sitting in the staffroom marking some test papers – with a lot of students in the classroom there were a lot of test papers – a quiet voice at the side of me said, 'Kemay welka.' Looking up I saw a boy about fifteen-years-old. He introduced himself as Robbel and he sat down.

'Can I show you my work?'

Putting my marking to one side I looked through many drawings. All of them were of the Crucifixion. Christ was drawn in close-up, talking to John and Mary from the Cross, being taunted by Roman soldiers and so on. Although the paper was screwed and torn and his pencils were clearly poor quality his talent shone through. The form, composition and detail were striking and he had captured the anguish and torment in the faces.

Talked about his ability, how long he had been drawing, where he drew and asked about his family and home. Not really sure about why he had come to me so I asked him directly 'What do you want from me?' Fully expecting a reply along the lines of 'I'll sell you these for ten nakfa each' I was surprised to see that he was puzzled by my question. 'You have already given me what I came for – encouragement.'

He collected up his drawings and went. I never saw him again.

It all nearly finished before it had really started. I had seen quite a few trucks loaded with cheering, jeering, gun-waving soldiers going down the road in the direction of Mendefera and beyond to the border. On the radio the early morning programme *Voice of Africa* was covering the Eritrean/Ethiopian situation in some alarming detail. Volunteers were all given a letter . . .

Dear volunteers,

I hope this letter finds you well. In relation to the news on the current situation of the Eri-Ethio border tensions I thought this would be a good time to share with you some updates from the Programme Office.

First of all we would like to inform you that we are following the situation very closely, from different sources and by liaising with other international bodies. Most of you must be following this on local and international news. The international news agencies are saying that there is movement of new troops around the border between the two countries and that tension has not calmed down since. At the moment nobody knows where this will lead. There is a possibility that any action – positive or negative that could be taken by one or both of the sides can lead to either a calmer or a chaotic scenario.

At the Programme Office we are making all possible preparations and plans to reduce the risk that could affect the volunteers' safety. We are considering future predictions that may require us to relocate part or all of the volunteers from their placements to other suitable areas inside or outside the country, according to what will happen on the ground. We are liaising with the relevant organisations for all volunteer nationalities when we prepare our plans. We are also very much aware of those volunteers who might be at higher risk than others. However, although we are prepared for such a scenario according to our assessment on the current situation it is our point of view that there is no need for such an action at the moment. We believe that staff and volunteers can continue doing our day-to-day activities as usual.

One of the key preparations we are making includes the updating of volunteers' emergency contacts in country and back home. Eritrea is a small country and most placements can be reached by car within a maximum of half a day's time. We also have a reasonably good idea how to spot volunteers in their placements. However, if we don't have your clear contact details, the direction to your houses and the details of your emergency contacts in Eritrea it can be difficult for us to reach you or pass on urgent information in an emergency. In such a situation you could be forced to carry more responsibility for your safety until we try to reach you. Therefore I would like to use this opportunity again to remind you that if you haven't filled in your Personal Record & Emergency Contact Form that we gave you during Induction Training this is high time that you send it to us ASAP. Out of 41 volunteers only 19 returned the completed forms.

We hope that the situation will not escalate to the negative but primarily all of us should take responsibility for our own safety. It is good to have all your essential documents and personal ID cards, personal effects, inoculation papers and other valuables in a suitcase of not more than 20kg handy all the time. Please find attached a list of suggested items to pack just in case you need to leave at short notice. If the situation changes to the worst we will immediately inform you of our plans and what action you need to take in your specific placements.

Finally I would like to reassure you again that we are prepared for a worst-case scenario but we do not want the tone of this letter to create more concern among the volunteers than is necessary. You should all continue with your daily lives and jobs as usual until you receive instructions from the Programme Office for any other actions. Please feel free to inform us if you feel unsafe in your placement for any reason.

Wishing you all the best

The Programme Office

Made for an interesting week back in Mai Nefhi. Every time a MiG buzzed the school – and one was so low it nearly took the roof off – I checked my bike tyres. That would have been an impressive sight, 50,000 Ethiopian troops chasing me on my bike up the road to Asmara.

December 2005 – Christmas?

Hannah said that Eritrea was a good place to escape Christmas.

In my home town, as in most towns and cities in England, Christmas cards are on sale from July, shops gear up from September, lights are switched on in October and Santa makes appearances from November onwards. This is the stuff that Hannah meant, the wearying commercialisation and alchoholisation of a special time. None of this in Eritrea.

One evening in mid-December I went to visit Teklu and his family who were my neighbours. Like Tesfai, my landlord, they lived in a traditional hudmo the construction of which had probably not changed for thousands of years. Simple shoebox-shaped affair open at one end with great logs supporting the flat roof which was earth-covered. Self-set grasses and weeds sprouted on the roof making the hudmos turn green following a shower. Inside was dark, sleeping chambers were built into the walls, bare floors, a few bits of furniture and a fire fuelled by dried cow dung. Didn't smell that bad – maybe I'd just got used to it. Of course the house was a mixture of many aromas – cooking smells, kid smells, animal smells and earthy smells to which I contributed my unwashed Englishman in Eritrea fragrance.

I was sat down next to the fire – welcome on a cool night. Behind my head stood a sleepy cow chewing to itself. A cow in the house is a good source of heat. It is also a good source of shit and soon after parking myself I heard the sound of cow dung hitting the floor.

Not a lot said during the evening. Usual stuff – 'how's the family, the land, the animals?' Long periods of comfortable silence, occasional tirades of Tigrinya aimed at various children by Teklu's wife, a laugh or two at my distorted attempts at the language. I felt accepted – not a bad feeling. Chewed away on my goat meat made fiery by the berbera and swigged the Asmara beer Teklu had opened.

Looking around the smoky room I took in the baby wrapped in a blanket asleep in his mother's arms, a couple of Teklu's tinies playing a game with stones, a dazzling star-filled sky through the open-ended hudmo, the cow, a few straggling sheep jostling outside and beyond them an old donkey, chickens scratching near the fire, Teklu's lined face and thought 'I'm in a Christmas card.' Not the snowy, robin, candle, Santa, glitter sort but the stable, manger, Madonna, ox and ass sort. The steadying thought, though, was that not one person in this scene was playing a part – nobody was reading from a script. The benches, pots, pans and donkey were no stage props positioned for effect. The fire was not artificial, nothing had been set up for cameras or an audience and certainly not for me. This was real, an evening that happened every night – minus me – and had been played out in hudmos for thousands of years. The absence of progress had removed the pressure of progress and peace and contentment – not frustration – flourished. Felt some privilege to have been a part.

The run up to the end of 2005 in Eritrea was not completely devoid of Christmas. The students in my Home Room had spent one break time chalking 'Happy Christmas' on the board but had no understanding of what Christmas represented either in the religious or commercial sense. A few shops in Asmara wrote a seasonal greeting on the window – the kind you guessed would still be there the following June (and they were).

I had been on the Saturday Hash a week or so before Christmas Day. The talk centred on the carol concert at St Mary's cathedral – some of the group were singers. One German lady in particular had been formally trained and she had put together a show to be performed by expats on the following Sunday evening. I couldn't make it as I had to be back in the village for school next day. Doug, the retired professor from Sheffield who was now working as a volunteer trying to introduce pig breeding to Eritrea ('Good luck with that mate') had a suggestion – he invited me to the final rehearsal in the cathedral that night.

After dropping off a few things in Bristol Pension I walked down the road to St Mary's. Taking my seat I realised that I was the audience – an audience of one. Great privilege. The carols were sung beautifully and the cathedral looked more spectacular than ever in candlelight. Mario – the Italian househusband – grinned at me mid-carol. His voice stood out a bit – the only singing he had previously done was on the terraces at Perugia football ground. He had told me quite a few times on the Hash he had once watched his team beat AC Milan in a cup game. I gathered this was comparable to, say, Chesterfield FC beating Manchester United at Old Trafford in the FA Cup. (It might happen one day). The strangeness of this 75 degree Christmas that wasn't Christmas and the concert made this a special hour or so. The closing procession down the aisle capped it all and was very moving.

Christmas Eve dawned unique. Forty nine previous family gathering-type Christmases crammed on my insides. On the outside was heat, unfamiliar food, people, language, clothes, customs. The usual city bustle – a total non-Christmas. The dysfunction of it all was stark and it bothered me a bit.

Buying *Eri-Profile* from the old girl outside the Post Office (as usual), downing a glass of tchai and a cake at Elsa's Café (as usual) and visiting the Internet Café (as usual) the dysfunction felt even more severe. Reflections on what my family would be doing now were vivid. Went to the VSO office, a few people about – Charlie, Rachel, Kaska and Miriam in her office. A nod in the direction of the time of year from Charlie who was talking about his first Christmas away from home - in Australia - and how difficult it was for him. After this experience his remedy was to drop all expectations, to let events like Christmas unfold and appreciate the new experience. A whole new mindset for me – alien to the business and educational standards set in the West where goal-driven aims and standards of expected behaviour are drilled in from birth. The value of having no expectation of events or people is an immediate release of tension. Being alert to anything said or done out of the norm and the innate desire to say or do something to make it conform is gone. What happens happens and is of interest in its own right. Not a complete convert – kids need the benefit of parents and teachers experience – but it's a great way to relax for a while. To have a day or two off with no expectations is a bit like an internal holiday. Experience provides the platform for understanding, communication, sound decision-making but referred to blindly can provide the building blocks of prejudice and a distorted view – obstructions to the here and now, clouds that cover the sun.

Other volunteers came in to a warm greeting. Some of them were infrequent visitors to Asmara. It was good to see them. That evening a party was to be held in the VSO office. There seemed to be a collective desire to satisfy the kind of 'need for Christmas' feelings I had been having. Canadian Tim (2004 intake) and his family arrived. The coincidental parallels with Kim and his family seemed odd. Both families from Canada, each with three children (Kim's a bit older but still in the one girl, two boys ratio) all working for VSO in Eritrea in 2005. Didn't know Tim well but here was my chance to create a bit of Christmas as I knew it. His children were all under ten-years-old and immediately the Christmases with my own three children growing up in England clicked into place – I had to do something.

'Come on kids, we're decorating the room upstairs for the party.' They dashed upstairs to the meeting room and I followed them. 'Draw anything you like on the whiteboards so long as it's Christmassy' which is what they did. The annual budget for marker pens was blown by the afternoon. After the drawing the paper-chain and hat making got underway. I occupied myself by drawing a few Santas, angels and reindeer on A1 sheets. After a few hours the room was finished and it looked great. I had a walk up to the roof on my own. It was a hot day. A woman was washing clothes in her big yellow plastic bowl down below in a little compound. The view over the city looked as spectacular as ever – no change there. However – at full volume – *Silent Night* was blasting out from the cathedral. Felt odd, odd, odd.

That night the VSO office was full with volunteers and HQ staff. Good session – plenty of village-experience sharing, plenty of laughs. Yohannes auctioned off the scribbled Santas, angels and reindeer I had drawn earlier. The bidding went up to a hundred nakfa. The singers – who had gone down well at St Mary's the previous Sunday – gave us a few songs. We all caught up with each other. The food was a highlight. Dave and Janet and John and Janet had bought a feast from the Intercontinental Hotel. The volunteers' underused taste buds all came to life. Pumpkin pie – never eaten pumpkin pie in my life. Hit the spot.

The Intercontinental Hotel is the only one in Eritrea recognisable as a decent standard hotel. Very grand – big place surrounded by flagpoles. Situated on the main road to the airport it is now called Asmara Palace. I am told the government took it over and renamed it after I left Eritrea.

Eat, eat, eat pretty much sums up that Christmas Day dinner. Most volunteers had been on basic village food since September so the majority vote had been to go to the Intercontinental. 200 nakfa (2 weeks' salary for a conscript teacher), buffet-style food. Fill up your plate. Eat. Fill up your plate. Eat. And so on. Apart from the gorging the other striking feature of the meal was silence. People just ate, lost in thoughts as tastes were recollected – turkey, beef, carrots, potatoes.

And then – on the bike back to Abarda. Christmas done it was a hot, sunshine ride back to a Christmasless village to prepare for tomorrow's Boxing Day lessons.

January 2006 – I'm Going Home

As I sipped my tchai I gave up. I was going. This was not a psychological ploy to take the pressure off myself, to release some magic that would make it all better. I gave up one hundred per cent. Didn't consider what would happen next, didn't think about what had gone before, didn't care. Not a rational decision. If I went back to England I went back to England, it was finished.

Spent a while just absorbing what it felt like to quit. Not familiar with this. Even as a kid was known for never giving up, being able to get stuck in and overcome the odds. Remembered looking at other lads' faces in school cross country runs being curious about the 'I've had enough' expression on their faces. Found that I could succeed against life's opponents – even those with greater ability – by working harder, sticking at it, getting up earlier in the morning ignoring physical, mental, emotional exhaustion. Sometimes a gift – sometimes a curse. Several times throughout my career, my life, this intensity to triumph had led to a blinkered living unaware of the big picture, not considerate of the impact on others or myself.

Over the last few weeks many of my classes had become a nightmare. I had lost control. In 9.1 the intense competition between Freweini, Muna and Aster to answer my questions first became so heated it led to fist fights. In 9.2 Dawit led the unrest completely fearless having noted the absence of a stick from day 1. 9.3 – my Home Room – were fussy, uninterested. They saw my attempts at using interactive methods as playing, not real teaching. They wanted to copy off the board – that was real teaching. 9.4 had some isolated successes with students like Tsegay who responded to challenging sessions with a variety of approaches. Problem was he, Biniam and Kifle had to resite themselves at the front of the class because they couldn't hear above the noise made by the others at the back. 9.5 and 9.6 were made up of the older ones. 'Some big boys in those groups' as Kasi said. Kasi had faced verbal and physical challenges from 'big boys' in his early years at the school. Isaak stood out from the crowd. He was one of only four or five Eritreans who I met who were taller than me (I am 5' 11''). A gangly man-boy he was taken seriously by the others despite his fluorescent lime green flip-flops. Like most of the others in these two groups of older students he was not just expected to chip in on the land but to take on the lion's share of the work ploughing, feeding cattle and driving the goats. As such Isaak, and the rest, usually came to school worn out and certainly not up for a spot of maths.

Had tried everything I knew obsessing every evening alone planning, evaluating, focusing on the group and individuals. Dredged up every lesson I'd delivered in England scouring for stuff that had worked. Did a great job in grinding myself down.

Had called VSO for help, but not in those words. Spoke to Bereket but hid the truth. Not a word about the real problems I was having in the classroom. In fact, not a word about the real problems was said to anybody. Asked for a move as 'I wanted to work in and experience all parts of Eritrea.' I figured that a constructive, progressive reason sounded better than 'for God's sake get me out of here.' He came down to Mai Nefhi and we had a talk over a cup of tchai. Strange session. He had already spoken to Meles about me – apparently I was doing fine. I must be a master at concealing disaster. He emphasised the perfectly reasonable view that the continuity of the students' education would suffer if I moved on after just one semester. He did agree to look for something else once my year at Mai Nefhi was complete. This was no comfort to someone who was struggling to get to the end of a class never mind the end of the year. And here we were in early January. The possibility of getting to July with the day to day chaos was unthinkable. Surprisingly, we finished our tchai with Bereket in tears. He had far more challenges in his life than I had – and these became more apparent as the year progressed – but at the time that was no comfort to me in a rioting classroom.

I had tried to reassure myself that it wasn't just me. During December there had been two whole-school meetings. Hundreds of students sat in burning sunshine for over four hours. The teachers gathered in the meagre shade offered by the thorny trees. All the address by Meles was given in Tigrinya. I managed to grasp a couple of themes. Whole school discipline and attendance were seen as greater problems than ever before. Had I just come to Mai Nefhi at a bad time? Or perhaps I was a primary cause of the school's heightened state of unrest? Further, funding had been cut by the Education Department. To meet this shortfall all students would be expected to pay one nakfa a week to attend school. This didn't go down well. Outraged muttering all round. A nakfa is a few pennies but if your family have nothing – well.

Anyway. I finished the tchai and I'd still given up. I'm going out the gate, getting on my bike and riding to Bristol Pension in Asmara. You can keep your school, keep the stuff left in my house, just not bothered. I'll see VSO and probably be back in England by the weekend. Somebody else will have to sort the mess out – I can't. There was one more class before lunch. I'll go in, let them do what they want (which they will anyway) and get off.

What happened next was not of my doing. I put nothing into the lesson but it went ok. Not perfect – but ok. Disruption was minimal. I didn't give any instructions so none were challenged. Wrote a bit of stuff on the board and they – most of them - copied it into their books. Went for lunch and was puzzled. I was still leaving though. But perhaps I'll stay for the afternoon sessions then get on my bike this evening.

Expected the usual bedlam that afternoon but it didn't materialise. Sure there was some disruption, some students asleep at the back and noise levels that did not indicate that much learning was taking place but the lessons didn't feel like they were gleefully being kicked to death.

Didn't do any lesson planning that night. No learning objectives set, no individuals scrutinised to see how I could temper their behaviour. Wondered what had happened. I had given up – no question. That had certainly not been replaced by a determination to succeed or a flash of inspiration or a sense of great support from others. What did remain was a curiosity to see what would happen next. Wasn't going to run off – just yet. Will take things cautiously, steadily. Will write a few pages out on the board for them to copy. Will tread carefully through each minute and see what it brings rather than trying to create it, enforce it. In this manner I found myself at the end of January, the end of the first semester.

Lying in bed one night sometime near the end of that first semester I was flicking through a Bear Grylls book borrowed from the VSO office. Caught sight of the following, 'When you're at the end of your tether sometimes that can be a good place to be. That's when there's more of Him and less of you.'

When your wife walks out after thirty years a pit forms. It starts somewhere around your throat and goes down through your chest and gut. Beyond that it continues into the blackness of the earth's crust. At bad times the fog closes in. The colour drains from bright sunny days in a very literal sense. Passing cars and people become shadowy. Looking down into the pit there is nothing but blackness. The pulling ache on your internal organs is accompanied by the growling, splintering, wrenching echoes from the pit. Guttural noises from the back of something's throat join in. As time passes the pit materialises less frequently. The problem with that, of course, is that when it does start to take hold again it comes as an even greater shock.

After a difficult day at school one Friday I was cycling to Asmara wrapped in thoughts of an awkward classroom and challenging students. As I rode I sought to distract myself by reflecting on holidays taken years ago with my family in England. Newquay, Scarborough, Brighton and Llandudno were all revisited in my mind. Without warning the fog started to cloud my head and the rock against rock grinding made me look down into the pit. Stopped before I fell off and lay the bike down. Sitting on the stony ground, head between my knees I concentrated on breathing till the pit gradually closed and the sun started to shine again.

Just read what I wrote here. Doesn't come close.

Some friends in the UK collected books to send me. The final count was over 2,500 – a great effort. These, along with books I had been sent in response to a letter I'd written to the *Derbyshire Times*, were to be our library at Mai Nefhi School. Managed to acquire an old, unused classroom which we built into something that was at least waterproof. Meles donated half a dozen empty bookcases and a few tables from the staff room so we were ready to stock the shelves.

Books are no problem – many people in England have a book or two they have read and want to pass on. The postage was another matter and this gave an indication of the kind of logistical challenges that major NGOs and, I suppose, international businesses in general have to contend with. The cost of sending 2,500 books from England to Eritrea was around £2,000. Undaunted the heroes back home raised the cash with quizzes, competitions, cake baking and numerous other fundraising initiatives.

Early in 2006 I got an email telling me the books would land at 9.25pm on the last Saturday evening in January. I knew this schedule intimately living about twenty minutes from the airport and being on the flight path. At that time

I had counted seven flights into the airport over the course of each week. Not a busy destination.

On the specified Saturday evening I bought a couple of bottles of Asmara beer from Mai Nefhi Hotel and took them home. I arranged a chair outside and made myself comfortable looking up at the Milky Way – beer in hand. Right on time the plane came over the mountains with its lights flashing.

'That's my books!' Good feeling.

It took three months to get the books released from the airport. Three months. Somebody had looked inside a fly leaf and seen a price tag of £19.99. The jobsworth had then done some calculations and worked out that I had to pay £1,000 in import tax. Thanks pal. Due to the efforts of Yohannes various meetings were held – none of which I attended – and he negotiated them down to £300. Thanks to VSO who paid up.

As the bus snakes its way around the rocky landscape Keren comes into view. A striking city surrounded by the sort of cone-shaped pointy-top mountains that kids draw. Kim – who was based in Keren with his family – had climbed one of the peaks with his sons. Must have been a hot day's work. Some climb, some view. From the bus the real eye-catcher though is the electric blue dome of the Orthodox church nestling in the mountains like a shimmering, vibrant egg vivid against the dusty backdrop.

I had met Janet and Kaska that morning at the VSO office and we made our way down to the bus station. Keren was served by many 'Governmental' buses in addition to the usual privateers. Very comfortable and not very full which was a rare experience for me in Eritrea. Children came on selling their wares. 'Soft, minty, mastika!' One young lad even had a few watches.

The bus stopped for a break halfway to Keren at a little café/eating house in the mountains. Rugged countryside all the way. Sheer unfenced drops next to the road. Unusually this driver seemed cautious and gave no cause for concern. I wondered how the private bus drivers who seemed to think adrenaline should accompany their journeys negotiated this way. Had read one of the few BBC reports from Eritrea just before flying out which covered the worst road accident in the country's history – over eighty people killed on a bus which had gone over the side and crashed down the mountain.

This driver did his job though and made it to Keren where we got off in the middle of town. The bus had stopped next to a great market building across the road from what looked like a camel sale. Had only seen the one camel in Abarda being ridden in stately fashion by a black-robed traveller so this was something different. Also in contrast to Abarda – where all the women wore the traditional white zuria and netsela (dress and shawl) – the women here were dressed in all the colours of the rainbow and a few more besides. One in dazzling pink, another in daffodil yellow, the next in deep purple – don't think there was any status indicated by the different colours, at least that was the reply I got when I asked.

Morven met us at a bar/café across from Keren Hotel which dominated the central square. We ordered the best yoghurt in Eritrea – it has a reputation throughout the country. Wouldn't argue with that – knockout stuff on a hot day straight from the fridge.

Morven cried a lot at Harborne Hall on our pre-departure training – I don't really know why but it did occur that if she got so upset in Birmingham how's she going to manage in Africa. Needn't have been concerned. That evening in Morven's house as we ate, drank and talked we learned that she is actually pretty extraordinary. Her casual, off-the-cuff remarks included beating Cambridge University ladies in a rowing team, playing the violin at the Edinburgh Festival with her band (for our entertainment she played a few of her recorded numbers on the computer) and being deputy head at a school somewhere in Scotland. And here she was now in Keren working with the Ministry of Education. Not certain but don't reckon she was much more than thirty.

In my twenty-seven years with Royal Mail and prior to that with Nat West I had never met people like Morven, people who had done so much at such an early age. Initially I thought she was a one-off – people didn't live such random, varied lives. Well they did and as I got to know the other volunteers over the coming months I realised that I was the one-off in this company. Nearly all had lived and worked in many countries – China, Spain, Malawi and on and on. Many had exotic careers – theatre directors, political advisers, development workers and on and on. Their ability to speak several languages was understood and accepted and, like Morven, most were only around thirty. Also like Morven, none of them spoke about their achievements with even a hint of arrogance.

Next day saw the sights of Keren. Good place for a few days' stay. Went to the British War Cemetery. Reflected on so many of the names on the gravestones being Indian. Stood among the graves and tried to picture the battle for Keren among the surrounding mountains in the heat.

After a walk through the market we went to the Madonna in the tree. Past some orange groves which were covered in ripe fruit we saw the tree. There were no other people – let alone tourists – in sight. At some point someone had decided to hollow the tree out and carve Mary into its innards. Squeezing into the tree and standing before the figure in the cool shade it's difficult not to experience great peace. Grateful to Morven for showing us. And – the rusty spiral staircase on top of the Keren Hotel we climbed on the way back to Morven's. Now that's a wobbly affair but worth risking it for the view.

That evening played with the kids in Morven's compound. Yes I can do handstands against a wall. One of Morven's friends from the Education Office joined us for dinner. Nice meal. Afterwards Morven showed us the photos she'd taken in Eritrea so far. She was a real snapper, some emotional stuff. Poverty, malnourished kids. The sort of thing you stop taking on emotionally after a while in the country, become hardened against I suppose, but when you see it framed in soft focus and accompanied by a beer and something sentimental like *'You're Beautiful'* by James Blunt it catches you a bit.

That night was hot. I slept on the floor in one of Morven's spare rooms. Nothing in it except me and the mosquitoes. Like the camels mosquitoes didn't turn up in Abarda. Seen pictures in books but didn't realise how big they were or how loud their droning buzz was as they slowly drifted round the room legs dangling. Remembered all the malaria stuff I'd covered with Grade 10 a couple of months ago. Four different types apparently – all spread by mosquitoes – and one of them kills you. Bit restless that night. Concentrated on the anti-malarials I'd taken and nodded off.

Woke up and checked for bites. None found which surprised me as there was nothing else to chew on in the room. After breakfast we all walked down to the bus station where I said ciao. Janet and Kaska were continuing their mini-expedition catching the bus to Hagas where Rachel lived. Met up with them a few days later in Asmara where they filled me in. Hagas was seriously hot, much hotter than a pretty hot Keren, but they had a great time. Had I missed out? Possibly, but I had found a rekindled energy for the task in Mai Nefhi High School and was eager to get back to the maths and the students. The journey back to Asmara from Keren was particularly memorable in that for the first time in many weeks I felt up for it. That short break in Keren had been a turning point. Nobody else knew it just as nobody knew of the challenges in my classes which is how I wanted it. The main thing was that I knew it. I had come up for air and it was good to feel oxygen in my lungs again.

In basic terms Nigdet is like a pub-crawl without the pubs. Instead of visiting the local you visit all the houses in the village where you are welcomed and given food and drink. It is the village Saint's Day – Abarda's saint was Gabriel – a great celebration. Along with the eating and drinking there is music and dancing. All villages have their Nigdets on different days usually between December and March. Much preparation goes into this. Each villager invites friends from the other villages. Stages are prepared, musicians practise strumming their koras, banging their koboras and bowing their wartas. Men brew and filter their alcoholic sewa and even more alcoholic mes. Women cook pancake-shaped injera, spicy zigny and not so spicy chiro.

As a teacher I was fortunately placed – students issue invites and you are encouraged to join them in their homes. I was honoured to go to many Nigdets. Adi Gabri was my first.

After finishing school Kasi, Fasi, Curvilla and myself headed off to Himbirti – over an hour's walk – where we, eventually, caught a bus to Adi Gabri. I could see this village in the mountains from my home – houses looked like dots half way up the side of one of the peaks. Looked a long way. Because it was Nigdet the bus was crowded and because it was Nigdet there was a real buzz, a good atmosphere. Roads not so good up to the village; the bus ground over big humps and strained out of dusty hollows lurching right or left depending on the incline. Pulled into Adi Gabri and everyone squeezed out. Kasi led the way to our first house. One of his students, Welday, had invited us. We were welcomed in with the customary shoulder-bumping and guided to seats by Welday's parents. Tin mugs of sewa were passed round followed by plates of injera piled high with goat meat. The next course surprised me – a plastic washing up bowl full of honey. Now honey is great but this was around two kilograms to share around between the four of us. Dipping our bits of barney in we got on with it helping things along with regular swigs of sewa. Not the done thing to leave anything you'd been served. We were also aware that the honey could have been sold for two hundred nakfa which would have been a colossal amount of money for this family. We had been truly honoured and there was no way we were going to insult the family by leaving any. That was house number one

Over the course of the evening five more houses were visited. Coming from the centre of the village we could hear the constant hypnotic Tigrinya music beating out. Sewa flowed, injera and meat were eaten. Noted that beef – we were given beef in one house – tastes a lot better than goat.

The warmth was tangible. I felt very privileged to be stuck halfway up an East African mountain in a hut made of stone and wood surrounded by such generous people. A real sacrifice was being made here for our benefit but to listen to the villagers the benefit was all theirs. Down below the dancing grew more frenetic as the cobora was banged ever louder. Then, an unexpected fantastic finale. From behind us somewhere in the mountains came a low roar which escalated to thunderous proportions – it was the 10.15 flight coming in to land at Asmara airport. Looking up at the massive airliner it felt close enough to touch. Coloured lights blinking it roared overhead against the backdrop of the universe and headed straight over Himbirti, Mai Nefhi School and my house in Abarda before finally coming down to land on the airstrip about twelve miles away.

It was a long, long walk home – no buses at that time of night. Remember the Milky Way, remember Kasi whispering sharply 'don't speak any English' as we passed a group of soldiers in the dark (he was wary of drunken soldiers) and reflected that I was part of something real, not an artificial touristy thing. Felt I belonged a bit.

Carlo was angry. 'Right,' he growled as he slammed on the brakes. We were driving back from the Saturday Hash in Carlo's Toyota Land Cruiser and had diverted through a village to get back to Asmara. A small boy had thrown a stone at Carlo's headlight and he was having none of it. Jumping out of the car he strode up to the boy, grabbed him around the waist and lifted him above his head with one hand. 'Whose is this?' came the roar. Dozens of villagers swarmed around shouting at Carlo and he shouted back. They pushed and jostled him to get the boy down. Carlo pushed and jostled back. With the boy now back on the floor a full scale shouting match took place naturally – as it was Carlo – peppered with profanities. Point made to his satisfaction Carlo got back in the car and off we went. Not a good day for Eri-Hash relations.

'I'm Chinese,' Carlo had declared when I first asked him where he came from. Right from the beginning it was clear that getting anything sensible from him was unlikely. Over six foot, sixteen stone, loud, aggressive and Dutch – that was the Hash organiser. Always taking photographs. He told many stories of previous Hash experiences usually ending with a fight. Listening to others it was clear this wasn't just an image. He had been locked up on many occasions for rucks with locals in Asmara's bars and amazingly was still in the country. His own accounts always ended with him protesting his innocence – 'I wasn't the one with the knife.'

He did his research on Hash destinations during the week driving to all points of the compass within a seven-mile radius of the city. Some of the walks were spectacular. The clouds billowing up the escarpment and enveloping us was like being in a cauldron. Plains stretching away to the Simien Mountains and Ethiopia looked endless. The echoing chambers of the gorge near my home in Abarda were eerie and foreboding. If it was worth a look Carlo found it.

There were some oddly curious Hash destinations. Once we headed off over the hills to the East where I was told that a Russian transport plane had crashed years before. Sure enough after a mile or so walking there it was – bits of fuselage and lots of unrecognisable wreckage strewn over quite a distance. There were also soldiers guarding it. Off went the Hash at a smart lick led by the nervous Americans who didn't want any part of this. Like a fool I stayed behind with Waldo, an Eritrean botanist, to explain what we were doing. Thankfully Waldo calmed them down and I managed to keep my freedom.

'That's dazzling,' said Janet when we stumbled on to an outcrop of quartz at least five or six yards wide and six feet high. The talk was of how this indicated that there would be gold deposits in the vicinity and, of course, gold is mined in the country. Didn't find any on that or any other Hash though.

Freweini had been among the first to welcome me to Abarda. She ran the little village shop and I was a regular visitor, usually to buy lamba (fuel) for my stove. Ten nakfa for half a litre seemed a bit steep as it didn't last too long and I only used it to boil water for tchai. The operation pouring it through the funnel was a delicate one – not a drop spilled. Stock on the shelves in the shop was sparse. There were always Maggi stock cubes and salt but fruit supplies were variable and often bananas were sold out. Yves Saint Laurent men's underpants were an unexpected item. Persuasive salesman? Ambitious proprietor not understanding her customer base? When questioned Freweini got a bit sharp. 'Why shouldn't I sell underpants?' My brain went into overdrive seeking to negotiate a dozen or so cultural sensitivities and settled for a lame 'no reason at all Freweini – very nice.' So how they came to be there remains another of Eritrea's mysteries. Anyway – they were on the shelf the first day I went in the shop and they were still there when I left the village. They're probably still there now – no takers.

Donkeys used to congregate outside Freweini's. I think it was because when someone had bought and eaten a banana on site they threw the skin to the animals to eat. Water-carrying was the donkeys' endless task and usually for many miles. Massive, flexible rubber containers weighed heavily on their backs. A maize stalk (minus the corn) was used as a fairly inefficient stopper. Donkeys were like any other animal in Eritrea – they served a purpose or were disposed of. Unlike other animals donkeys were never eaten. In fact Eritreans are disgusted at the thought. This was the worst experience recounted on *Bana Radio* after Donard's Eritrean colleagues had returned from a trip to China. The concept of 'pet' in Eritrea was unknown. Donkeys, sheep, goats and cows satisfied a need or they went.

One of the big lads from school – Zerra – approached me as I was walking back up the road from school. 'Can you buy my cow Teacher Kevin? Not expensive.' The cow had swallowed a length of rusty wire that was mixed up with its feed and it had lodged in its throat. Despite half the village having a go at removing the wire it was stuck, well and truly dug in and the animal was suffering – I could hear it. Nobody bought the cow so it was killed and eaten – a sad and unwanted feast.

By now I had become accepted in the village and used to sit with neighbours talking about the day. I knew Dawit more intimately than most. Each morning I used to pass him standing completely naked in the cow's water trough washing himself down. 'Selam' was responded to with 'Selam' and we both carried on with our business. When Dawit was dressed he never wore shoes which was unusual in Abarda. The charity distribution service did a reasonable job here. Touching his bare feet was like touching a plank of wood. There was never any pain felt treading on sharp stones or thorns, many footprints over many years had made footwear unnecessary. I considered it must be similar to camels' mouths when they chewed on spiny cactus. I never did take up his offer to have a go at walking barefoot.

I was comfortable in the village, and also knew the surrounding area pretty well up the road to Kt Mewli which was similar to Abarda except they had a police station. Never went in but Kasi had friends there. When a big lad wanted to fight him in school his response was 'Ok, let's fight. You may win, you may lose but either way you will be reported to the police in Kt Mewli.' That was enough to make sure no fight took place.

Down the road there was always a little gang of chicalistas (puncture menders) who I got to know well as I visited them regularly with my bike. Going out of the village Mai Nefhi Hotel stands isolated on the right and to the left of the road is nothing but scrubland until you hit the school and beyond that the college. A few miles further on is Himbirti and after that the mountains.

On hot afternoons when there was no school for some reason Abarda was quiet except for an occasional radio – always the bump, bump, bump of Tigrinya music. Berbera was laid out in front of houses to dry in the sun and often supplemented with droppings from passing birds. Women washed clothes in their colourful plastic bowls about four times the size of washing up bowls seen in England. None of this went on in my house which had basically become a study where a spot of lesson planning took place. There wasn't much room for anything else. One tiny bed, my old table which by now was covered in candle wax as we had plenty of power cuts in the evenings and a rope which served as my wardrobe with a few shirts hanging on coat hangers. Next door was a toilet – well, hole in the ground and that was it, self-contained and easy to maintain.

'God must have been knocking on your head,' said the fellow bike-rider to Asmara. Used to happen quite a bit – being joined by a villager as I rode to the capital. Used to tell each other our backgrounds and the 'head-knocking' quote was his response to my explanation about why I was living and working here. Always enjoyed that journey. Never rushed it and a steady pace used to see me in the city in an hour and a half. After passing through Adi Guadad I always focused on the airfield to the left which was used by military and civil aircraft. Thought I was done for one day. The runway pointed straight at the road and the five MiGs would regularly be taking off right over my head as I passed. (There had been six MiGs in the Eritrean Air force but I was told by volunteers who'd been here a while that one had crashed into a mountain.) This particular day, with the MiG-crashing story in mind, one jet didn't seem to be lifting as it thundered towards me. I actually shouted 'pull up, pull up!' and thankfully he did. I had slightly distorted ringing in my ears for the rest of the day.

If I ever go to Asab I'll do it that way – bus there, fly back, maximise the experience. Asab is one of two Eritrean ports on the Red Sea, Massawa is the other. Serious journey to get to Asab. Well over two hundred miles from Asmara through mountains then across the Danakil Desert down the finger of land that forms the southern part of Eritrea next to Djibouti. Mel had been assigned by VSO to Asab in September but was withdrawn fairly quickly and re-sited in the capital. The tension on the border with Ethiopia was rising and she would have been right in the firing line with little chance of VSO being able to get her out safely.

Kim, Barbara and their family plus a few other volunteers had spent the semester break in Asab and I bumped into them when they got back. Sounded like they'd had quite an experience. The bus journey was long and hot – the further you go south the hotter it gets. The Danakil rivals Death Valley in America for the title of hottest place on earth and 45C+ is the norm. It's not possible to get to Asab in a day so Kim and the family slept overnight under the stars. On the edge of the desert in the open air are rows and rows of beds – take your pick. 'Where's the toilet?' asked Barbara. The bus driver responded with a wave of an outstretched arm 'you can use the whole of the desert.'

Asab itself sounded a bit like Massawa – a place crying out to be developed. Its position, on the border with Djibouti and Ethiopia, right on the mouth of the Red Sea which is virtually a highway in seafaring terms could open up north-east Africa but, then, the border is closed and hardly any ships are allowed to dock. All this is enforced by thousands of armed Eritrean soldiers. Asab is a tribute to the stagnation resulting from Isaias' No War, No Peace policy.

Although the bus journey sounds like one of those things that has to be done once in a lifetime the emphasis is on 'once' and I can understand why the volunteers opted to catch a plane back. It's not expensive and there are small aircraft that connect Asab with Asmara. Can't vouch for their airworthiness but Kim said it was fine and the flight was memorable in itself.

Charlie, Sandy and Phil joined us. They had also headed for Asab during the break and supplemented Kim's account with tales of paddling in the Red Sea under the Milky Way in the middle of the night. Topping it all they had been shot at by the soldiers and had to run for it. Apparently bullets make a whizzing noise as they approach. Getting Mel back to Asmara was probably a good move.

February 2006 – Human Tragedy

Bahgu, the nun, had her arms folded on the desk in front of her. Her head rested on her arms. I guessed her eyes were closed. She was not going to contribute to and wanted no part of the chaotic class in which she found herself. At that point I knew I had to take the final step and for her sake if nothing else I was determined to see it through.

Since the semester break in Asmara and particularly Keren I had regained a little perspective, had recovered to the point that my feet felt they were at least on the ground if not striding determinedly forward. A measure of control had been exerted in the classroom partly by my improving Tigrinya. By no means could I converse but I had practised basic phrases I could use in the classroom. Cof bel (sit down), segum yelen (no problem) were key. I had noticed that when invited to dinner at an Eritrean household protestations and excuses in English were ignored. Even when there was a pressing meeting elsewhere or a bus to catch, the exhortation to join the family for a meal was impossible to refuse. Mixed in with this was the care not to offend by turning down a generous offer. However, the word 'programme' had been taken on as part of the language. 'Thank you very much but I have a programme' carried weight and was usually respected. Similarly 'sit down' in the classroom did not register (irrespective of volume) but 'cof bel' did. Using Tigrinya to call the register – hade, kelete, celeste instead of one, two, three actually drew applause when I first tried it. Now that hit the spot.

More importantly I had tempered the gung-ho approach to teaching. The interactive methods encouraging whole class discussion, students being given the chalk to write on the board – attempts for them to construct their own knowledge rather than me pouring it into them like water into a jug – were reined in and talk and chalk, usually without the talk, dominated. It had been unrealistic for me to expect students to embrace a form of teaching which they had never encountered before without its inherent freestyle being seen as 'not real teaching' and weakness on my part. Over the coming months I planned to use chalk and copy when I felt the need to regain some control while letting out bits and pieces of a partnership, interactive methodology in a progressive manner – the rate determined by how quickly the class 'got it.'

They certainly hadn't 'got it' in this lesson when Bahgu had had enough and withdrawn from the proceedings. With her head down on the desk she might have been praying, or sleeping or dead for all I knew. I did notice drops of water on the desk which I took for tears. I had taken on the language issues and teaching technique with some success but I had shied away from the discipline problems because I had witnessed that the only disciplinary measures that had been administered in their school lives and at home involved beating, slapping, punching or kicking. Usually I didn't know what the misdemeanour was due to my inability to gain any real proficiency in the language. Many times I would see a teacher, most often Meles, walk up to a student (girl or boy didn't make any difference) and scream a tirade of

Tigrinya at them. This was followed by a punch to the stomach or a slap across the face. If they went down a kick or kicks often followed.

I was never going to touch a student myself. Never. Maybe it might have been understandable if I had having attended a school in the Sixties and early Seventies where sticks and slippers were regularly used on backsides and across palms. I even remember once being 'officially' caned by the Head Teacher. The act was made 'official' by being logged in a big book and was therefore seen as different to the random beatings. It didn't feel any different. Worked out a plan – I needed an example and I somehow suspended my revulsion at what I was about to do.

Awet was a big lad who clearly did his stint on the land with the plough. He was a ringleader, a source of trouble in the classroom. For the first time I had decided to involve other teachers in the challenge I was facing and knew it was likely to end in pain for Awet. That morning I went into class without a word and wrote on the board in big letters: RABASHI TO MELES. Rabashi meant nuisance, trouble causer. They all knew what Meles meant.

Started the lesson and within minutes Awet was on his feet shouting across the room to another lad. 'Cof bel' had no effect. A second order was ignored, no effect. Approached him, pointed to the staffroom and said firmly 'Meles'. Awet looked at me as did the whole class. Three days went by – at least it felt like three days – before

Awet grinned. That was enough for me, I gripped his arm and moved him out the door and we were marching to the staffroom. I later learned from the Indian teachers that all the classes they were taking – and probably all the Eritrean teachers classes – stopped. The students were transfixed. 'What is no-stick Teacher Kevin doing?' During the 100-yard walk to the staffroom Awet made two attempts to struggle free and he nearly, but not quite, succeeded. I intended to shove Awet straight into Meles' office and let events take their course. We didn't get that far. As we approached the staff room Futsom and Solomon came out. They completely ignored me and 'got in Awet's face' forehead to forehead, treading on his toes and growling viciously in Tigrinya – the spit spraying Awet's face. Awet started to shake, tears ran down his cheeks and his legs collapsed beneath him. There was no kicking which surprised me. After a few more minutes of fearful language from the two teachers Awet was left slumped on the ground. Orders must have been given because he didn't move for more than an hour.

I am neither proud nor ashamed of what I did. I offer no excuses. Awet could easily have been given a severe beating and I anticipated that this is what would happen. I was told later in the day that Meles was in Asmara. The probability of the beating would surely have increased if he had been in school. Or would it? Wondered many times after why Futsum and Solomon didn't use the kind of physical violence they used regularly in their own classrooms or outside in the compound. Was it my involvement – not in a creditworthy way – that stopped them? Maybe they didn't want to hurt one of 'their own' on behalf of a foreigner. Don't know. Do know that having witnessed the incident maintaining discipline in my classes became less and less of an issue, teaching and learning became possible and Bahgu stopped crying on the desk.

Knew something was up the moment Meles broke his barked address to the assembled students and headed to his office. It was late February 2006 and to that point the day had started the same as all the others. Clear blue sky, bike ride to school, shouted 'kemays' along the way. Stood with Meles, Kasi and Fasi watching the students pile through the gate, Meles blasting on his referee's whistle every now and then. Students formed their usual rows and columns in front of the flag. Teachers adopted their usual positions, me at my top left corner where I could keep an eye on my Home Room students. Remember seeing an airliner high above which must have been late – or early? – having taken off from Asmara airport. One student, Elsa, noticed it too and grinning looked at me with a little wave and said 'bye-bye Teacher Kevin.' Could have read all kinds of meaning into that but didn't bother. Put my index finger to my lips – 'quiet Elsa.'

With Meles' disappearance into the staffroom it wasn't just me who thought something was up. The Indian teachers responded with a shrug when I glanced sideways. They were in the dark as much as me. Low murmurings among the crowded students, teachers tightening grips on sticks all round.

The speaker crackled over the compound – Meles' voice emphasising every word. The murmuring grew among students and teachers alike. A couple of muffled wails. Where expressions had been relaxed they were now tense.

'What's he saying?' I asked Kasi.

'Eritrea needs more soldiers – they're going to take them to Sawa.'

Sawa is the biggest military training camp in the country. Every young Eritrean goes there or to one of the other training camps for an indefinite period of time. *Eri-TV* often shows the parades at Sawa and Isaias addressing the thousands of battle-dressed recruits. Helen Meles' gigs for the troops are also broadcast – *everyone* dancing and clapping and singing along for the cameras.

I had heard many stories about the brutality of Sawa where beatings, kickings, solitary confinement and all kinds of unimaginable torture was commonplace. Mehawi was particularly descriptive. Before receiving his posting as a teacher to Mai Nefhi the previous year he had been in Sawa. His stories of abuse and torment were all about 'getting his thinking right' and 'making a man' of him. Some real imagination in the techniques used – the perpetrators clearly enjoyed coming up with new methods. Mehawi particularly remembered some misdemeanour being punished by a 'water carrying exercise'. He was ordered to empty a large tank of water into another tank twenty yards distant using a Coke bottle top. It took him four days with only snatched bouts of sleep – he recalled it clearly. On completing the task he was told he had misheard and should not have emptied the tank. The next four days were spent putting the water back again with the bottle top. After that he quite appreciated being confined in a cell. Last email I got from Mehawi he was in Angola probably wearing the Arsenal shirt I sent him. A couple of years after I left Eritrea he had done it – crossed the border.

Meles' announcement was echoed throughout high schools in Eritrea. Kasi wasn't quite accurate in his interpretation – only students who 'looked' 18 were going. No good looking for non-existent birth certificates. The soldiers were coming to take them in three days. During those days I was approached several times by desperate students usually with crazy requests like 'please give me your visa' or 'get me over the border Teacher Kevin.' Their lives were being diverted down paths they did not choose. There was no alternative. They would not live where they chose, they would work all their lives where they were told to work doing what they were told to do. Some soldiers who have served time at Sawa are told they are going to be teachers. Their names are put in a pot and chosen at random for placement. Being near to your family is not a consideration. Actually it is in the negative sense – separation from families is deliberate to promote loyalty to the State not your parents and siblings.

The Indian teachers were concerned what this meant for them – so was I. The need for more troops signalled heightened tension at the border with Ethiopia. Kasi would seek me out early morning to see if anything had been broadcast on the BBC. It did make uneasy listening when the Eritrean government ordered the UN helicopters to be grounded along the border. 'How are we supposed to do a surveillance job without helicopters?' seemed to be the response.

Three days after the announcement five buses turned up at the gates of Mai Nefhi High School. Students were ushered on them . . . It was a fairly quiet exercise. Soldiers with Kalashnikovs, mothers in tears, fathers stoical.

Samuel, a big lad, asked for my phone number. I gave him VSO's and said goodbye. He was emotional. I tried to reassure and encourage him. 'Work hard, be strong, look after those who are not as strong as you' and – moving into lies – 'I will see you when you get back, I'll be here, I'm not going anywhere.' It felt that the need to offer him comfort at that moment was more important than the need for me to be honest.

That weekend volunteers were buzzing with the events of the week. The Keren volunteers said there had been a few small violent protests which had been crushed. Similar stories from Dekamhare. No protests in Mai Nefhi, violent or otherwise – perhaps a bit more accepting in the villages.

March 2006 – More Human Tragedy

A brick wall had been sighted as far back as October and I was heading straight for it. With no syllabus the only point of reference I had for anything that looked like structured teaching was the dog-eared maths book Meles had given me. Nor was this a helpful text with some A-level topics mixed in randomly with the kind of material taught to thirteen-year-olds in the UK. This wasn't a great problem as I reorganised the subjects myself. Nobody was looking over my shoulder to say this had to be taught to a certain timetable. No, the brick wall came into view as I realised that the material I was to teach would run out about three months before the end of the school year. Meles and Andi offered little – 'start at the beginning of the book again.' Didn't bother asking Ambes. In his usual alcohol-influenced state I don't think the question would have registered. In truth a problem which would have been seen as catastrophic in England wasn't that major in the scheme of things out here.

Wanted to do a good job with the teaching though. Big deal for me. Wasn't here to get stuck into the country's economic, health or political challenges but did feel I could chip in a bit on the education front. In particular I wanted to get all my students through the national exams and more importantly plant some seeds in young folks along the lines of 'there's something in this maths other than copying off the board.' If that connection, that buzz could be felt by even one student I knew that could lead to greater things. I knew it because I'd got the buzz from maths at school and without that initial spark which led to the necessary qualification I would not have even got to the VSO interview never mind on the plane to Eritrea.

So in March I ran out of stuff to teach. I should have addressed this earlier but the demands of class management and Eritrean life generally had taken my time. I sat in the British Council library one Saturday morning determined to sort it. As I looked through the window I watched two eagles circling above. Next to me a young lad was watching a video about *Changing the Guard* at Buckingham Palace. The sound of a heated discussion could be heard downstairs. My bits of Tigrinya enabled me to pick out certain words and what I imagined was the gist of the exchange. Lots of distracting stuff and I was still like a kid fascinated by incidents that were nothing to the locals but served as a constant reminder that 'Wow – I'm living and working in East Africa.'

In my mental wanderings I recalled a telephone conversation with a teacher before I had flown out. VSO give you a few names of people who have just completed their stint overseas, the idea being to give them a ring to get a flavour of VSO work – key points and tips from someone who'd been there and done it. The character I contacted had just got back from Ethiopia and was completely relaxed about the whole thing. Had spent most evenings after school in the bar chatting with locals. Missed classes in school, missed days in school when he felt like seeing the sights or going for a bike ride and saw the placement as a 'bit of a break.' He had never been to Eritrea. I had no intention of going down this easy-going route – the work-ethic was far too ingrained – but did appreciate having the casual approach to reflect on. Decided to make my own mini-syllabus based on my knowledge of the UK system and using the GCSE and A-level books I'd brought out with me. Integrated topics with what I'd already taught and left the British Council feeling pretty good about things, the brick wall had been crashed through.

Mulu spoke quietly and in a measured tone, there was no emotion, no drama. A broken life recalled in an unbroken flow. Her Tigrinya was interpreted into English by another sister – her voice matching Mulu's in volume and intonation. Mulu had seen her father, mother and brother killed in the conflict and together with her sisters, had been raped. Pain on top of pain on top of pain. Tell her you've got a problem paying your gas bill. Mulu had joined the Catholic Church and was training to be a nun.

I was pleased to accept Kasi's invitation to walk to the Catholica in Himbirti one Sunday afternoon. I particularly wanted to meet Mulu and Sinait who were both in my Home Room. Every morning the Head Sister at the Catholica drove them to school along with four or five other school-attending nuns. Other than the buses their Land Cruiser was the only vehicle I regularly saw on the road in Mai Nefhi. They were the only people who were driven to school. Mulu and Sinait hardly spoke in the classroom. When I tried to bring them into a discussion or asked them a direct question they would answer shyly or just smile. At break all the nuns congregated together and were very visible in their pristine navy and light blue uniforms in a sea of grubby green-jumpered students.

It was a good walk that day – hot and dry as usual. It was about four miles to Himbirti from Abarda. Long stretch down the shimmering road past my empty Sunday afternoon school, the sprawling college and the three peaks which rose out of the plain. 'There are shiftas (bandits) in the mountains,' Amanuel had told me one day. Kasi couldn't confirm this but if you could imagine a place where bandits might live that looked like it would fit the bill. Didn't see one car, bus or human being on the road that afternoon – a totally inactive landscape except for one twister. The dust-devils were a fairly common sight in this area. About twelve feet high the show-offs among the students used to jump through them as they weaved their way crazily across the school compound. Out the other side the lads were covered in dust – they were dishevelled before they had jumped in so not much changed there. The twister we saw that afternoon was no dust-devil – must have been 150, maybe 200 feet, high – a thin, wiggly column that thankfully kept its distance. Try jumping into that and you might end up in Sudan.

Got to the outskirts of Himbirti. Usual white, box-shaped houses and shops. One or two kids about but otherwise no signs of life. Mad dogs and Englishmen (and an Indian) etc. Made our way up to the Catholica which overlooked the village. White compound walls and grey steel door which we banged on a few times. After a couple of minutes a Sister opened up and after the cheek to cheek greeting we followed her through the large compound to a small, cool, ice-blue painted room where we sat down. A few pictures were on the walls of Catholic dignitaries and another of the Good Samaritan. While we sat recovering from the walk Kasi told me he had been here several times over the years particularly during his first year when he had found the going a bit difficult.

After ten minutes Merhawit came in with Mulu and Sinait. I was pleased to see them and they seemed pleased to see me. They poured us a glass of red wine – this was a different place to the usual village visits.

The Sisters talked about their work which centred around helping villagers in difficulty. They took on household jobs such as washing clothes, cleaning and cooking when people were too sick to look after themselves. Don't know if they actually supported families financially – didn't ask. Did ask how Mulu and Sinait arrived here and that prompted Mulu's horrific account about her family. Sinait had a similar story. Seemed to me that they had to take on this life of sacrifice and servitude to orientate all their faculties outward to others. What hope could there be if the focus was inward where the sights and sounds of your witnessed experience was unimaginably gruesome?

That afternoon we learned that the Catholica was to have another visitor – the head of the Eritrean Catholic Church who was coming over from Asmara – and he had just arrived. He was greeted warmly by the Sisters and us and we all sat down in a large circle under the compound trees. Our existence was briefly acknowledged and briefly discussed but the focus of the attention was the Cardinal and the business he had come to discuss whatever that was. After an hour or so we made our move. Before we left, however, Mulu took us to a small chapel in the compound. Tiny door, inside were seats for maybe fifteen people – a church in miniature with small stained glass windows. Naturally there was a blessed, peaceful atmosphere. 'Beautiful,' breathed Kasi. I was a bit distracted by the fairy lights around the altar. Yes, fairy lights. These were of the musical variety and an electronic version of *'Rudolph the Red-Nosed Reindeer'* was struggling to get to the end of a verse despite a dying battery and a few non-functioning notes. Nobody in Himbirti would have any inclination of what a reindeer was or that this tune was not really Christian or that it wasn't customary to be played on a hot day in March or that maybe this decoration might not be appropriate in this setting. So what? This had been a memorable afternoon for all kinds of emotion-twisting reasons spent with memorable people. Nice setting, pleasantries exchanged, horror recalled. An overwhelming awareness that life just goes on no matter what. People behaving 'normally' when their experience is anything but.

On the walk back to Abarda I wondered if becoming a servant of the Church and the community had been a conscious decision on Mulu's part or if it had just happened. It didn't have to be that way, both Mulu and Sinait could have picked up guns as many other Eritrean girls did. During later conversations Mulu told me that she had been taken in by nuns while still a small girl and that clearly had shaped her future, pointed her down a certain path. She was a product of her environment. 'What if you had been taken in by a family of fighters?' No reply, but I just caught the wince that said 'enough questions.' My inquiries were causing pain and had gone on too long.

Mai Nefhi Hotel was a sanctuary for me. During the first few months in Eritrea it was a welcome refuge where I could either evaluate and assess the challenges of the country and the classroom or, if I was exhausted by the day's events, I could let the brain wander where it wanted – pure escapism.

It was a beautiful place in an Eritrean sort of way. You could see it from the road between Abarda and the school – about twenty minutes' walk from my home. The surrounding landscape was harsh and stony – grey, sun-bleached stones – and rough thorny bits of scrub. The building stood alone block-shaped, stark, softened on one side by a few eucalyptus trees and a row of bushes. These were populated by what seemed like thousands of crickets. As the sun went down the rhythmic insect volume went up to piercing levels. Someone had made an effort at the back of the hotel. A nice sun terrace and a couple of wooden shelters that overlooked the spectacular Mai Nefhi Dam.

Two big dams supplied water to Asmara – one to the north and Mai Nefhi to the south. Used to think that living a stone's throw from two highly strategic targets – the dam and the airport – I was not best placed if the

Ethiopians invaded. The hotel grounds led straight to the dam wall towering perhaps three hundred feet above the water. While the girls were cooking my nightly pasta I usually took two strolls. One went along the dam wall to the other side and back. There was only a flimsy fence between me and the sheer drop to the water. The second went down the steps to the small waves lapping at the cliff sides. This provided me with a factual awareness of the country's water supply as the steps were marked in metre levels showing the depth. In September 2005 the level showed at twenty six metres. By June 2006 it had decreased to eighteen metres. With my regular walks I watched each metre down as the months went by. Kept me occupied while I waited for the pasta.

Never saw many people at the hotel but those I did see left an impression. The first time I talked to Mai Nefhi College students was sitting on the sun terrace one Sunday evening. They had been teasing the handyman's muscular pet baboon which was tethered by a chain to a not-very-secure stake. Nasty looking creature – all teeth and fleas. Often saw it throttling itself with the chain as it contorted its body trying in vain attempts, thankfully, to escape. The three students were surprisingly open with me. They had jumped over the college wall to come for a beer at the hotel. Genuine risk, if they had been caught beatings, imprisonment and even torture would follow. They asked about England, they talked of getting out of the country, they had absolutely no idea why I should have come to Eritrea. During the school days I often saw students from the college making a break for it running across the school grounds. They were usually caught as they tried to scale the high wall on the other side of the compound. The guards would grab a flailing leg and drag them back. Once on the floor the usual treatment was a stamping. The captives would then lie face down in the stones often with a boot at the back of the head not daring to move.

Occasionally older teenagers would come to the hotel. One evening I was sat on the top step leading down to the water. I had said 'hi' to two young couples who were chatting together in one of the shelters. After a few minutes admiring the view one of the girls came over and sat down on the other side of the bush next to me. Had a little natter. 'Do you come here often?' sort of stuff before she stood up and straightened her clothes. Hadn't realised she'd been urinating in a crouched position. Casual eh? Could have been worse. At induction we were told that you could tell a woman from the Rashaida tribe as they urinated standing up.

Some evenings I was too exhausted to walk down the steps to the water. Had visions of me being stuck at the bottom not having the strength to get back up. Needed the break this place offered. Remembered music used to play in my head as I walked slowly across the top of the dam wall. For some reason 'Electrolyte' by REM was a recurring melody.

Another slightly unreal mental state surfaced when I used to think about sport. I was in real 'for God's sake fill your brain with something nice to help forget the strain of the day' mode. Used to miss sport while I was in Eritrea. Not just the events themselves but the structure sport gives the year. Special occasions to anticipate: Six Nations Rugby in January followed by the start of Flat Horse Racing then Boat Race and Grand National. Then moving well into spring with the FA Cup Final and then summer with Wimbledon, British Grand Prix and Open Golf. Football starting again in August and so on. Was going through one of these mental ramblings one evening when I realised it was the second Thursday in March – Cheltenham Gold Cup day. Then thought 'I've missed the big race.' Then thought 'no I haven't, there's a three-hour time difference – the race is probably underway at this minute and I'm stood here on Mai Nefhi Dam in East Africa.' Weird stuff. Got to watch myself.

The soldiers stopped me walking across the dam wall. A camp was set up in March. They were a friendly crew always up for Premier League football banter. They probably wondered about me. 'Why does he walk down all those steps every evening to look at the water? What's so interesting about the dam?' In the end they put a makeshift barricade made of dry grey branches at the start of the wall. Standing in front of the barricade I looked across to three soldiers who were staring at me, waiting for a reaction. Silently, in my mind, I asked 'Why?'

Silently, in their minds, they replied, 'Because we wanted to.'

As the school year progressed and things were starting to move in the right direction I used to see the hotel as more of a meeting place rather than a refuge. Had one or two encounters that made an impact.

Big fat bloke staggered over to me as I was finishing my Asmara beer on the hotel terrace. Bloodshot eyes, slurring – drunk. 'I'm Hagos.' He talked a lot about the conflict and particularly about battles around Mendefera. I pricked my ears – my next placement was going to be Mendefera and I'd never been there. Might learn something. As it turned out if I'd wanted to defend Mendefera against the Ethiopian Army I was in good company. I learned all about the high ground which offered views across the plain and, thus, early sight of advancing troops. Got an overview of the wooded areas which offered cover and on which routes to expect tanks. After an hour made my excuses and left. Described the conversation to Donard the following weekend.

'You've met Hagos the Tapeworm,' said Donard.

'Hagos the what?'

'Tapeworm – the Ethiopians called him that because they couldn't shift him when they attacked Mendefera.'

Hagos was apparently well known in Asmara. He had been an officer in the conflict and was renowned for his defence of the towns in the south of the country. It was clearly nothing special to have sat in a bar listening to him reminiscing about his heroic exploits. This was his nightly pastime and anyone in earshot was fair game.

I came to realise that Mai Nefhi Hotel was a kind of bolthole for dignitaries who wanted to meet up but didn't want the attention they might attract in Asmara. Off for the walk down the steps one evening I was confronted by the biggest Afro hair I'd ever seen. The owner wore shiny robes – dark green with golden swirling patterns. He seemed to know something about me as he greeted me with 'Once we were enemies – now we are friends!' I responded with 'Yes mate, good to be friends,' thinking 'who the hell are you?' Turned out he was a Libyan politician who talked as if he was close to Gadhafi. The Tamoil petrol stations in Asmara were the evidence of trade between the two countries and he was here to tie up a deal with the Eritrean government. Friendly chap.

The chattering and giggling could be heard a long time before the origin of the chattering and giggling came into view. Bright sing-song tones – uplifting. I had just finished my pasta at Mai Nefhi Hotel and as there was nobody around to talk to save a few soldiers over in their camp I started reading the *Guardian Weekly* I'd picked up the previous weekend in Asmara. The sound of the voices carried a long way across the barren landscape and I looked up from the newspaper to see three walking trees on the near-horizon. As the trees approached over the brow it became clear it was three girls carrying sticks on their backs for their families' fires. The sticks were long and grey and were arranged vertically on their backs so that they towered high above their heads. In many areas I had seen sticks carried horizontally across backs. Not a stick-carrier myself so wouldn't know which method to recommend.

The girls stopped in front of me and one said, 'How are you?' in steady, clear, over-pronounced English before they, and I, burst out laughing. I guess they were about eleven or twelve dressed in long, colourful, flower-print skirts with bandana-type scarves tied over their hair. For about ten minutes they gabbled in Tigrinya with a few bits of English thrown in for my benefit. I responded by gabbling in English with a few bits of Tigrinya thrown in to show I was making an effort. Talked about our families, school and villages – day-to-day stuff.

With cheerful bye-byes said they left as they had come – chattering and giggling. In the midst of poverty and deprivation with an uncertain future it was joyful to witness the complete uncrushability of the human spirit and how it had been given a voice in the simple words and demeanour of the three friends. Nothing out of the ordinary had been said, nothing out of the ordinary had been done. In these circumstances that's what felt extraordinary.

Children died in Abarda. UN figures show that getting to five is an achievement in Eritrea. That morning I had come out of the gate of my compound to go to see Freweini in the village shop. Looking up the dusty track I could see across the tarmac road which split the village in two. On the other side was a large expanse of flat ground about the size of a football field which had a few small trees dotted here and there offering little shady spots. Overlooking this area was the Orthodox church which was ornate and imposing. Dotted around the wide expanse of dusty, barren earth, some under cover of the trees – some standing in the full sunlight, were groups of three or four women chanting quietly or standing silently in prayer. Tewelde, a student in one of my classes, had died earlier that week – this sacred scene marked one of the stages up to his burial. Didn't take that photograph. About as sad it gets.

Struggled coming to terms with the villagers' resigned approach to sickness and death in the beginning. The diagnosis part of the medical process seems to be missing or distorted. The most common response I used to get to the question 'what did they die of?' was 'Nefas (the wind) changed direction that night.'

In my part of Eritrea the practice when someone dies was to pay a visit to the family home. Nothing is said but men are greeted with the customary shoulder-bumping handshake and women with the cheek to cheek kiss. You then sit quietly for fifteen to thirty minutes before leaving – a silent, respectful tribute. Did this too many times.

The Indian teachers had started speaking in Hindi in the staffroom – always a bad sign. At lunchtime there were some angry looks exchanged and a bit of squaring up in a doorway between Kasi and Aman. Meles got involved and after a couple of behind-closed-doors meetings an uneasy calm was restored. On the walk back home that evening Kasi told me that some of the young Eritrean teachers and even some of the older students had been making suggestive comments about Madam Latha's bare midriff. She always taught in traditional Indian dress – brightly coloured, flowing satin with beautiful embroidery. Stood out a mile from the traditional all-white simple Eritrean zuria. Today's costume was a bit more revealing and had drawn unwanted attention. Not a serious episode but it was typical of the little clashes that happened fairly regularly. Good thing was that next day all seemed fine – Madam Latha covered up a bit and everybody got on with it.

I, along with all the other teachers, was given a voucher for a gas canister which could be used for cooking. By now I had totally abandoned any ideas of creating culinary masterpieces so I kept it simple and gave the voucher to Kasi. I'd done this with my UN ration card. I had actually stood in the queue in Asmara the first time and picked up my cooking oil, salt, pasta and a few other items. After staring at them for a few minutes and deciding I didn't really want to fill the house with lamba smoke I went off to Mai Nefhi Hotel. Cooking? Forget that.

Used to wonder about the Kasi-Ruta relationship. Kasi looked worried as we took our regular lunchtime walk out of the school gates and down the road past the college. His wife, who he had not seen for years was coming to Eritrea to visit. Over the next few weeks he tried everything he could think of to stop her but to no avail – she was due to land at Asmara airport on Saturday. Ruta, the maid, slept in Kasi's room sometimes when I was visiting. She had her own single bed on the opposite wall from Kasi's. The day before Kasi's wife landed, Ruta moved out. The day after Kasi's wife flew back to India she moved back in.

You could get a decent game at the bowling alley in Asmara. Just up from Barti Meskerem Square the facilities were okay. Janet's sister had come to Eritrea with her husband and we all went for a game. Didn't do badly but Kim took the honours – reckon he'd been practising. Highlight of the evening was not the contest but the pin-replacement gang. Nothing automated so a group of lads sat above the pins with little legs dangling. As soon as the second bowl struck down they jumped and feverishly scurried around restacking the pins before climbing back on their perch. Worth the entrance fee just to see them.

April 2006 – Getting to Grips

Always found this story difficult to tell. Just as difficult now as when I told Joe, Barbara and Carlo a few weeks after it had happened.

Meles used extreme violence to maintain order in Mai Nefhi High School – I witnessed this on many occasions. Big lads much taller than him literally cowered in his presence or ran and tried to scale the walls of the compound before he could catch them. His aura was actually enhanced by the fact that his physical size was unimpressive. To see a short, ten stone wizened old man growling down at a strong eighteen-year-old lad writhing on the floor at his feet was more disturbing than if he had been a hulk.

Perhaps the secret was his cold demeanour. His violence was of the snarling kind but also clinical and calculated. He knew how to hurt and dispatch most effectively usually without leaving a mark. He demonstrated this strange attribute one morning during a conversation with me about what he had eaten for breakfast. An ailing, diseased mouse struggled slowly towards us on the floor of the classroom – don't know what it was suffering from. With no more than a glance and without breaking the flow of his speech he carefully cracked its skull with his foot. After another five minutes' chat he went about his duties without any reference to the incident. Then again – as a 'party man' – perhaps the real reason for his power lay in the fact that he could call in the soldiers at any time and the students knew it.

This particular day, after the anthem, I went into 9.6 – the big boys – to teach. The atmosphere was different, quieter and I noticed a lot of papers ripped up and strewn on the floor under the desks. After a few minutes the Deputy Head – Biniam – strode into the classroom. He was a short man but very loud. Ignoring me he started to address the class in sharp-toned Tigrinya. I only witnessed what happened next just the once during my time in Eritrea. The students started to answer back. Loudly. I had no idea what this was about but I did know that this would have consequences. The Deputy walked out.

Asked Guosh what was happening. She explained that a window had been broken in the room the previous day and the Deputy Head had been to tell them to bring one nakfa each to pay for a replacement. They were outraged as another student from a different class had broken it from outside and this had led to the protest.

The next morning at the same time, again a few minutes into the lesson with 9.6, Meles walked into the room. Not a word was said. Clicking his fingers he motioned to the door. In silence the forty or so students filed out and knelt on the stony ground straight-backed, shins and bottom touching the ground, thighs uppermost. Futsom and Andi led me away in the direction of the staff room. Meles started at one end of the line. With all his strength he stamped his heel down on the thigh of the first boy who keeled over in agony. Maximum pain, minimum observable injury. The lower leg served as a cushion to reduce the chance of the thigh bone being broken. This was a callous attack. Then the second. Then the third. The first girl was fifth in line. By the time Meles got to her she was sobbing so much he punched her in the face. At this point some of the students further down the line were wailing and two boys in the middle made a run for the wall. Immediately Meles, Futsum and Andi were after them. I went to the kneeling students. 'What can we do about this Teacher Kevin?' said Habtom. 'Don't answer

that Teacher Kevin – you have done nothing wrong,'
shouted Tsegay. But I had.

I had witnessed this act and done nothing to stop it. Okay,
later I discussed it in the staffroom trying to persuade, to
influence to say this is not right. In my house in Abarda
alone I rationalised knowing that if I had stepped in and
grabbed Meles I would definitely have been kicked out of
Mai Nefhi and possibly on the next plane out of Eritrea.
There is also the weird possibility that if I had attacked
Meles the students would have protected him by
attacking me such was the indoctrination, the acceptance
of violence as a means of control. 'Teacher Kevin – have
this stick so you can beat us.'

No more excuses – I should have decked him.

I had told this story over dinner to Joe and Barbara at
their house one Saturday night after a Hash. Carlo was
there too. There was a genuine interest in volunteers'
stories as this was the closest they came to life in the
villages and the schools not being able to get out of
Asmara themselves. Quite often my stories, like this one,
shocked too much – not really suitable after a nice dinner
over a glass of red wine. Bit too graphic, too painful, too
real.

Carrying a big stone into class I kicked off with . . .

'Question – what's the most famous equation in the world?'

Blank looks – what's the crazy white teacher going on about now?

Undeterred, 'Come on – what's the most famous equation in the world?'

Tsegay was one of the earliest to get this approach. Students contributing in class, playing an interactive role, building their own education didn't feel right for most students. How could it? Copy off the board at school, plough the field when I tell you at home, pick up that gun when you become a soldier. Tsegay did his usual thing of getting out of his seat near the back and taking up a position on the front central seat about three feet in front of me. The wonderful thing that happened as the year progressed was that the numbers doing this increased until it wasn't necessary as all were paying attention. Tsegay's eyes were fixed on me. After a bit more cajoling it was pleasing to get a few responses.

'Pythagoras?'

'$y=mx + b$?'

'Sine = Opposite over Hypotenuse?'

'Thanks for that but what about $e = mc^2$?'

The discussion built around Einstein, and generating power and nuclear bombs leading to my prompt 'What's energy?' Blank looks again. 'That's what we get when we eat injera,' said Freweini. Good to see the girls chipping in just as much as the boys.

'True – that's a good example, but what kind of brain takes energy and mass and throws in 'c', the speed of light, to come up with an equation that can calculate the amount of energy?'

Tsegay – 'That must be a genius.'

Me – 'Yup'

Back to the stone I had brought in. 'Ok then – how much energy in this stone?' Tsegay, Rigbe and quite a few others estimated its mass then scribbled furiously, 'Nine billion joules.'

'That's a big number. So, you're telling me there's enough energy in this stone to light Asmara for a few months – years then? We'd better get down to Isaias Afewerki's house and tell him we've solved the energy crisis.'

Further discussion about the dangers associated with extracting energy – perhaps getting nine billion joules of energy out of a stone wasn't that easy after all.

This is why teachers teach and in this country, any country, you hope that one day the ones who question and use their brains overcome the ones who accept and see their guns as a solution. Asking the right questions is usually more important than finding the answers.

On another day I saw Getachew, Zera and Hailezghi doing calculations near the flagpole during break and realised that they were replicating something we had done in class. They were estimating the height of the pole using the measured length of its, and their, shadows and applying a bit of maths ratio. (There had been an odd coincidence the day before when I had taught this to my classes. My opening line – after I'd took the class out into the compound – was going to be 'Now then, we can't climb the flagpole as it's too high but how can we use maths to estimate its height?' That very morning during the anthem the flag snagged as it was being raised – the one and only time this ever happened. Meles called for a volunteer and one kid was up the pole in about five seconds to free it. Typical.) Anyway, it was good to see students actively doing a spot of maths and using their own initiative. 'Could we use this to measure the height of St Mary's Cathedral in Asmara, Teacher Kevin?' 'Of course,' I replied. Afterwards, imagining them dodging the traffic on Harnet Avenue to measure the cathedral's shadow, I thought my response should have been a bit more cautious.

At last, my lessons had started to look like lessons. I had regained perspective, tackled the disciplinary issues that had gone on for too long, recognised the need to adjust my pronunciation and intonation and, critically, had started to build an appropriate relationship in the classroom. Respect for the subject, environment and each other was growing and the marriage of syllabus and students was taking place. None of this could have happened without the realisation that the first thing to manage in the classroom – perhaps in any situation – is yourself.

It's no good me pretending that model lessons were the norm – they weren't. The challenges faced by every teacher in every country featured every day but a level of normality had been achieved if you can call lessons being buzzed by low-flying MiGs and the occasional goat popping in to scatter its droppings on the floor normal. The times I stood at the back of the grimy classroom late in the school year scanning students quietly at work before glancing out of the window across the compound and beyond that to the mountains were special moments. Sometimes it's not necessary for a bit of success to be accompanied by fireworks.

'There's no meat in this,' said Janet as she ate her pasta in Mai Nefhi Hotel. Don't know why but I was a bit indignant. 'Yes there is.' Kaska joined in supporting Janet. 'Trust us – there's no meat in this sauce.'

'Really – no meat?'

This revelation had completely undermined my dietary programme. Janet and Kaska – along with every volunteer except me – had become fairly accomplished at cooking, sampling the different meat, vegetables and spices the country had to offer and producing meals that not only kept them fed but tasted pretty good. Unfortunately I needed a tin opener, a freezer and a microwave and these were in short supply in Abarda. Had a go back in September at boiling some cabbage leaves I'd bought from one of my students on Himbirti market. It tasted like boiled cabbage leaves. Tried boiling eggs but for some reason when I peeled the shell off most of the egg came with it and it disintegrated into a mess. Bananas were okay when Fiori had some in the shop but there's a limit to how many bananas you can eat at a sitting. Gave up on the cooking. Lied to myself that I was too focused on the lesson planning and didn't have time. Truth is I couldn't be bothered. As a result I was an outsider during the lengthy volunteer discussions on how much berbera to use in a dish or whether chiro was easier to prepare than hades.

Managed to stay alive in the village firstly due to the kindness of the Indian teachers who used to invite me into their homes for tchai, barney and rice after walking back from school. Secondly, I used to walk to Mai Nefhi Hotel every evening on schooldays and have what I thought was a meat-filled spaghetti bolognese. Janet and Kaska's blunt assessment of my unwitting vegetarian diet had been a shock.

I had a bigger shock when I was getting dressed one Saturday morning in Bristol Pension. Alga had put me in room 14 as my usual room 12 was taken. Room 14 had a wardrobe with a full-length mirror and I caught a glimpse of my upper body. My ribs were sticking out visibly. Standing up I didn't recognise myself – what was in front of me was not the picture I had in my head. Sunken cheeks, spindly legs and the aforementioned ribs. Got dressed and had two buns instead of one in Elsa's café that morning. Rationalised a bit over my second bun. I had not felt sick or weak since I'd arrived so the lost weight wasn't that harmful. Decided I'd be okay. After all I hadn't missed – and didn't miss – a single day in school because of sickness. When I got on the scales back in the UK I discovered that I'd actually lost two stones dropping from just over twelve stone. There was something else I was also struck by as I stood looking at myself in the mirror – I was white and I'd forgotten.

Used to try and fill up in Asmara at weekends with pizza and buns. Took some bits back on the bike to Abarda which I bought at the Import-Export shop. Once I bought a big loaf of bread wrapped in a plastic bag. The intention was to share it with the Indian teachers at lunchtime the next day in school. Tying it on the back of the bike I rode back to Abarda one Sunday afternoon. Didn't realise that the hot sun on the plastic bag had turned it into a breeding ground for mould. Next day the Indians handed me back the green-bottomed bread with a look that combined disgust with sympathy and gave me an extra share of their rice obviously thinking I was in dire straits.

The seeds of paranoia regarding what I ate were planted by the Eritrea VSO handbook which contained the line 'Be careful with food hygiene as all Asmara's hospitals are full of people with diarrhoea.' Perhaps I'd taken things a bit far.

My approach to the water I consumed was equally disciplined. Intended to do great things with water. I'd read about filtering water through sand to cleanse it, had heard about the benefits of boiling water to kill bacteria and had bought some purifying tablets from England. I was going to do all three – the bugs weren't going to get me. Unfortunately I was just as lazy with the water as the food and the vision of a filtration plant never materialised.

Kasi and Fasi took me one afternoon to meet Filimon who had a water purification factory halfway between Abarda and Mai Nefhi School. Filimon gave us a tour. The factory looked in pristine condition – all clean shiny pipes and an enormous blue sixty feet square, three feet deep plastic bag from which girls were filling big plastic containers (the familiar jerry cans) and plastic bottles. I recognised Gebrella, one of my Home Room students. She was the thinnest student, person, I met in my time in Eritrea. Never tried it but I reckon if I'd attempted to put my two hands round her waist my finger ends might just have touched.

The machinery was Swedish so Filimon must have been working closely with the government to get agreement for all this. He was doing fine selling the water all over the country. I had seen the bottles of Mai Nefhi spring water on shelves in Asmara and in plenty of village shops. The good news was that he would sell us jerry cans of water direct from the factory. Kasi and me used to call every two or three days to tie the precious containers to the bike – some for all of us. I bumped into Filimon a year later in Asmara after I'd left Mai Nefhi. He looked really down. The government had hiked up his taxes so much he'd had to close the factory. Wondered what had happened to Gebrella.

Towards the end of my time in Abarda the Mai Nefhi water factory seemed to be functioning erratically. Often we would bang on the doors and get no answer. Big problem. Kasi and me met the Director. Kasi reckoned that because the Mai Nefhi college lecturers used the Mai Nefhi School canteen we should be able to use their shop and buy jerry cans of water from there. Meles took this one up and following a meeting with the college Director told us he'd got agreement to the proposal. Bit of a walk through the college to the shop; we used to go in twos and threes making our way through the hundreds of students.

One particular day, however, I went on my own only to be confronted by a big lad who started shouting in my face. He didn't actually touch me but it was close. A crowd of students gathered round – we were surrounded just like two kids about to fight in a school playground. Managed to get the gist of what was being sprayed in my face.

Basically, it was 'Stop taking our water you so and so.' Didn't want any part of this but had no thoughts of backing down – needed the water badly and there was an agreement in place. After a while with me trying to explain about lecturers using 'our' canteen and no break in him shouting things were on a knife-edge. Could have got really nasty. Recalled the power of just using the term 'Director' in school and tried it here. Shouting for the first time – 'You!' (pointing at him.) 'Me!' (pointing at me.) 'Director now!' (pointing somewhere, anywhere.) Although his shouting continued the look in his eyes showed that my command had worked. He was looking for a way out. I hadn't got a clue who the Director of the college was or where his office was but that didn't matter. The lad walked off still shouting in an attempt to save face and the crowd dispersed. Thank God.

In April the books which had arrived the previous January courtesy of the good folks of Royal Mail were finally ferried to the school in a tuc-tuc driven by Biniam, the Deputy Head. It was a little three-wheeled affair and he crouched in the tiny cabin with the books piled up behind him. Four big lads were recruited and soon all the books were stacked in the room we'd prepared. Over the next few weeks books were arranged on shelves in subject order, one shelf for maths, one for geography and so on. A few good-sized maps had been stuffed in with the books and these were hung on the walls. It looked great.

After we'd finished I peeped through a window of the library. A group of the lads who had helped with the sorting and shelving were sat in a circle around a child's book, the kind where you pressed a button and it made the noise of the animal on that page. They were fascinated and took turns to press the button. All very orderly.

Some of the books were Christian – kids' bible stories. One of the boys handed me a few he'd found. I was aware of the government's strict oversight of the church. Only Orthodox, Catholic and Lutheran churches were permitted in the country. The Seventh Day Adventists where Yohannes attended was closed down while I was there. A few weeks earlier, in a naïve attempt to get support for the library, I had gone into Christian bookshops in Asmara and asked for donations. Predictably, I was blanked. Showed Meles the books the boy had handed me. 'Our government may have a problem with these,' he said taking them from me. Never saw them again.

The library was strictly monitored. It took over a week for the Deputy to log every book by hand on large sheets of paper. Once logged Kasi, Fasi and me started a Reading Club at lunchtimes. The usual keen students were there – Tsegay, Fiori, Gebremeskel, Rigbe were regulars and they were usually joined by up to six or seven others. We had some good sessions but did strike a bit of a problem which may be familiar to experts in this field. The reading levels were around typical eight to nine-year-olds in England. However, the subject matter for this age group was not appropriate for a seventeen to eighteen- year-old teenager. On the other hand teenage/adult books were written in English that was too advanced. I can't be the only teacher who has bumped into this problem. Fasi said he had learned written English by reading 'trashy novels.' Didn't try this in the Reading Room.

It might be sweet to have dozens of nicey-nicey stories to relate about loving, close relationships built with locals but that isn't the case for anyone living and working in Africa. Once you become accustomed to the hardship the realisation dawns that people are the same everywhere. This isn't apparent when the BBC shows pictures of wide-eyed, malnourished kids. Personalities are hidden behind the trauma generated by a starving child. Living in a village – when the TV cameras have moved on – has to have a day-to-day routine, has to accommodate the different characters and behaviours.

Some people you naturally warm to, some you don't. There is honesty, jealousy, craftiness, respect, lying, boredom, arrogance, sacrifice, decency – just like in every community on the planet. People can be aloof, sneaky, affable, caring, aggressive, dismissive, servile – just like in every community on the planet. This is the reality of daily life in the village and you are part of, and contribute to, the day's unfolding dramas.

A mate, Bob, had sent me some sweets from England in a parcel containing all kinds of stuff. One lesson Azieb answered a question correctly in class. 'Well done Azieb, have a lollipop,' and I gave her one of those hard, sweet lollies that cost a few pence in England. She licked it a few times and gave it to Elsa who had a lick. She passed it to Tesfai who did the same and so on. The lollipop went all the way to the back in this fashion and then across to the next column of desks for others to have a taste.

Stood at the front of the class this show of generosity caught me off guard. I was touched by the unselfishness, the camaraderie – sharing the prize, looking after my brothers and sisters. Nice story.

Nonsense.

Visiting Azieb and her family sometime after the lollipop-sharing incident I recalled the episode over the glass of tchai I had been given. Something along the lines of how wonderful it was to see children sharing and thinking of each other. Azieb was puzzled. 'I didn't like it so I gave it away,' she said in matter-of-fact tones. 'Did anybody like it?' I ventured. 'No. Too sweet.'

It dawned that I'd romanticised the situation and missed the reality. They were recoiling from the sweet taste – without any facial expression – and were trying to get rid of the lollipop.

I tested the different taste bud thing out a few times after that incident. Habesha children generally don't like chocolate or sweets – the sort of thing given to English children as a treat. I never found one that did anyway and this seems to be apparent with the Eritrean children I have since got to know in the UK. Possibly the taste mechanism is affected at an early age by the berbera the children are fed. Common sight to see toddlers chewing on chilli pepper in the village. Probably better for them than sweets.

'Just another ten minutes,' I said to myself. 'It'll be alright.' I knew full well it wouldn't be.

Kaska had invited me to her home in Adi Guadad. I always thought this was a fortunate placement for her being only a few miles from the capital and yet still a village. Like all capital cities Asmara was swallowing surrounding towns and villages and thus extending its boundaries. Being Eritrea this was a slow process but Adi Guadad was thriving because of its proximity to the hub.

Kaska was from Poland with a few years' experience in education. She was fluent in several languages and had put in the hours to master Tigrinya and the local customs. Her presence, dynamism, intelligence, determination and desire to involve herself fully in the local community meant that she 'belonged' in Adi Guadad. Well known throughout the village she became very close with the families near her house to the point where she didn't need invitations to pay visits or to give invites for people to visit her. It was pleasing to see she had reached this informal state of being able to drop in unannounced.

Kaska, Dave (retired bank manager from Newcastle) and Rebecca (teacher from London) took things to a different level as volunteers by building themselves into a strong team. Most volunteers worked by themselves or in partnership with Eritreans. True, these three had some advantages, in particular they lived close together and close to Asmara. Also as teacher trainers/support they didn't have to schedule their lives around a strict school timetable as the volunteer teachers did. That freedom coupled with the access to Eritrean decision makers, resources, communications and transport meant they could progress initiatives successfully and really benefit schools and communities. They made contact with the Pestalozzi Fund who awarded them £30,000 to help fund their work and it was good to see them make such a contribution to the country.

Kaska had pushed the boat out and I was treated to injera, zigny, chiro – you name it. Great time catching up with her and some of her Adi Guadad neighbours who had popped in. 'Perhaps another ten minutes,' I said to myself again. Stupid. I knew to the minute how long it would take me to get back to Abarda on the bike. Give or take five minutes I knew exactly when the sun would go down. I knew there was no moon that night and, of course, I knew that there was not a single street light on the long road between Adi Guadad and Adrassi, Adrassi and Kt Mewli, Kt Mewli and Abarda. Not a single light on my bike either.

Eventually I said my goodbyes and thanked Kaska for what had been a great get-together. Outside I pushed the bike across the stony ground to the main road feeling some trepidation at the journey I was about to make. It wasn't just a possibility that I might have to negotiate total blackout conditions, it was a certainty. Didn't want a puncture to add to the challenge so was careful over the rough ground to the tarmac. Adi Guadad is a bustling place – much bigger than my village. Lots of people around here but I knew the road and the small villages on the way home would be deserted. With the sun already setting behind the three peaks beyond my home I pressed my left foot hard on the pedal and swung my right leg to mount. Next thing I was on my back looking at the sky with the most crippling pain in my chest. The chain had slipped, the bike had hit the ground and the ribs above my heart had slammed down onto the end of the handlebar which was pointing straight up. I laid in the middle of the road shocked by the pain. Couldn't breathe. Couldn't move. If a bus had trundled up the road in the dusk at that moment I was probably a goner.

Something even stronger than the excruciating pain overtook me – anger. On the opposite side of the road had been a queue waiting at the bus stop. As I hit the ground they erupted in laughter at my expense. It only lasted a few seconds until it dawned – as I lay motionless

– that this could be serious. A couple of men came over to help me up. I brushed them away and managed to struggle to my feet gasping. Deliberately ignoring them and the watching crowd with a face set like thunder I put the chain back on, slowly got on the bike and rolled down the road consumed by agony and resentment.

Just managed to get past Adrassi when my screwed-up eyes could see no more – I was almost riding blind. It would have been completely blind if someone had not left the lights on in a few houses in Kt Mewli. On the brows of the undulating road glimpses of the lights gave me a bearing. The occasional crunch of the stones as I veered off the tarmac was another indicator. With these pointers and my memory of the twists and turns I'd negotiated many times in daylight I thought 'I'm going to make it.' Then I went over the handlebars.

A herd of cows had decided to wander across the road. Never saw a thing even as my face hit the side of the stinking cow. Not too much pain from the impact but alarmed at being in the middle of the unseen but noisy beasts. Using the bike to shield myself I slowly edged forward and managed to escape a trampling.

Walked a bit – just as difficult as riding – biked a bit. Got through Kt Mewli and felt a bit closer to home. Only three miles to go. Thankfully the road smoothed out with less troughs and peaks and the few lights on, in Abarda this time, guided me home. I collapsed on the bed and undid my shirt. A six inch bloody scrape down my chest from the

Adi Guadad accident. Not a good night but the heart was still intact – was pleased the ribs had done their job.

Power cuts are part of everyday life in Eritrea. The lights can go out anytime morning, afternoon, evening and for anything from five minutes to five days and, just like sitting in your prison cell in Eritrea, there is no indication of how long it will last. During April 2006 in Abarda (and in the rest of the country as well according to other volunteers) matters became extreme. Between seven and eight every evening the fluorescent tube flickered and died and my room went black. There wasn't much to do with the light on so – with it off – life in any form that was recognisable ended. The torch provided some relief and I had quite a few batteries but after a short time the eyes weren't focusing properly. In the dim light the little stock of candles came in handy but whatever they were made of wasn't healthy. In the smoke-filled room coughing uncontrollably the lesson planning suffered but there was no choice – the teaching had to go on.

After screwing up the eyes to produce something like a lesson plan there wasn't a lot to occupy the time. Read a bit – the VSO office had quite a few books and, although normally not much of a reader, managed to get through a book or two. No TV of course and the radio was usually a source of irritation rather than entertainment with erratic signals meaning I couldn't always tune into something in English or anything else for that matter. I once managed to get reasonable reception in English of a Manchester City game one Sunday evening but that was a one-off and I gave up trying after seven o'clock. For some reason reception in the morning was fine – *Voice of Africa* was listenable and occasionally there was news about the heightened tension on the Ethiopian/Eritrean border which could have been critical given my location. The previous November I listened intently as things had got particularly edgy and the UN were making noises about pulling out and letting the two armies get on with it. The Indian teachers and even some professors teaching in the college used to stand at the school gate in the morning looking out for me keen for an update on the situation – information from any source was valuable in this country.

So, what to do? Really, after some stretching days in the classroom I needed a break, needed to relax. The walk to and from Mai Nefhi Hotel helped the brain to unwind as did the little chats with locals along the way but I was soon back home with an evening in the dark stretching before me. In the blackness the senses were fully disabled – zero external stimulus. Didn't want to go to sleep at seven o'clock as that would destroy any remnants of a waking-sleeping pattern that was left given that the nightly disturbance caused by noisy worshipping Orthodox Christians and Muslims and even noisier animals had done me no favours at all. Needed to work hard to retain some sense of normality in abnormal circumstances. The only thing left in such situations are your own thoughts.

Had seen a couple of years earlier a programme about Terry Waite and John McCarthy who had been kidnapped and held hostage in a poorly-lit room for years. McCarthy talked about how he planned a garden in his head to fill the hours, days. He imagined where to position certain plants and detail such as fertiliser and pest control. Helped to keep him balanced so I thought I'd give it a try, not with a garden but with a Rock Festival. Spent hours lying on the bed in the dark picking headline acts – the Beatles on day one, Led Zeppelin day two and the Stones on day three. Support acts were carefully chosen and deciding on the playlist was spread over a few nights. Best and worst England teams (football and cricket) were up next using players from the Sixties to present day.

Strange conversations were had in Asmara at weekends when the power cuts were at their most frequent usually prompted by the question 'what do you do when the lights go out?' Ann had quite a good one focusing on three S's – shooting stars, satellites and storms. Sitting outside looking up at the night sky which with no electric light around whatsoever was, of course, vibrant she would while away the time looking for the 'three S's.' The flashes from storms many miles away in Ethiopia were, apparently, particularly worth looking out for but I never saw any.

Did use the thinking time usefully one evening. Really wanted to spend some time evaluating the problems I had in the early months at school and this was a good time to do it. Considered that this kind of situation was likely to happen in the future as I was starting afresh in Mendefera the coming September. More than that, though, I wanted to generalise, to come up with basic tenets which might provide a touchstone when the wheels were falling off in any circumstances not just in school. Not mind-blowing stuff but I got to the point where I was comfortable with the following:

1. Always keep cool.
2. Keep busy.
3. Take rest, having a break is not running away.
4. Look at the big picture.
5. Look at the long-term.
6. Talk to the right people – you know who they are.
7. Pray, always pray – and remember that praying is as much about listening as speaking.

On one seriously dark night I heard a noise in the room. 'What the hell is that?' Strange noise – sort of heavy fluttering with little bumps every now and then as the thing hit the walls. 'It's a bat,' I reckoned. Did they have vampire bats in Eritrea? Wasn't taking any chances going to sleep with that flapping around. Flailing about in pitch darkness with a rolled up *Guardian Weekly* I hit something and I heard a small but definite thud. Stood still for a while. Silence. 'Gotcha.'

Difficult to describe the guilt I felt the next morning when I saw on the middle of my old table, with wings perfectly opened, the most enormous, beautiful purple and red butterfly I had ever seen – dead. The butterfly that went thud.

'Don't forget me Isaac Newton, don't ever forget me!' I was sitting on the bus to Adi Guadad when a crazy man got on. Seeing the white face he made straight for me. Over the next ten minutes I was subject to a tirade of all things British – well he thought they were British anyway. It was not aggressive or abusive but it was loud. Squeezing up to me ever closer I had the lot belted into my ear: Margaret Thatcher, Tony Blair, William Shakespeare, Bobby Charlton, Winston Churchill, John F Kennedy (didn't like to correct him), Princess Diana – they all featured somewhere. And Isaac Newton – he thought I was Isaac Newton.

Not surprising that Asmara has its share of characters given its history – learned to take these incidents in my stride, nothing really violent. I think Alga and Donard must have had a brush with the same bloke who'd collared me on the bus. Both had been grabbed from behind in a bear hug on the same day while walking down Harnet Avenue. Donard's response had been to shout, 'leave me, leave me' and it seems the crazy did just that. Perhaps he just wanted a cuddle.

'Don't worry Donard – if he does it again me and Eddie will have 'im,' I joked.'

'Thank you Kevin – I don't think that will be necessary.' Donard had a gentle way of putting you down.

Alga's bear hug had been a little more serious and needed the assistance of two soldiers to prise him off. Telling the story she wasn't too bothered as there was plenty of help to hand and I think she'd probably have sorted it out even if there wasn't.

Don't know if it was the same bloke but one evening in Bar Zilli a man on crutches seemed to be after a fight with somebody, anybody. The bar tender took him on – looked a bit comical as he ducked several times to avoid the crutch swung at his head.

I suppose the chap who ran in front of my bike as I was riding through Asmara and grabbed the handlebars could have caused a nasty accident. Luckily I managed to stay on and he ran off down the road. Bit of a shock that one as it was totally unexpected and the mind was wandering as it does riding through the capital. Don't need to concentrate too much in the city as there are few vehicles and those that are there rarely top thirty mph.

Used to think I was one of the crazy gang myself sometimes. Lenny Henry once told a story about his mother who had ended up in Dudley during the Sixties after emigrating from Jamaica. Apparently there were very few other black people there at the time so when she did see a black face she nodded and said hello. The fact that she was greeting a perfect stranger who may have actually come from Sierra Leone was not a consideration. Found myself doing the same thing to white faces in Asmara and actually met some interesting folks that way. Spotting a white face coming towards you in the distance amid a sea of black faces it would seem bad manners not to greet them. Weird. However, having shook hands with a perfect stranger, it led to me sharing a cup of tchai with, among others, an Italian artist, a Russian engineer and a Jewish archaeologist. All sorts of waifs and strays pass through Asmara (even British maths teachers) and some of them even spoke English.

Thought I'd better put something about homesickness. It passes.

May 2006 – Examinations all Round

Thought someone had had an accident in the classroom when I heard the groans. Had gone into school early that morning to go through some of the books in the library. Nobody else was about so it was down to me to help whoever was suffering. Burst into the room and interrupted a couple of students involved in a frenzied sex act. Their faces were a picture as they frantically adjusted themselves and ran out. Mentioned the incident to Kasi, 'Happens all the time.'

It was true, used condoms were a regular find on classroom floors. Not nice. The big problem for village teenagers with designs on each other was how to get close. Families of six, seven even ten children in every house, villages teeming with folks, no covering undergrowth to speak of, eyes and ears everywhere. Empty classrooms before school started became a favoured venue. The used condom discoveries increased to such a level it was decided at a staff meeting to hold sex education talks for all the girls – not boys for some reason. This meant that all girls were taken out of maths, English, science classes for 'the talk' while the boys doubled up and trebled up to continue with their academic classes. 'How are they going to fit in the room?' Well somehow they did. The biggest class I took was seventy six students – I know because I did the register. Had to take a deep breath before that lesson. 'Get it by the scruff of the neck. Don't let this one go off the rails.'

Went ok. I had prepared a very interactive discussion-based lesson so needed to be on top of things. The material was based on arithmetic progressions – A- level material in England. The hook was the first demonstration – 'stand up Tesfaldet.' As he stood I shook his hand and bumped shoulders in the usual manner. 'Question. If everybody in this room shook hands with everyone else, how many handshakes? Segum yelen (too easy) what if everybody in the world shook hands with everyone else how many handshakes?' Bit of discussion concluding 'a lot.' I carried on. 'How can we find the exact answer to these questions in ten seconds?' And off we went. Enjoyed that one.

Countdown (the daytime television programme in England) provided the basis for another big-class lesson. Standards of mental arithmetic are generally higher in Eritrea than England because students don't become brain-lazy by having well-meaning parents giving them a calculator at five years. Became a bit of a specialist in finding props to use in the classroom. Gets the attention right away. Bike gears were used to illustrate ratio, a bendy wire coat hanger became a parabola. Tedros liked the word 'parabola' so much he used to repeat it over and over again in a deep voice. Eventually it became, and possibly still is, his nickname. Maybe there will be generations of 'parabolas' – it all started here.

Another stand-out session had nothing to do with maths. Meles, along with all other Directors in Zoba Maakel had been given the directive to test all students' eyesight. When this was disclosed at a staff meeting I expected a band of opticians to be visiting. Not so. Home Room teachers would undertake the testing and provide documented results for collation. No equipment or guidelines were issued so one evening I made a few eye-charts of the kind you get in Specsavers back home. Big letter A at the top, two slightly smaller letters below and so on. Next day I drew a line on 9.3's classroom floor about six feet from the wall, gave the eye-charts to

Mussie and Fiori and they got on with it. A 'fail' was any student who couldn't read below the third line. Not very scientific but got some paperwork back to Meles. The whole episode triggered the realisation that there were probably dozens of undiagnosed conditions afflicting hundreds of students in the school. Every class would undoubtedly have children who would be considered 'special needs' or having 'learning difficulties' in England and here there wasn't a classroom support worker in sight. The enormity of the task — teaching effectively in Eritrea — seemed even more overwhelming.

Highlight of my medical involvement, though, came when I carefully administered vitamin drops — two per open-mouthed student — when the health authorities decreed that schools should take on this task. We only did this once before the drops ran out. God knows what medical benefit two drops of vitamin supplement provides.

Knew the end of year exams were coming up so I asked Meles when I would be getting the papers. 'You prepare the papers,' came the reply.

So, the exam paper was mine. Not so difficult as I'd covered the old Eritrean school maths book and gone on to use material from both GCSE and A-level books I'd brought from England. As far as standardisation went I was in the dark but eventually produced something I thought would fit the bill. Forty questions covering the whole year's work – this was handed to Teame the administrator to copy three hundred times on something I recalled from my old school days in the Sixties – I think they were called banda copies and came out bluey-purple smelling of chemicals.

I had done a lot of testing over the year; found that it gave focus to the lessons – something to aim for. It also gave me lots of mind-numbing marking sessions. In the VSO office I listened to most other teaching volunteers complaining that it was impossible to test fairly with so many in each classroom and often three to a desk. It was inevitable that students copied from each other. I put some effort in to address this with half the class outside while the others did the test. After twenty minutes, swap over. Made a bit more space in the room and allowed, mostly, one to a desk to be possible. Once I allowed whole class tests to be sat and relaxed regarding the copying noticing that it was happening but not intervening. Was surprised to note that the results of these tests mirrored the non-copy test results. Those who couldn't do the maths couldn't copy very well either.

The final exams were not relaxed at all. Disciplined affairs held in strict one-student-to-a-desk classrooms. Invigilation was undertaken by pairs of teachers. There was no supervision of your own subject exams. Looking up from the paper was not allowed and I saw teachers tear up several papers and expel students from the classroom after they'd flashed only a brief sideways glance at a companion.

The Eritrean teachers used quite an effective technique to ensure that students knew they were being watched at all times. Every few minutes the teacher would break the silence by lightly tapping five times with their fingernails or a pen on the chalkboard. It was enough to keep the focus and maintain order without disrupting the concentration and I got into the practice myself.

Gezae was a good student and I felt sorry for him the day he was kicked out of the classroom by Fasi and Madame Latha. Don't know why there were three of us invigilating that session. It started badly – I think there must have been some history with this group. Within a few minutes of 'eyes down you may start the paper' Madam Latha started shouting at Gezae. He must have felt some injustice at being attacked in this manner as he protested. Immediately Fasi started hitting him with his stick and Madam Latha's shouts turned to screams 'We know what you're saying – we can speak Tigrinya!' Meles strode in. All the other rooms were silent so the outcry had been picked up immediately. Gezae was ordered out the door and was chased across the compound by Meles swinging the length of rubber hose pipe he favoured that day.

Once the exams were over the students disappeared and the school emptied. After being handed the three hundred completed maths papers I shut myself away for the best part of four days in my house in Abarda. Quiet, hot, self-disciplined days. The toil was eased by noting each students' achievements and I was pleased to see that the results reflected pretty accurately the respective abilities based on what I'd seen in class and the test results over the year. Compiled a few statistics for myself. Girls did as well as boys – 10% groupings starting at 40-50% were populated roughly in a normal distribution while 9.5 and 9.6 did better overall than 9.3 and 9.4. 9.3 and 9.4 did better overall than 9.1 and 9.2. In other words, generally, 'older' looking students did better than 'younger' looking ones. There was evidence that many of these students would do well in maths lessons in the UK. Although it was good to see the marks in the nineties from Rahwa, Rigbe, Tsegay and other 'stars' it was particularly pleasing to see that all my students had managed a pass mark – some only just – but they'd all done it. Combining the maths results with other subjects it became clear that all my grade 9s would progress to year 10 next year.

Rani – a small, excitable Indian teacher – attempted to distribute marked papers to students in the compound. Total bedlam. He disappeared beneath the crowd of clamouring students only struggling free after a few minutes. He pushed his way to the staffroom steps and gave up, throwing the papers to the crowd. The poor guy staggered into the staffroom cursing the mob at the top of his voice. This wasn't going to happen to me. I walked into an empty classroom, shut the steel door and dragged a table across it. The table was to act as my 'shop counter.' Behind me I arranged more tables in rows and dealt the exam papers out in alphabetical order. Opening the door I stood behind my desk and in reasonable fashion gave out papers.

I took a similar approach to giving reports to parents a couple of days later. Went even more smoothly as Bisrat helped me this time. Some parents signed as they accepted reports but most had to press their thumbs in the ink pad and make a mark. When the ink ran dry Bisrat took to scribbling on thumbs with a biro. The mark was pretty unintelligible but don't think it caused any problems. It caught my eye when only five blank spaces were left, only five thumbprints to go. I counted them down to myself. As the last mum pressed her thumb on the page it dawned that the year's work was done. It was the end of the placement in Mai Nefhi – the previous January it had been impossible to visualise this moment. Walked back to Abarda. Time to get ready to leave.

Alga often talked about her meetings with the Eritrean Tourist Board and how frustrating it was. Tourists don't go to Eritrea. Tourists don't know Eritrea exists. Real challenge for her. Leaving aside the visible signs of a military dictatorship in power, armed soldiers on street corners, nothing in the shops to buy, poverty, disease and the constant threat of war breaking out this is a special, even unique place. Maybe it is made even more special because of the challenges it faces on a daily basis.

Asmara is a diamond of a city but I had to leave it and contrast with other cities in the West before it dawned on me why – people live there. Twenty four hours a day, seven days a week, on the main thoroughfares, on side streets next to the Ministry buildings, around the big churches, up the road from the President's Palace people live there – right in the centre. This gives Asmara the feel of a community. Seems like everybody knows everybody. People greet each other, ask how their families are doing. Even volunteers who only come in for the weekend like I did get known. The nice problem associated with this is that it takes a while to get anywhere as you are constantly stopped in the street and asked 'how's things?'

Harnet Avenue cuts Asmara in two. About a mile long with the President's Palace at the top and Barti Meskerem Square at the bottom it is dead straight and lined with towering palm trees. There are bars and cafes on either side all with seats outside which gives an indication of the climate in the city. Asmara is on a plateau over six thousand feet above sea level and about fifteen degrees north of the Equator. This makes for days that are generally blessed with what many English folks would describe as perfect English weather. From September to May seventy five degrees, blue skies, not a cloud to be seen and fresh air – humidity not a problem. Some rain in

June, July and August ('winter') – sometimes causing floods particularly in August. First sight of children literally dancing in the rain singing 'mai, mai – good for Eritrea!' is a little strange for English people.

Soldiers sitting in groups outside the Post Office and the Municipality (City Hall) are sometimes friendly, sometimes cool. The President's Palace where foreign dignitaries are welcomed is guarded inside and out. It doesn't register when it happens in the movies but when a soldier points a Kalashnikov in your direction and twitches it a couple of times indicating that you need to cross the road as he doesn't want you near the palace it's real and you respond. Odd how after a few times it becomes an acceptable part of the day. Don't know if the guns are loaded but, of course, you don't want to find out. Common sight in Asmara is young lads walking casually down the road with little fingers linked. When soldiers do this in Asmara it makes for a curious vision of cuteness mixed with brutality. No bike riding near the palace – you get off and push – and no photographs. Kaska and a friend were a bit too close when they were clicking away and spent a few hours in prison. It's not the few hours that's the problem it's the not knowing during that time if it's going to be a few hours, days or weeks. People disappear in this country and that thought is always somewhere at the back of your mind.

The striking architecture in and around the centre of Asmara is a legacy of the Italian colonial period. Seems like they had a passion for making buildings look like other things. The Ministry of Education looks like a capital 'F' on its back. I was told this was a reference to 'Fascist'. A petrol station is shaped like an aeroplane and a pub like a ship. Somebody had some fun drawing up these plans.

My favourite building was situated just behind the Post Office – the pristine, ice-blue and white residence of the French Charge d'Affaires. Never went in.

Got to know Daniel's bar on Harnet as they have a television and, therefore, Premiership football. Usually it was free entrance but they charged ten nakfa for big games like the 2006 FA Cup Final. Good crowd – black, white, Eritrean, English all pales into insignificance of course when the football's on. Only the shirt colours matter. Don't know if Arsenal have undertaken a promotion campaign in Eritrea (of course not) but they are by far the best supported team out there. Talked to many Eritreans about this thinking it might be because they field a number of African players but no, it seems their flowing style of play is the attraction. Got this response time and again. Only once saw the confrontation between rival supporters that is a feature of football in England. During an Arsenal v Manchester United game trouble flared up in the bar resulting in a door being broken off its hinges. Seems all the aspects of football can cross boundaries.

Volunteers stopped going in the American Bar. On the noticeboard in the VSO office Claire had pinned a piece of paper detailing an incident. Apparently a few volunteers were sitting on the pavement seats outside the bar when some children approached them asking for handouts. The manager didn't want his paying customers disturbed so proceeded to drive the kids away, in one case kicking a girl after he had pushed her to the ground. He lost a lot of business that day. These violent examples were isolated though – a cup of coffee or a couple of beers in Asmara's bars is usually about as relaxing as it gets.

I enjoyed visiting the Post Office as it gave me access to and allowed me to touch base with my family. Aerogrammes were only three nakfa and got to my family within a week. The building is old and impressive with a quiet bustle. The political situation is to the fore in the paintings on the wall depicting a loving father handing Badme to his tiny son. Badme is the village that is occupied by Ethiopia and Eritrea want it back. Hence, the uneasy No War, No Peace policy and the thousands of soldiers facing each other on the border. Never visited but was told that Badme is a tiny village like any other in this part of Africa with not much in the way of natural resources. One political commentator described the situation as 'like two bald men fighting over a comb.'

The wrinkly old lady sitting on the floor outside the Post Office door selling *Eri-Profiles* was a pal. Seemed to take to me. A smile from a stranger is a big deal when you feel a long way from anything familiar. Used to sit down and listen to her ramblings for ten minutes on Saturday mornings before I went to read the newspaper in Fiori's café. No idea what she was saying but that didn't matter to her or me.

Eri-Profile is the national newspaper, the government's mouthpiece. Filled with articles about the 'final and binding' agreements about the border being ignored by the enemy, the influence of the decadent West and the glory of the Eritrean Cycle Racing team it was not much of a read. A bit more riveting, if two weeks out of date, was the *Guardian Weekly* which I had subscribed to before flying out. Global viewpoints with a bit of sport on the back pages. Not the sort of thing to replace the newspapers back home but it fuelled the need to feel at least a little connected to the outside world.

St Mary's Catholic Church on Harnet Avenue is spectacular. The delicate statue of the angel on the roof catches the eye and you can climb the clock/bell tower if you can find a trainee priest to take you up. Phil, Janet and Fiona had been up the previous day. They got the timing wrong and the bells nearly deafened them on the hour. With this in mind I checked my watch and followed the lad up the steps – many steps. There's not much in the way of health and safety consideration at the top which makes for a very open panoramic view of the city and beyond. The spectacle is heightened by the adrenaline generated by the awareness that a life-ending fall is probably imminent. The little priest had obviously done this many times before and was delighted at my caution (fear) as he strode around the parapet protected from the two hundred foot drop to the concrete by only a small rusty fence.

There is a small kindergarten open to tots in the church. Before flying out a good friend had kindly given me £200 to use in the country. Kay had left it to me to decide where it would do some good. I gave it to the pastor who ran the kindergarten at St Mary's. Not very creative on my part but it satisfied a few concerns. Firstly, I wanted to get rid of the money pretty quickly – didn't want to lose it, didn't want it stolen. Secondly, I wanted an audit trail (Kay is an accountant) and I knew the pastor would log the donation and give me a receipt. Thirdly, I didn't want to waste it by risking it on a scheme of my own which might not come to fruition. Bit pragmatic but I know the cash went to benefit children's education and Kay seemed happy with the outcome. I visited the kindergarten a few times afterwards and saw the books and equipment bought and where they mattered – in the hands of the children.

St George's is the ex-pat church in Asmara. Only went a couple of times for by the time the Sunday evening service started I was back in the village getting ready for school the next day. When I did go it was always full. I met a Cornish vicar and his wife in the VSO office one day. Happy couple. They had only been in the country two weeks and were being deported for asking the congregation of St George's to pray for the people suffering in the Israeli-Palestinian conflict. The government spies had reported back and, for a touchy minister, that was enough. The vicar and his wife thought it was hilarious that they had beaten the record time for someone of their calling being kicked out which had previously been a month. I wished them well.

Shops in the city are nothing to write home about. A couple of import-export shops, one curiously-stocked souvenir shop (wooden giraffe, lion and hippo ornaments none of which live in Eritrea) but plenty of photography shops and hairdressers. Dave Wright reckoned this was a vanity thing – looking good and taking pictures of yourself – 'legacy of the Italians.'

Got to mention the flowers in Asmara. After a while in the country the vivid banks of yellow, orange and purple nasturtiums and petunias that grow in the gardens of the Eri-wealthy are taken for granted because there are so many of them. VSO office was in a 'nice' area – embassies, hotels and the like. Looked a picture. In February there is a crowning glory just up from Africa Pension. Sixty feet high, a jacaranda tree blooms dazzling violet. There are plenty of others in the area too and the blossom even makes a vibrant carpet when it falls off in March.

Plenty of flowers but not many statues as the government doesn't believe in them – policies not personalities. There was an empty plinth in the middle of the Hotel Nyala roundabout. Simple, cheap plastic sandals called Kongo's had been worn by soldiers throughout the conflict. In honour of the vital role the sandals played a statue of the footwear was erected but then taken down again. Icons don't figure in Eritrea.

The people are what makes Asmara tick though. All the cafes, shops, ministry buildings and churches are alive with the characters who live on the doorsteps. These are not museum pieces but are given life by the masses. The single best example of this happens every night on the steps of St Mary's which is known as 'the meeting place.' Hundreds of people gather in this area on warm evenings and get together for no other reason than they want to get together. Although friends do move on to city bars and restaurants the steps are a venue in themselves and provide a colourful statement of what Asmara is about.

There you are Alga – Asmara travel brochure for the next Tourist Board meeting.

June 2006 – End of Term

Exams over, results distributed, paperwork done – it was time for a party. My Home Room students in 9.3 had got together and asked Meles if he would leave the school gates open one Sunday afternoon so they could have a party in the classroom. This group had an advantage over the other five grade 9 classes because some of the students – Bahgu and Mulu – were nuns. These two had asked the Sisters at the Catholica if they would provide food and drink for the get-together so everything was in place.

It was a tough decision whether to go or not. That Sunday afternoon – the last before I flew back to England – Sporting Adulis were playing Asmara Beer United at the Asmara Stadium. I'd been a regular attender over the previous months but decided to give the football a miss, get on the bike and go back to the village a bit earlier than usual. Rode back with dark thoughts about the party being 'all talk' and expected the school to be deserted leaving me with nothing to do except regret missing the match.

I could hear the familiar bump, bump, bump of Tigrinya music before I got to the school gates and headed for my classroom. Every one of my students was there and the welcome bowled me over. Fiori and Gebrella put flowers behind my ears, Bahgu served up injera and meat, Sara gave me a bottle of Fanta (don't know where they'd got that from) and I was sat down behind a desk to eat and drink. Habtom was in charge of music and he did a great job on the CD player. (Like the Fanta, no idea how they'd got hold of batteries.) I handed out two disposable cameras I hadn't used and Elsa and Mehari clicked away as students posed. They were all dressed in their finery – flowery dresses and colourful cardigans. Aklilu must have fancied himself as a model as he stripped off his top and demanded that Elsa take his picture from all sides as he stared menacingly into the camera.

Eating over I was dragged up to dance or in my case wobble in an ungainly fashion. Outside various students were taking it in turns to ride my bike around the school compound. This had been a no-no over the year – nobody was allowed to touch the bike – but this was my last day in Mai Nefhi. 'Go on then, take the bike.'

Next day Fish came in the VSO truck to take me and my furniture (bed and table) to Asmara where it was put in storage to await my return in September. Janet and I had booked to catch the 5 am Egyptian Air flight the next Sunday morning so I had a few days in the capital before heading off. In the VSO office I caught up with Phil and Claire who brought me up to date with the news. Most of the volunteers had left by now – it was late June – but I had quite a bit I wanted to do this final week. I also had visits to make to various government offices to get the necessary paperwork needed to be allowed to get on the plane. This was serious stuff – no papers means turned away at the airport and wasting the cost of a ticket. The worst example I heard of this was an American who had worked hard to get all the documents needed. He'd actually boarded the plane but the flight was delayed. Sitting on the runway midnight came and went, his exit visa expired and he was ordered off. 'Protest as much as you like – off.'

In the middle of this last week I caught the bus to my placement for 2006-2007 – Mendefera. Out of the city, past the airport, through Adi Guadad and past the right turn to Mai Nefhi the bus headed south into the unknown territory of Zoba Debub – well unknown to me anyway. Noted half a dozen villages and some spectacularly shaped mountains. Eritreans don't climb mountains – seemed a waste. After about an hour and a half the sign MENDEFERA was spotted at the roadside and this signalled the end of the journey. One checkpoint remained. Looking through the window I noticed the soldiers had a baby hyena tied to their shelter with a bit of string. This was the first hyena I had seen and I made a mental note that if there are little hyenas here big ones will not be far behind. Need to double check the compound gates are locked at night.

Didn't do much in Mendefera that day. I didn't know anybody and I had planned for this trip to be an unannounced affair, just wanted a feel for the place. Mendefera had grown to become the capital of the zoba. The region's government offices had been sited there and the population had increased dramatically in recent years. Had a little look round – main street with shops either side, usual white block buildings, two incredible churches one on either side of the road. On the right a striking white, half-size replica of St Mary's in Asmara. Looked like a rocket about to take off. On the left a traditional Orthodox building with a massive multiple-arched doorway.

Went back to the bus station, put a rock in the line and had a tchai at the café while I waited. Didn't get far with my attempts to converse with the waitress or the two men sat at the next table. No English? Not used to seeing white faces? Couldn't be bothered? Back on the bus I was glad I'd made the effort and bounced on the ropes, taken away the newcomer nerves. When I returned in September I wouldn't (quite) be a first-timer.

I'd just picked up my flight tickets when I bumped into Martin on Harnet Avenue. Martin was an Indian teacher at Mai Nefhi, an overweight bloke with black curly hair and a big moustache. He taught physics in the school and I remembered him particularly for two specific incidents. Firstly, his disbelief when Mehawi told him the earth was not flat during a tchai break and secondly, for having his stick taken off him and snapped by a student in the compound. Martin didn't live in Abarda with Kasi and the others but commuted from Asmara. He was regularly late and his classes were often seen hanging about outside the classroom in the mornings waiting for his bus to turn up.

He invited me to his home for something to eat. Martin lived on the top floor of Den-Den High School in Asmara. I'd passed the school hundreds of times on my bike but never been inside. After many stairs we got to the top and I was confronted by what can only be described as slum conditions. Looking down the long corridor it was clear that many Indians and their families lived here. It was crowded with half naked, dirty children running between equally dirty washing that had been hung out. The place was a mess. Looking inside the rooms as we passed rubbish seemed to be piled everywhere. Martin's room was at the end of the long corridor. Over tchai he explained that he lived here and endured the conditions and the rigours of the daily commute to Mai Nefhi school because he was desperate to get employment downstairs in Den-Den – working and living in the same building would solve all his problems. He never was offered a job there.

July 2006 – Home for the Summer

Ronaldo scored and England were out of the 2006 World Cup finals. As the ball hit the back of the net Cinema Roma erupted. Two hundred Eritreans jumped out of their seats dancing, shouting, screaming – you'd have thought Eritrea had just beaten Brazil 3-0 in the final. The sheer, ecstatic outburst was unconfined. Janet, Eddie, Tony and me sat silently for a full three minutes. Had to do something, had to try and balance the joyful scenes going on around me. Made a silent – if slightly pathetic – protest by just standing up with my arms crossed and stared at the distraught England players on the screen. After a minute or two, 'Come on Janet, let's go.'

In the Eighties Norman Tebbit had made some remark about how watching reactions to cricket matches revealed where people's hearts were in relation to nationality. I'd actually seen this in practice at Headingley years earlier when Pakistan had beaten England in a one-day international. Third generation Pakistani friends with broad Yorkshire accents went delirious as the winning run was struck. Here it was a little different, England were the bad guys, America's poodle, the West – and they'd got beat.

In all my time in Eritrea I was never once on the receiving end of any overt racism. The only flicker of this was passed on by Kasi as we had walked back home after school one evening and he told me the lad who'd just past us muttered the word 'colonial' in my direction. Didn't hear it myself, if I had I would have laughed. Colonial!

Kasi had kindly invited me to his house one evening a few weeks earlier to watch England play Trinidad and Tobago in a group match. Three Eritrean lads – Solomon (unofficial Head Boy at Mai Nefhi), Filimon and Gebremeskel – joined us and Kasi turned on the match. Passes going astray, missed chances – not a great game but England scored a couple near the end and were going to qualify. The goals had been applauded politely by the students but that was nothing compared to the leaping, whooping celebrations as Trinidad and Tobago scored in injury time. Sorry lads – offside. They sat down looking a little embarrassed to have shown their true colours. All kinds of stuff mixed up with these displays of emotion by young people. Reckon if I had asked them to explain their reactions they might not have been able to fully understand themselves.

My first year in Eritrea was over. Janet and I left Cinema Roma and headed back to Bristol Pension which was just around the corner. We had booked on the same flight and were both keen not to miss it so arranged to set alarms for two o'clock. Managed a few hours' sleep before the bell went, dressed, jumped in the pre-booked taxi and in fifteen minutes was stood at the gates of the airport on a cool night. Going home for the summer.

I recognised the girl on the check-in desk 'Hi Rigbe – how's the new house?' A few months earlier I had been pedalling up the road to Asmara. Just past Kt Mewli there was an old man stood at the side of the road. 'Come, come.' Now, what does he want? Didn't really fancy being diverted. I was enjoying the steady ride as the brain was coming back down to earth following the week in school. I suppose someone might have had an accident – I'd better go with him.

Sitting on a pile of stones not a hundred yards from the road were a group of folks all eating, drinking and talking – looked fun. My bike was taken from me and carefully parked and two girls pulled me by the arms to where they had been sitting. 'Come, come.' Sometimes it's best just to go with things in Eritrea and see what happens. Seated in their midst I was given piles of food and a tin cup of sewa so I got stuck in. The old man kept to his task going back and forth to the roadside pulling in more and more strangers who were similarly made comfortable on a stone where they were fed and sewa'd. Nobody was really fluent in English but Rigbe was up for having a go so we had a chat over our injera. Apparently I was a guest at a traditional house-building ceremony. Rigbe, who told me she worked at the airport, and her husband were to be the new occupants and the old man was her father. The stone had been delivered and the builders were ready to start but we had to bless the new home-to-be first with a get-together. Okay – Asmara can wait.

This wasn't the only time I had been pulled in while on my bike. Not long after the new house celebration I was riding along, this time on a Sunday afternoon on the way back from the city, when a soldier clicked his fingers and motioned. Hmm, wary of this one. The Kalashnikov across his back might have had something to do with that. 'Come, come.' I'd heard that before. Following him up the track a little way I was led into a large brown tent packed with people. Unwittingly I had been invited to a baptism this time. Fair enough – pile up the plate and fill up the cup. Other volunteers had been a bit cynical about this kind of thing figuring that it was some kind of status symbol having a white face on the photos. Not sure about that – in my dirty, holed trousers and shirt I didn't reckon I was much of a catch.

The girl serving the food was very pretty and I smiled and thanked her for the injera. The soldier who had led me in noticed this and said, 'Do you want something?' and nodded in the direction of the girl who had continued serving others.

'What do you mean?'

'If you want her I can talk to the father.'

'Get outa here – she's only about twenty,' I replied catching his drift and trying to highlight the fact I was old enough to be her Dad, maybe even Grand dad, and wasn't on the lookout for 'something' at all.

'Might be expensive but you'll be able to afford her.'

This bloke wasn't giving up easily, perhaps he was on commission. Then, of course, you get into all kinds of silly conundrums like 'I don't want the father to be offended and get some idea from the soldier that I think his daughter is ugly.' After some careful words I managed to get the message across that I was quite satisfied to have my dinner and that was enough, thanks. Let's talk about football now please.

Need to be careful who you smile at in Eritrea.

Over the past few months dreams in Abarda had often revolved around fish and chips. The lack of food and the extreme nature of sensations on the tongue – either bland (barney, spaghetti) or explosive (berbera) was affecting my sleep pattern. When I got back to England and made my way to the local chip shop I was surprised to find that my taste buds woke up not to the taste of cod or chips but to vinegar. Hit the spot.

Another vision which had regularly come into sharp focus – particularly as my departure time approached – was that of the in-flight meal on Egyptian Airways. When it materialised somewhere over Sudan I made the most of it. The arrangement was critical – no rush. Chicken something-or-other was surrounded by bread roll, butter, plastic pot of peas and carrots, knife and fork, paper napkin and for afters – a chocolate pyramid. Nobody could have interrupted that meal and it will stick in the memory for a long time.

September 2006 – Mendefera, a New Town

'Travel permit please Woldu,' I asked handing over the application form. Having got back to Eritrea after the summer break my first stop was the Ministry of Education on Harnet Avenue to secure the paperwork that would get me past the checkpoints between Asmara and my new home in Mendefera. 'Call back later in the week,' was the best he could offer. Although I was keen to get to my new placement, meet the people I'd be working with and start the teacher-training I wasn't too bothered about the delay and had expected Woldu's response. Anyway, a few days would allow me time to catch up with the VSO staff and the others of the 2005 intake of volunteers who, like me, would also be starting their second year. The new volunteers would also be around and it would be good to see Alga and Mama at Bristol Pension again.

This overlap of volunteers was a great way to ensure that accumulated knowledge about Eritrea – from a foreigner's perspective – was passed on effectively. We were all in the same boat and the bonding in these circumstances was natural and beneficial for the organisation and volunteers alike. The folks who'd done a year had the experience and the new folks had the energy, passion and innocence. That was definitely true of the 2006 intake. Steffan was particularly high on Eritrea (this place can do that to people) and by the end of the first week seemed to have covered half the country on his bike and photographed every smiling kid he'd passed. Like us the year before the new folks were holed-up in the Lion Hotel and we all got together in the evenings in the rooftop bar. Had some good sessions fielding the predictable questions about the country and VSO staff while we found out where they were all going to be placed.

'Got the travel permit yet?' Woldu gave me a gormless grin and shrugged. 'What's the problem Woldu?' Woldu gave me another gormless grin and shrugged. This went on for three weeks. THREE WEEKS. Of course during this time I didn't know I'd be stuck in Asmara for that long. After the first week I called into the Ministry to pick up the permit every day. Same response with no indication of how long it would take. Maybe it would take a month, six months. Maybe I wouldn't be granted a permit. Maybe I'd have to find some work in Asmara, return to Mai Nefhi, go back to England – who knows?

Being Eritrea this situation naturally led to time drifting into days of limbo, days that were distinctly odd and some days that were inspiring and rewarding. The 2005 group of volunteers disappeared off to their villages or hadn't arrived back in the country yet, the new volunteers were involved in their induction training and I was kicking my heels waiting for Woldu. Never did find out the reason for the delay.

The limbo days consisted of getting up in Bristol Pension, picking up an *Eri-Profile* from the old girl outside the Post Office and going to Fiori's for a breakfast bun and tchai. After that a quick check in the VSO office for mail and a session on the computer in the internet café. The rest of a limbo day was usually spent in the British Council library doing a spot of maths and trying to plan for the teacher-training workshops I was going to be involved in if I ever got to Mendefera. The British Council library was as a library should be – calm and peaceful. Unfortunately the mindset was 'let's get on with it' and 'calm and peaceful' wasn't really the ticket at that time. Enjoyed meeting up with Abraham, the librarian again. He put an American or English film in the video cassette at 6.30 every Saturday evening and I – and sometimes other volunteers in Asmara for the weekend – used to turn up for the show along with a few Eritreans who saw this as another way to pick up some English. Not sure what they picked up from *'Brassed Off'* with broad Yorkshire accents throughout but I understood it fine.

As the days passed I found myself desperately trying to fill them usefully and tried things I'd not done before. The

Tigrinya film at Cinema Impero was a bit like a filled-out *Neighbours* episode and I picked up from other volunteers that this was typical. Given my ignorance of the language I occupied myself during the film by trying to spot buildings and views I recognised in Asmara – all the Eritrean films seem to be made in and around the city. When that interest waned I cast my eyes upwards and admired the Italian-sculptured ceiling. Real old fashioned type of cinema – took me back to when I was a kid watching *The Nun's Story* (no idea why my parents thought that was suitable for a four-year- old) in Grassmoor Playhouse. In those days all pit villages in Derbyshire had their own cinema. Present mixed with the past – strange experience.

Strange became decidedly weird when I bought a ticket for the German Oktoberfest show at Cinema Roma. The Germans in Asmara held a beer festival in the Intercontinental Hotel every year. The show in Cinema Roma was really a rehearsal for the real thing. Sitting in a sea of blond and grey hair watching an oompah band accompanying grown men slapping each other's leather-clad bottoms in time is not really my cup of tea. Went down a bomb with the sober German audience so the actual event at the Intercontinental played out before a drunken German audience must have been a riot.

The unwanted free time allowed me to reflect a bit on the previous summer in England. I'd listened to some of the others who'd been back to see their families and heard them talking about shedding a tear in supermarkets stocked to the roof with every kind of food imaginable. The stark contrast and sudden and relatively easy transfer from an African village where families are faced with the daily challenge of trying to feed their children to a world where the biggest challenge is whether to have salmon or beef for dinner had hit hard.

Not leaving the tap running while we were brushing teeth – we'd all agreed to do that before flying home the previous July. Clean water was precious and needed to be conserved. Realised that I'd managed to stick to this resolution in England for about three days before the 'take it for granted' approach took over. Didn't bump into the famous 'wallpaper conversation' I'd heard about. It goes like this – live for a year in a tiny box-house with neighbours who have nothing and where children have no shoes and can't get any medical care and then resite yourself to an English pub and listen to a couple arguing passionately about whether to decorate the living room with floral or striped wallpaper. As a consequence you are hit with the frivolous nature of what most in the West occupy themselves with most of the time. Had a little nod in this direction when I was out with some friends the previous August in a restaurant in Sheffield and there was an intense discussion about what you were and were not allowed to put in your blue – as opposed to your green - dustbin. Thoughts wandered a bit to the ragged kids in Mai Nefhi who were ushered on to the bus for their military training and I couldn't really get into the blue dustbin debate.

Mai Jah Jah is a special location in Asmara – a bit of a jewel. It surprised me that although I'd had a year in Eritrea I hadn't discovered this place. Heard a couple of volunteers talking about this café that sold 'proper' ice-cream at the top of Mai Jah Jah. Got directions and had a walk up there one day. Just up from Barti Meskerem Square the road opens out to a large palm tree-surrounded area. Leading up the hill is a decent road and a beautiful stepped waterfall probably about a hundred yards long. No water of course but the steps were tiled in eye-catching colours and the view from the top over the city was a stunner. St Mary's Catholic Cathedral really was made to crown sights like this. If the water was turned on – and this never happened during the time I was in Eritrea – the whole picture would have started to justify some of Alga's Tourist Board claims about the city. The ice-cream in the café was nice as well. Nick the recently appointed ambassador and Brian – Head of the British Council – were in there sharing ice-cream with some friends. It was that kind of place – a long way out of reach for the locals.

The day I went to Himbirti on the bike was very special for a number of reasons. In the third week of 'permit-waiting' I decided to visit Mai Nefhi and some of the villages I'd known in my first year. Never knew what to expect with this kind of adventure. Sometimes it was a non-event, sometimes it was a complete one-off experience of the kind that sticks in the memory for a lifetime. It started well. Just past Gordaif on the Mendefera road the flowers started and they went on and on and on. 'Where did they come from?' Lining both sides of the road all the way down to the right turn I needed for Mai Nefhi there were thousands of small pink flowers on stems a couple of feet tall. Did I miss these last year or didn't they bloom? Yohannes had told me that the rains in August had been pretty good and maybe this had triggered the spark into life. Stopped at the junction to say 'hi' to the chicaleestas who had mended many a puncture on my bike for me. Sat down on a stone and had a tchai with Nuguse and Samuel who could repair a 'bucco' in less than three minutes for one nakfa. Their corrugated iron shelter provided the shade and I told them about my future home and work in Mendefera. 'Lots of dust in Mendefera,' said Nuguse without the slightest hint of irony as we sat in the dust sipping our drinks.

Told the lads I'd see them on the return journey and set off on the road down to Adrassi, Kt Mewli, my 2005/6 home Abarda and beyond this to Himbirti. Most of this road was a gentle downhill slope so it was an easy ride with plenty of time to gaze around at the scenery I'd got to know very well. Stunning place. Open plains with the small villages dotted here and there – mountains in the distance. Passed Adi Hamushti (Village Five) so called because there were only five houses in the village.

Remembered going with Kasi and Fasi to a short, sharp Nigdet there the previous February.

In Abarda I called in on Kasi, Curvilla and Ruta – I knew they'd be home as, from last year's experience, I knew the students wouldn't be turning up at school for another week or so. Good to see them and catch up on what had been happening. Fasi had left to start work in Qatar, Kasi was putting paperwork together to try and get work as a professor in the college next door to Mai Nefhi School. $13,000 a month salary paid to professors by the UN was very tempting and he had big ideas for his daughters back in India which would require a lot of finance.

Took a while to find Fiori's house in Himbirti as I'd lost my bearings a bit but the villagers soon put me on the right track. The house was full and they were pleased to see me. As well as Fiori and her little brothers and sisters there was her aunt and uncle who lived close by. They'd all been working hard throughout July and August and the crops harvested from their little patch of land should be enough to keep them fed. I gave Fiori a few photographs of herself and her friends I'd taken in school the previous year. I'd had them enlarged in England and the whole family were overjoyed with the simple gift. They insisted I take some photos of them outside the house holding the photos so I did. Energised by the tchai and barney but mostly by the welcome they had given me I set off back to Asmara. It was sixteen miles on a gently rising slope but it didn't feel like it. That's what decent people do – make you feel you're going downhill when you're going uphill.

Made a couple more visits to different folks during the last few days before Woldu gave me the permit but really I was filling time and ready to go. Some volunteers were actually placed in Asmara and had found accommodation in the city suburbs. Popped over to Paradiso near the football stadium to see Katy and Margaret. Margaret had finished her year in Ghinda and had shacked up with Katy in the city. Margaret was out and Katy was close to tears – Margaret was driving her crazy with her bizarre ways and there had been numerous clashes over the sort of petty things that can happen when two people live together. Katy was particularly disturbed by Margaret's tendency to hide the pots and pans under her bed for some reason.

In Bristol Pension there was actually somebody else staying there for a few days. Mark was a wind farm engineer who was in the country doing some preliminary studies for the UN. Another global traveller who saw opportunity rather than nuisance factor when posted to the other side of the world. Didn't trouble him with my tale of woe waiting for the travel permit to Mendefera. It's all about perspective.

And there it was – a bit of A4 with the heading TRAVEL PERMIT on Woldu's desk. No messing about. Back to VSO

office where Fish was sat on the rooftop drinking tchai –
'Come on Fish, get the truck. We're going to Mendefera.'

Vijay and Nina were a lovely couple. Vijay was standing in
the doorway of my new home in Mendefera when Fish
dropped me, my table and my bed off in the compound. I
had never met Vijay before, hadn't a clue who he was and
never found out how he knew I was going to live and work
in Mendefera. He helped me carry the furniture into one
of the rooms as a dozen children watched us. I had the
compound to myself. There were three rooms I could
choose from and an outside toilet. With the stuff inside
Vijay explained he had contacted Eyob the landlord and
told him the broken window in one of the doors had to be
fixed – and a few days later it was. He had also arranged
for the well to be filled. This was a luxury. My compound
had a purpose-built concrete pit about six feet deep and
Vijay told me a water tanker went round Adiga Berai (my
district) filling wells up for twenty nakfa. I took the bit of
corrugated iron off the top of the well and was delighted
to see it full of clear, sparkling water. The dead lizard
floating in it took the shine off a bit but I had no intention
of drinking it anyway. This well was the solution to my
clothes, washing, and toilet-flushing challenges.

Thanked Vijay for what he had done and he invited me
round that evening for dinner. Vijay and Nina lived on the
other side of Adiga Berai and I carefully picked my way
through the usual white block houses following the

instructions Vijay had given me. Plenty of 'Selams' with locals along the way and a nice, warm evening as the sun was going down. It felt like a good start to my time in Mendefera. Nina had cooked about five courses and they tasted great. Over the meal Vijay gave me a lot of information about my new town and this proved invaluable over the first few days. After the meal they put on a video of their traditional Indian wedding – very colourful, very beautiful. They had only been in Mendefera a year. Vijay had taken up the chance to teach in Eritrea and earn some decent UN money which he intended to invest in a family home back in India. He taught at St George's – the only High School in Mendefera and they seemed to be making a good life for themselves.

Goodnights said I ventured out into the darkness to go home. Over an hour later I was completely lost. Like a fool I had not taken note of any landmarks or really given much attention to which direction I was going. It was pitch dark and I kept bumping into figures that grumbled at me in Tigrinya as I trod on their toes. Dogs raced around howling – hoped they weren't rabid. Only one thing for it – got to find my way to Vijay's house and ask if he'd take me home. It was getting late by the time I found their house. All the lights were out, probably fast asleep. After what this couple had done for me I felt terrible at what I was about to do but did it anyway. I banged on the steel door of their compound for a full five minutes shouting 'Vijay! Vijay!' Vijay, along with the entire population of Adiga Berai, woke up. Without a word of complaint, which of course made me feel even worse, he took me home. Felt like a little kid which, in this new place, is what I was. Once again, the stark realisation that I needed to learn fast.

Some mornings Habtom, my neighbour gave me a lift on his bus from Adiga Berai to the PRC (Pedagogical Resources Centre) on Tibor, most times I walked as he was usually on an early run. The walk to work was just over a mile and was a good opportunity to get to know the folks and for them to get used to seeing me around. Regularly called in to see Josef in his little shop – bought biscuits and bananas when he had them. Friendly bloke with a dozen kids. His shop, like many shops in Mendefera, was pockmarked with bullet holes – this region had been the site of many pitched battles during the long years of struggle. Crossing the main Asmara-border road which cut through the middle of Mendefera I either took the road up to Tibor, on the high plateau overlooking the town, past the soldiers' barracks or the one that went past the bus station. Tibor was a wide expanse of flat ground littered with bombed-out tanks left over from the war. The view back over the town was always worth a glance. High ground rising on the other side of the main road dominated by the white St Mary's lookalike church with my home beyond that. Walking across Tibor then in and out of the classroom buildings of

Frei Kalsi Elementary School the plain opened out and stretched all the way to Ethiopia. The Simien Mountains shaped the horizon in the distance. Never saw them clearly as there was always cloud covering on the peaks but mightily impressive all the same.

My office was part of the PRC compound which also comprised Belay's office and a large classroom used for teacher-training workshops and meetings. The Frei Kalsi canteen was the socialising venue on Tibor just as the Mai Nefhi canteen had been at the High School the previous year. Belay – the PRC Co-ordinator – and me used to share tchai and a bit of barney with Kibrom the Elementary school Director and any number of teachers. After work the walk home tended to be slower than in the morning. I was no longer teaching kids in the classroom so the demands of lesson planning and evaluating wasn't an evening fixture anymore. Had a bit more spare time. The other reason for strolling home was, of course, weariness. Much hotter in Mendefera and therefore more tiring. I had a thermometer and measured the temperature (in direct sunlight) at 43 degrees one day. In the same way that it was good to bump into people coming to Tibor so it was on the return journey. Dembay was a restaurant/bar just off the main road and this became my usual eating place on the journey home, never did get round to cooking for myself. Sometimes I dined alone and read the *Guardian Weekly* or talked to the waitresses as I ate my pasta. I continued to trust my choice of staple food as the main reason I didn't get too many of the two hundred different types of diarrhoea. Sometimes I was joined by teachers I had met in schools or Mussie who worked in the little hospital up the road as a porter. He was always well dressed and always on the lookout for an advantage, an edge. Bit of a Del Boy character he was very open about homing in on white faces to strike up relationships. I was an obvious target being the only one with this feature in Mendefera. He told me his last 'friend' had been a Canadian woman who had visited the town for a few days. Don't know what she was doing here. Mussie had cornered her in Dembay and was now a regular emailer to Vancouver – him asking for money, her sending it by Western Union. Mussie lightened the day and I looked forward to seeing him.

Brkti (roll the r's and you've got it) was a frisker at the library in Mendefera, nobody got past her with a book stuffed down their trousers. She had failed some exams in Sawa where she had been posted for her military training and had been sent home for a few months before her next call-up. While she was waiting she had been assigned the security duties at the library and was in situ on her chair at the door during opening hours always on the lookout for the next frisk – and there were many young lads who were happy to be frisked. Listening to Brkti's tales from Sawa gave the strong message that girls were treated no differently to boys during their training. The sacrifices made during the wars had put women on an equal footing in the eyes of the military and there was no letting up either during the training or in terms of punishment for misdemeanours.

Letemichael used to tend a small charcoal fire in a metal furnello (tin box) at the side of the road going up to Adiga Berai. Maize cobs were roasted on this for a few minutes and sold for three nakfa each. Often burnt and black it was just about edible and I saw it as my dessert course after the pasta in Dembay. In the firelight Letemichael used to do a spot of maths on bits of old cardboard. As I crunched my maize I used to nudge her in the right direction with her sums. Despite the private tuition she never once let me off paying for the maize. Fair enough.

Picked up a jerry can of water from Josef and headed home. Usually it was dark by now but this all changed within a few weeks of me arriving in Adiga Berai as we were granted street lights. Well, a fluorescent tube every hundred yards anyway. No matter, it did the job and my frequent falls and sprained ankles were a thing of the past.

Being a bit more developed than the villages Mendefera had other facilities as well as street lighting. A Post Office meant that I could send aerogrammes to England without having to take them to Asmara. The town also boasted two internet cafes and this meant I could communicate with my family on a daily basis not just at the weekend when I went to the city. One internet café was in an ordinary looking white box-shaped house. By mistake I once turned in a block too soon and stood facing a family having their dinner. Two men, a woman and three children all stared at me in mid-mouthful. I stared at the bemused faces wondering where the computers had gone. After a full five-second frozen moment I turned round and walked out. Not a word was said. Reflected on what would have happened in England if a foreigner had barged into your house while you were having lunch, stared for a while and then walked out again. Worst of all only a week later I made exactly the same mistake again and we played out the same little ritual once more. Thought by now they were probably used to me – 'it's alright, it's just him again.'

October 2006 – Trainer?

Government buses travelled the Asmara to Mendefera route. These were pretty new – a step up from the old privately-owned wrecks that serviced the villages. Disciplined boarding usually featured due to the presence of police in Mendefera bus station. The use of the rock line was strictly adhered to as the police officer stood at the head of the line and barked at each rock in turn whatever is Tigrinya for 'whose is this rock' and the rock's owner then boarded.

On every bus journey I took from Mendefera to Asmara there were always at least two checkpoints usually manned by at least five soldiers. The first checkpoint was between Mendefera and Dbarwa. The bus always stopped and a young soldier would get on. Looking down the bus he chose the people whose identification he wanted to see and signalled his intention with an almost silent click of the fingers. The power the uniform conveyed meant that there was no need for volume or even the slightest show of aggression. The minimalism of the action, of course, made it all the more impressive to watch as paperwork was duly handed over to be checked.

On my second journey he clicked at me and I handed him my papers. Taking no notice of these he motioned for me to get off the bus which I did. The bus drove on. The soldiers thought this was quite funny. My questions about the time of the next bus and how far it was to Dbarwa were ignored. I waited in the dust at the side of the road for an hour not just for a bus but to show them they had not inconvenienced me (which they had). I also thought that my plight might embarrass them, make them feel bad. No chance, forget subtlety with Eritrean soldiers. It took nearly three hours to walk to Dbarwa in the burning heat.

Caught the next buses from Mendefera to Asmara with some trepidation. The soldiers were a concern. It was about thirty five miles to the capital over rough terrain and baking tarmac roads that wound up serious mountains to the cooler Asmara plateau. The solution came in the form of a tiny girl called Winta. Winta was one of the little urchins at the bus station selling small items for the journey. The call was always 'soft, minty, mastica!' (tissue, mints, chewing gum.) I bought eight mints for a few nakfa, I think she overcharged me. On the bus I offered the sweets around until all the folks in the seats near me were sucking away furiously. The bus driver climbed in and we were on our way.

As we approached the checkpoint I was prepared to accept whatever happened. I had no prepared speech, no plan to avoid being ordered off the bus. If you want to do it soldier, get on and do it. The soldier got on and spotted my white face sticking out like a white face. He smiled, clicked his fingers and motioned for me to get off the bus. Immediately my new mint-sucking friends piped up. The broad translation must have been along the lines of 'no, no he's with us' and from those who had seen me around the town 'memher, memher' – he's a teacher in our town. The soldier shrugged and moved on to the next click. Winta made quite a killing on mint sales that year.

It was good to meet up with the Hash group again at Alpha supermarket. Things had changed, people had moved on. Carlo's wife, and therefore Carlo, had gone back to Italy and Barbara, the German Ambassador's wife, had left with her husband so Brian offered to take the reins as Hash leader.

Brian was a surveyor at the Ministry of Public Works so he was used to travelling the country overseeing road and bridge building. I say used to because he had just been confined to Asmara by the government, travel permit refused. This effectively stopped him doing his job and his frustration showed. It was obvious he would not be in Eritrea for much longer and was actively contacting acquaintances around the world looking for a new post. In the meantime his lack of employment meant that he had plenty of time during the week to get the Hash food and drink and research our Saturday destination.

Nick had now taken on the full duties of British Ambassador following Mike's departure and he occasionally came on the Hash. Listening to conversations between him and Brian was an education in how these international travellers lived. Once they were discussing their respective work in Thailand – Brian had lived there around 2001 and Nick a little later.

'Do you know the Apollo Hotel in Bangkok?'

'Yes of course – stayed there a few times – nice swimming pool.'

'It is – I used to take a dip there myself.'

This intimate knowledge of the world – talking in the same way that I might discuss a local pub in Sheffield with a mate – never failed to impress. It was an insight into a world I had never known and the Hash was made up of people with this kind of background and experience. Planet Earth was just a global village and its nooks and crannies seemed to have been thoroughly explored.

On the other hand the group were still keen to hear my stories from the villages in Zoba Debub. Few were permitted outside the capital – Americans particularly had to maintain radio contact with the embassy at all times – so someone who lived and worked in a village was a prize. Felt honoured but after a while became a little cynical at the level of interest shown. At no point was I ever directly asked for information that may be 'useful' to an external government and I never sought to pass on anything that I thought may be of value. My innocent ramblings about what had happened during the week were no more than that. However, I do believe the volunteers' presence spread around the country from Nakfa in the north down to Adi Quala on the border with Ethiopia gave an indication of the state of play around the country and that in itself would have been worth knowing in some quarters.

The Eritrean government might have had some justification for restricting Brian's movements around the country. He used to laugh that he had logged the positions of every bridge in Eritrea on to his GPS – 'sure-fire future pension if Ethiopia ever needed a bit of strategic information.' He invited me to his home once for a beer after the Hash. An enormous photograph of his wife and son standing on a bridge in Scotland expanded to cover a whole wall. Told me he had taken a lot of stick from his wife's family over the years for his absence. Travelling the world as a surveyor leaves little time for family life. 'I know what they mean,' said Brian 'but it's what I am, what I was when we married. Can't change now.'

During a 'city' Hash (a walk around parts of Asmara itself) we had a look at the Red Sea school which Joe from the US Embassy told me was the location of the American spy station in the Seventies. Hundreds of Americans were employed in the country at the time and quite a few are now surprised in the US by grown Eritrean sons and daughters who they had fathered and forgotten years ago. Joe and Barbara invited me to stay at their home a couple of times on Saturday nights after the Hash. They had a wonderful house. The shipping container standing outside which had been used to bring their furniture was bigger than my home in Mendefera. All the material bits were in place – flat screen television, luxurious sofa, oak dining table, beautiful ornaments – the lot. Contrast my creaky bed, the old table I had bought from the market and the two bricks I used for bookends.

One Sunday morning after a night at their house I got up early – just after half past five. I needed to get the bus back to Mendefera to work. Nobody about, I dressed, tiptoed downstairs and opened the fridge door to see if I could find something to stuff in my mouth for breakfast before I set off. I'd just had a week visiting teachers in a school in a particularly remote area. The families had little to eat, children in rags some with distended bellies. With this fresh in my mind the contents of the fridge hit me – it almost felt physical. This was a place of plenty not just apparent by the amount of food but the range. Various packets of cooked meat, any number of different cheeses, milk and so on. On the surface next to the sink were packets of chocolate biscuits and four different kinds of cereal. I left Joe and Barbara a note on the fridge door thanking them for their hospitality. I appreciated their generosity and seeing the lifestyle they enjoyed but it wasn't what I had come to Eritrea for and I was comfortable living and working as a volunteer.

On my way out I said a cheery 'Good morning' to the guard in his sentry box – big mistake. He had been dozing on duty and nearly jumped out of his skin. His automatic reaction was to point his Kalashnikov at me – my automatic reaction was to put my hands in the air in true 'stick 'em up' fashion. Legacy of too many Clint Eastwood films in my early years. Backing away down the path with what I hoped were soothing words I managed to get round the corner in one piece. Not good having an adrenaline rush as dramatic as that so early in the morning.

Brian had inherited Carlo's ability to find curious places to visit. One time after driving a couple of miles outside the city we got out and walked round a small pond. Took less than ten minutes and we never lost sight of the cars. More adventurous walks were usually found in villages south of Asmara just off my road – the road to Mendefera. We were not always well received by villagers and I could understand their reaction – a group of well-to-do foreign strangers striding through their village without any real attempt to build a relationship. In some cases kids threw stones. I don't think this was done in a nasty way but just to provoke a reaction. They certainly got a reaction from Jim who used to shout and swear at them usually along the lines of 'kicking their asses.' Not good. Felt a greater allegiance with the villagers than with the Hash at these times and understood why some volunteers steered clear.

Belay and me had walked the few miles to Mendefera Elementary School. We had organised an observation and I was looking forward to getting inside the classrooms. I'd sat in on a few classes giving brief feedback to teachers at the end of lessons with a formal report to the Director to follow. I'd wanted to do things this way. Considered it necessary to get a feel for strengths and improvement opportunities before I started putting together training workshops for the teachers. It was good to be able to build on my own experience teaching in the UK and Mai

Nefhi where the demands of the timetable had restricted the time available for me to visit other schools.

'This is a ball,' said the teacher as she held up a bottle.

'What is this?' she continued still holding up the bottle.

'This is a ball,' chorused the children.

And . . .

'This is a bottle,' said the teacher as she held up a ball.

'What is this?' she continued still holding up the ball.

'This is a bottle,' chorused the children.

I called the teacher over and quietly pointed out the mistake. She looked at me in disbelief and glanced at Belay hoping for confirmation that what she had been teaching for the past three years was correct.

This was not an isolated case and was perhaps predictable given that many Eritreans are taught English solely by Eritreans who in most cases have never spoken to anyone whose mother tongue is English. Neither television nor cinema is freely available so exposure to English is limited and mistakes creep in, are replicated and multiply. Similarly written English is poor and it is rare to see a sentence that doesn't contain spelling mistakes. Plenty of material for training workshops and made notes along the lines of 'invite the English teacher volunteers to Mendefera to take workshops while I deal with the maths.'

Halfway through the morning Belay decided he would like a photograph of me with some kids. I grabbed the nearest little girl and held her up for the picture with half a dozen others squeezing up close to make sure they got in the frame. Click.

A larger group of children on the other side of the compound raced up and demanded to get in on the act. Belay took a few steps back to make sure he caught them all. Click.

A couple of classes full of children spotted what was happening. Out they came and gathered round. Click.

By now the whole school, including teachers, were determined not to be left out.

Click.

I really enjoyed visiting schools and observing lessons. It was a good way of getting to know many teachers and students in the area very quickly. They, of course, got to know me and I was invariably made welcome. As always the informal stuff, the chats over lunch, the jokes shared over a glass of tchai in the canteen were often the most revealing not just from the perspective of the school but also the country.

'What is that?' In the staffroom Claire, who had taught in Adi Gaul the year before, had hung up a bath mat with a picture of Mickey Mouse on it. The teacher with the question had never seen Mickey Mouse – nobody in Eritrea had. I suppose a mouse standing on two legs in red shorts is a bit confusing when seen for the first time. When I looked at the picture through his eyes Mickey Mouse doesn't even look like a real mouse but you don't question these things when you are drip-fed Disney cartoons from when you are a baby in the West. I don't think I helped his understanding much with my rambling explanation – how do you tell someone who has never seen Mickey Mouse, or any cartoon, what Mickey Mouse is?

After this incident I used to test Eritreans' awareness of all things that are part of the fabric of life in England. Didn't find anyone who had heard of The Beatles or Elvis. George W Bush was known, as was Tony Blair. He did me no favours at all by visiting Ethiopia – the enemy – not long before I went to Eritrea. Some footballers were known but only if they played for dominant English Premiership teams. Princess Diana was the one, though. The striking aspect of this fame was not just that everyone in Eritrea knew Diana – they spoke as if they loved her. Oh – and Bob Geldof, he drew a complete blank.

Claire had been at Adi Gaul for a year and listening to the teachers she had clearly been liked and done some great work. Irish Claire was all energy, bright, bubbly – life and soul. I remembered her talking about what she was getting up to in Adi Gaul Middle School the previous year. (She had now moved to a placement in Asmara.)

'Dust? Dust? My classroom is covered in dust? All Eritrea's covered in dust!' This had been Claire's exasperated (edited) response to the Director after she had spent the whole weekend with some students cleaning and painting a classroom and he had sniffily remarked on the dusty floor while ignoring the pristine walls. He knew where he stood with Claire after that.

It had been a long bike ride that morning to get to Adi Gaul – at least five miles over some rough ground. Didn't expect the lush growth on the plains and realised that some parts of Zoba Debub were a 'garden of Eritrea.' Saw fields of carrots, cabbages and maize all looking healthy and felt pleased for the people in that area.

Due to the distance Belay and me set off back to Mendefera early. There was no lighting across the plain and the way was unmarked. Riding back I could understand VJ's reaction as he told the story of Claire regularly setting off to walk from Mendefera to her house in Adi Gaul as it was starting to get dark. As I bumped my way across the stony, pitted track I shared his amazement. Cycling in daylight was difficult, walking across this lot in the dark must have been a nightmare.

Belay was well known in the area. He had been a School Director before moving to the PRC and seemed to be playing the system well. The fact that he could walk to the PRC from his home in Mendefera in ten minutes was an indication that he had managed to get things a little bit organised for himself – no daily grind on the buses to get to work for him.

Girma, Shewa and Solomon were the official School Inspectors of Mendefera and they reported to Yacob. All, predictably, ex-fighters they ran their office tightly and inspected secondary schools and elementary schools across the region. Understandably I learned a great deal about the education system in Eritrea from them and they supported me throughout my time there. We got on well – good friends.

Shewa and I headed off across the plain early one morning to have a look at Adi Mongonti Elementary School. Two mountains of the pointy kind a child might draw marked where we needed to bear right and after a couple of hours we were at the school gates. The school was on the outskirts of a typical middle-of-nowhere Eritrean village. Goats, chickens and plenty of Claire's dust everywhere. I'd particularly looked forward to this visit as the School Director was spoken of with some reverence due to her exploits in the conflict.

Saba, the Director, welcomed us in and we stood to one side as the students sang the anthem as the flag was raised. Noticed that elementary children belted out the anthem as if their lives depended on it and the kids at Adi Mongonti were no different. In fact, they were definitely the loudest I'd heard almost screaming the words with hand on heart as Saba and her team scanned the gathering. I contrasted this volume and passion with the Mai Nefhi High School students who were of the mumbling variety.

As well as noting the lusty singing it was clear from the ragged school jumpers that these children were from very poor families. Some of the volunteers used to have competitions to spot the jumpers with most holes. This kind of daftness deflects from the tragic circumstances and helps get you through the day – a sobbing volunteer is no good to anybody. Students' jumpers are handed down from sibling to sibling and kids in village families have a lot of siblings. The little boy that stood out must have been the youngest in his family. The collar, cuffs and lower section of his jumper were all held together with five strands of wool, I know because I counted them as he proudly sang his heart out.

It was easy to imagine Saba with a Kalashnikov in her hands. She was tall and strongly built and very direct in her manner. Shewa and me observed a few lessons then we joined the Director for lunch. Lots of injera and meat – maybe in our honour? – and we listened to how she had won the bike race the previous weekend. Bike races were held in Mendefera every Sunday morning around the town. Crowds used to gather to cheer the riders on and Saba had built a reputation competing against and sometimes beating the men.

As we ate the food Elsa, Saba's daughter, joined us. The value of having parents who were renowned ex-fighters was demonstrated again as we learned that Elsa was a stewardess on Eritrean Airlines. Clearly this kind of job offered opportunities to escape the country and claim political asylum abroad. Only people who had backgrounds demonstrating total loyalty to the Government were given these jobs and the obvious conclusions could be drawn – these were 'card-carrying' people who were loyal to the Party.

Bereket had managed to get out of the country during the summer. Donard updated me and was a good source of information as he had witnessed the escape.

Donard had been assigned to work in the city not as a trainer but as project manager setting up a programme for teachers on *Radio Bana*. The idea was to make a range of teaching methods, materials and ideas available to as wide an audience as possible. He even interviewed me for one broadcast. As part of the research during the preliminary phase Donard, Yohannes and Bereket had flown to South Africa where a similar project had taken off with some success. Only trusted Eritreans are allowed this kind of passage but even the trusted Eritreans can't resist the opportunity when it is handed to them and Bereket took his chance. 'I'm not going back.'

Predictably, this route is seen by many as another method of escaping the country and an awful lot safer than dodging the thousands of soldiers on the border who are quite happy to pull the trigger if you don't stop. Eritreans choosing this course spend years building up an image of loyalty to the President. People I met actually went on government missions to other countries and returned just to build up this trust. Then, biding their time, picking their moment another mission comes up. 'Oh they've been out before and come back – we can rely on them' and off they go never to return. The Eritrean football team has done this a couple of times which is why the country doesn't compete on an international level anymore.

There is usually collusion with family or friends overseas – once out of Eritrea you probably don't know anyone in the country you find yourself in and, worse, you have no money. A brother or sister in the States can be a big help. There is another serious complication – you have left your family and friends back in Eritrea and they come under the government's microscope being subjected to interrogation and often much worse. Bereket received many emails detailing the precarious position he had put his family in. That he knew this would be the case and still went ahead gives an indication of his desperation.

Over the next couple of years Yohannes did the same as Bereket. So did Yakiem, a Programme Manager and Miriam, the Finance Manager. These were all people in positions of status in Eritrea – not subsistence farmers scraping by in a village. They were seen as respected pillars of the community by an ever-watchful government.

Doesn't matter how elevated you are if you don't have freedom you are not really alive and they knew that.

November 2006 – Trainer!

Every white visitor to Eritrea gets it on a daily basis – gangs of kids shouting 'You, You, You!' or 'Tilian' (Italian) which is a throwback to colonial days.

It can feel strange living in a country where you know you only have a flimsy knowledge of the language. Forget shades of intonation, sarcasm, innuendo –relations have to be created using big, bold brush strokes leaving no room for ambiguity. I'd decided early on during my time in Eritrea to greet in an over- the-top manner – hugs, shoulder-banging, cheek to cheek stuff with the women. I'd overdone it in the beginning with an actual kiss on a woman's cheek. She let out a shriek which was followed by embarrassed laughter and an apology from me, only husbands kiss their wives. However, better to be thought of as an overfriendly but harmless idiot than a cold, untrustworthy, secretive character and, of course, the more friendly gestures offered the more these were reciprocated. Reckoned this approach was much more likely to lead to a sharing of cultures than being cool and stand-offish. Why on earth would I go to another country and try to limit discourse? Might as well stay at home.

Also, the *faux pas* that inevitably happen are more likely to be forgiven if relations are on a friendly footing. 'Oh it's just him – he's from England.' Misunderstandings happen the other way as well. The phrase that had irritated me more than any other in Eritrea was 'What is THIS,' as voiced by countless kids to me as I approached. The emphasis on 'THIS' as in 'What is THIS (walking towards us) in England would have been insulting to anyone and it really grated. On a visit to an elementary school with Shewa I realised where the phrase had originated and that I had been wrong to feel denigrated.

We were sitting at the back observing an English class and as the teacher held up a cup she said 'What is THIS?' The class dutifully replied 'THIS is a cup.' Next, 'What is THIS?' – teacher holds up a ruler. 'THIS is a ruler.'

I saw this routine in many elementary and middle schools. The kids greeting me with this phrase were not being disrespectful or condescending but showing off the three words of English they had remembered to an Englishman – they were actually trying to impress me.

Keep it simple, keep it broad brush, and don't make snap judgements.

Felt we'd had a bit of success in Mai Nefhi High School building the library, stocking it with the kindly donated books and extending this to Reading Room sessions. Wanted to send an update/thank-you to the folks in England who had contributed so I spent a few evenings in my house writing an article for the *Derbyshire Times*. Also thought I could put down another request at the same time. As follows:

Under the headline 'CHESTERFIELD-BORN TEACHER KEVIN APPEALS FOR YOUR HELP AGAIN' the Editor penned an introduction:

'Back in January of this year volunteer maths teacher Kevin Morley appealed to *Derbyshire Times* readers to help him provide books for a library at a school in Eritrea. You responded magnificently. These books are so valuable, I know because I visited the school recently and peeped in the window of the library to see many students avidly reading them,' he told us. 'Now Kevin who was born and brought up in Chesterfield is asking if YOU can help him provide basic support for children at a school in another part of East Africa. Today we publish his appeal in the hope that you might be able to give underprivileged children a step up the education ladder.'

> – and my bit under the headline 'GIVE FIORI THE TOOLS TO LEARN'. . .

'You may have read my letters printed in the *Derbyshire Times* at the beginning of this year when I asked for some books for a library I managed to build at my school. The request prompted Derbyshire folks to send me over two thousand books which kept the lads down at Asmara airport quite busy for a while. These books are so valuable. I know because I visited the school recently and peeped in the window of the library to see many students avidly reading them. You did that.

'I've moved down south now to a small town near the Ethiopian border. This is a bit different – more shanty town than rural village. Living is just as hard, there are just as many noisy kids and the effects of extreme poverty are just as obvious.

'Conflict, disease and drought denies these children their education. This doesn't just mean they can't do sums or read and write properly. Nor does it just cost them their chance of a job when they grow up – it can cost them their lives. If you don't go to school you don't get taught what a landmine looks like or learn how to stop getting AIDS or how to avoid becoming a child soldier. Until you learn the hard way.

'Right now there are over forty million children in the world living like this. What do we think we are playing at? Schools are destroyed and teachers killed. Pens, paper and a bit of chalk can be impossible to get hold of. There can be as many as two hundred in a class – sometimes sat under a tree because there isn't a building. Seventy children is common and in many cases taught by a teacher who hasn't had a day's training. Tell these folks you've got problems.

'The kind of numbers I'm quoting are an outrage. They are also vast – so vast they become meaningless. Fiori isn't meaningless though and she is one of these numbers. Fiori is about 17-years-old – she doesn't know for sure as we don't have birth certificates out here and birthdays are not celebrated. In her straight-talking way she told me that I was okay once – 'for a maths teacher.' She'd do alright in Derbyshire.

'Fiori's dad died in the conflict six years ago and her mother died of an unidentified illness this year leaving her with five younger brothers and sisters. What do you do when this happens not in a magazine story or on telly but in reality? Can you imagine?

'Well Fiori gets on with it setting the kids on with jobs and getting them off to school on time before coming to school herself because 'I am a student' and she's proud of that. There is spirit, strength and basic human decency in what she does and she has never asked me or anybody else for a penny. In fact she welcomes me when I visit with a cup of tchai and a bit of bread because 'I am a guest in her country.' No. Fiori is not a meaningless number nor, as the figures quoted show, is she a one-off in these kind of circumstances.

'Many families in the world suffer from extreme poverty and hunger. Some 1,500 children die every hour of the day from causes they would not die of in Derbyshire. Half a million women die every year during pregnancy. Twenty times that number suffer injury and permanent disability after giving birth. AIDS has become the leading cause of premature death in sub-Saharan Africa. 'Malaria and TB kills as many people each year as AIDS across Africa and Asia. And always there is the constant threat of war.

'I'm trying to chip in a bit by setting up and delivering a programme of training which will benefit teachers in twenty schools and, in turn, thousands of children. The building is in place but could do with some equipment. I don't want anything complicated that breaks down – not much in the way of spare parts out here. What I do need is pens and paper. If you can stick a few biros and a writing pad in an envelope and send it to me I will put them in the hands of teachers and students and we will take it from there.'

I remembered the class in Mai Nefhi School when sharing the lollipop was not as nice an act as I'd first thought. Another 'real kids' – as opposed to 'Ahh kids' – incident happened early one morning in my house in Mendefera.

Yordanos was a little girl about six-years-old. Bright face, active, often carrying her baby brother Futsom on her back in the traditional way. Never saw her (or any other baby-carrying girl) trip or let their siblings fall. She used to walk into my home at breakfast time and we'd share the four or five biscuits I'd bought to start the day. She ate very quickly, and always seemed ravenous. This was a pleasant time as she'd sing songs she'd learned at school (in English) as she pottered about my room. A more uplifting soundtrack to breakfast than the radio.

'Dubana has red shoes, Dubana has red shoes,

Dubana has red shoes, red, red, red.

Dubana has blue dress, Dubana has blue dress,

Dubana has blue dress, blue, blue, blue.

Dubana has black hair, Dubana has black hair,

Dubana has black hair, black, black, black.

Dubana has white teeth, Dubana has white teeth,

Dubana has white teeth, white, white, white.

Dubana has brown skin, Dubana has brown skin,

Dubana has brown skin, brown, brown, brown.'

And another one . . .

'Hade is one, kelete is two, celeste is number three.

Abarte is four, hamushte is five,

Hade, kelete, celeste, abarte, hamushte.'

One morning I was tidying something and making the tchai. When I finished I sat down to eat and realised that the biscuits had gone, Yordanos had eaten them all. I told her off with a stern voice and a very serious expression. 'I share my breakfast with you and you take it all!' – and so on.

She went home – a bit upset.

Now. Not for the first time I pondered on what I had become. I had got past the hungry African kids' faces on Christian Aid adverts and was dealing with Yordanos just like any other child. I had reprimanded a malnourished girl for taking my biscuits. 'Not right to take things that aren't yours,' etc. Felt bad that she'd left in tears and was glad she came back the next morning with the usual smile on her face. This time she only ate half the biscuits.

After a month or so of visiting schools and observing teachers and students I put together a programme of training workshops using what I'd seen in the classrooms for guidance. Started off using core material to illustrate themes that I was familiar with – maths. Once up and running the intention was to invite the volunteer English teachers with a view to holding combined workshops. In broad terms it was necessary to address two areas, the focus-plan-delivery-evaluation cycle and interactive teaching. The first workshops were planned for my own PRC so travelling problems weren't an issue for me and knowing the room would help. I also arranged to start mid-morning so teachers travelling in from miles away could be accommodated.

Andom had brought a few sticks to demonstrate angles in response to my request to bring 'show and tell' props that could be used to describe concepts in the classroom. Thank you Andom. Up next was Bisrat who used a ball to talk about circular measure and she extended this impressively to bring in some ideas on planetary motion. Thank you Bisrat. Thought to myself 'this is going well.' I should have been more cautious when I asked Debesay to show the group what was in his box. I'd already heard scratching noises so guessed it wasn't an inanimate object. Out flew the pigeon straight up to the beams overhead. Not a bad idea to use the bird to talk about how long it would take it to get to Asmara if it flew at fifty mph and it would definitely get the attention of a class of students. During this workshop it proved to be a bit of a distraction refusing to come down no matter how much Debesay cooed. Predictably, its habit of occasionally aiming droppings at the teachers below was a little off-putting as well. Despite the wayward bird I got an encouraging response from the teachers at this first session and they chipped in plenty of ideas to contribute to future workshops.

The Frei Kalsi teachers came along to one of the first workshops. This was deliberately planned to get me into the swing of it with a friendly audience. I knew most of them from the canteen where we all had tchai together during break in the mornings and afternoons. Had to laugh at Tgesti. During a tchai break at the workshop she asked whether I was married. Very direct woman was Tgesti. Tall, middle-aged with gold canine teeth (not unusual in Eritrea) she was another ex-fighter who had been in the thick of it when Ethiopia attacked. Told her I was divorced and my wife had gone. 'Is she still alive?' she demanded to know. Me – a bit surprised at the question – 'yes.' 'Well that's alright then,' came the response as she carried on drinking her tchai. Now that's what you call a pragmatic view of divorce.

The first series of workshops had gone well so the delivery plan was extended. The problems apparent in the English classes needed to be addressed. It was never going to be possible to take on everything in the time available but at least it would be a chance to flag up major recurring themes for the Eritrean teachers to take forward themselves. With that in mind off I went to the internet café and shot off emails to Kaska, Rebecca, Dave, Eddie and Janet – 'come and join me.'

I also wanted to take the show on the road so Belay got in touch with his contacts in other PRCs. The idea was to get to remote schools that couldn't really be expected to send teachers on marathon journeys across country. With the possibility of using the bikes – although the rough terrain was always going to be a challenge – it might just be possible to hold training workshops in one or two far-flung areas.

Finally I contacted Charlie who was teaching in a school right on the border in Adi Quala. Listening to him talk in Asmara, on the few occasions he made it to the city, it sounded like his place was worth a visit. If I could hold a workshop for the teachers at his school and also get a feel for the town that would be a good weekend.

Yohannes passed a book round at a VSO workshop. Graphic illustrations showed the different ways young girls' genitalia are cut by local women. In simple terms the belief is that this stops girls becoming sex maniacs lusting after men. The book described the different methods that are used by different tribes in different parts of the country. Over centuries the custom has developed into a highly technical practice and over time has attained respectability in local communities. 'This is our culture. I had it done, my mother had it done and my mother's mother had it done. My daughter will have it done.'

Female Genital Mutilation needs to stop, the question is how does that stopping start.

I think I probably saw more dead wild animals in Eritrea than live ones. The women were giving whatever this creature was a right pummelling. Walking down the road to Gyro Fiori (small roundabout with a few flowers) I saw a group of women throwing stones at the ground. After a while one of them got on her knees, raised a big rock above her head and smashed it down. Curious, I crossed over to where the women were. Could just about make out that the bloody mess on the ground had once been a snake.

'Do you always do that to snakes?' From the giggling responses I guessed that none of them spoke English.

'Temenai?' (I knew the Tigrinya for snake.)

'Ooer,' they nodded.

Thinking that was about as far as this conversation was going to get I went on my way to my office on Tibor. I mentioned the crushed snake to Belay. He confirmed that, yes, women killed all snakes that were spotted around the town. 'Why wouldn't they? Some are poisonous and there are many children playing outside.'

Charlie in Adi Quala had told me that one of his students had been killed by a snake that bit him. A group of boys were playing football and one of them went to fetch a stray ball that had been kicked into a pile of rocks. His friends told Charlie that the boy then threw the ball back before sitting down. They carried on with the game. After they finished they went over to the boy who they thought had just been resting and he was unconscious – later he died. Maybe if they had known what had happened and immediately raised the alarm he could have been saved.

No lions, no giraffes, no hippos in Eritrea. A few elephants remained but very little else in terms of 'big' animals. Ostriches lived in the Danakil region and hyenas came down occasionally from the mountains and that was about it. Never saw a fully grown hyena let alone a pack but did come across some evidence that they lived on the outskirts of Mendefera when I was walking with Tgesti back to her house. Just outside her village was a half-eaten donkey – I could smell it from fifty yards away. She told me that a neighbour had lost the battle with a small pack of hyenas that had attacked his animal and we ought to get a move on as they would be coming back to finish off what was left.

Never realised that grasshoppers are determined creatures. Marching in single file they crossed a road near my house. A bus came by and squashed a few unlucky ones. No messing about looking to tend any wounded – the others just carried on marching straight over their flat colleagues.

Birdwatchers would probably appreciate Eritrea. Bob sent me a book from England– *Birds of East Africa* – and I passed it on to a boy who seemed very interested. Without the book I managed to identify the soaring kites which seem to be widespread across the country and also an occasional scruffy- looking pelican on one of the small dams that fed Mendefera. Apart from that it was guesswork. Surprising sights were quite common. The most ordinary looking grey sparrow-like creature would take off and reveal a flash of electric blue or scarlet as it darted away. Don't know what they were called – shouldn't have given the book away.

December 2006 – England for Christmas

Brian was preparing to leave Eritrea for Australia and we were on his last Hash. This was going to be a problem as we would not only lose Brian but his eleven-seater Land Rover. Carlo and his Toyota were long gone so transport was going to become an issue.

For a finale Brian took us to Carrotti which I was told was famous for growing carrots. Not sure if this was a wind-up I nodded and smiled – 'yeah, yeah'– but sure enough when we arrived there at the side of the road, with bunches of carrots in hand, were gangs of kids who had spotted the white, and therefore rich, potential customers coming up the hill.

This was a craggy place north of the city. I remember it started well chatting with Hazy – an Israeli naturalist who was renowned for rediscovering the Eritrean elephants when it was thought they had all died out. 'I was looking at some trees when a grey trunk curled around a branch.' Seemed simple but I suppose that's how these things happen.

After a fairly lengthy walk beside and between some steep cliffs we got back to the cars and broke out the food boxes. A young Eritrean girl had joined the Hash a couple of months earlier and was now a regular. Over a ham sandwich we talked and I discovered she was training to be a journalist. Skirted around questions about how difficult it is to work in the media in what is widely reported in the West as the 'most repressive state in the world' but did discover she was actually the daughter of Meles, Mai Nefhi High School's Director, who I had worked with during my first year. Now, this could have just been a coincidence but the talk of spies in the congregation at St George's and even in the VSO office had recently been at fever pitch among volunteers. Gave me something to think about – I'd better behave myself.

Another incident gave us all something else to think about. Bill from UNMEE had lost his two sons. Bill was a friendly bloke who regularly turned up at the Hash with his kids and a big dog in the back of his pick-up. The boys, around ten-years-old, were lively on the Hash usually hunting under stones for scorpions to put in the food box. Lots of energy – always running. Nobody had seen them and this Hash had been over some rough terrain. More seriously – it was getting dark. We split up and set off in different directions to search, shouting their names as we went. After a while I couldn't hear the other groups calling any more – I had set off alone. Standing quietly, straining to see if there was any response to my voice it occurred that this could be a real problem. After another ten minutes I headed back and was relieved to arrive at the cars and see the boys with the group. They had decided to catch a passing bus to see where it went and not told anybody. The fact that the bus headed off towards a village somewhere in the mountains in the opposite direction to the Hash didn't worry them at all. In fact, looking at these two, that probably added a little excitement. They had looked around the village for a bit, returned to the bus and got off at the Hash cars on the return journey. Fearless, carefree kids they will be grown by now and no doubt at the South Pole or on top of Everest. Their village excursion seemed like a big adventure to me but – as seems usual in the community I found myself in – it was all seen as no big deal, bit of a laugh really.

About a dozen volunteers had turned up for the big international game at Asmara Football Stadium – Eritrea v Swaziland – and the match was a sell-out. The day was unusual for a number of reasons. During my first year in Eritrea I had regularly watched the games at the stadium. Ten nakfa for three games running consecutively was a bargain. Had been a supporter of Adulis, who played in blue, and took a dislike to the Asmara Beer team who played in red. Watching football as a detached spectator is not what it's about – you've got to have a team. At those local matches on Sunday afternoons there were about two hundred fans all sitting in the stand to keep out of the sun and I was the only volunteer, only non-Eritrean, in attendance.

I didn't get to the local matches in this second year as the journey to Mendefera was a bit far to be a comfortable bike ride. The buses had to be negotiated and that could make for a long day. No time for watching football, at least not in Asmara. There was a TV in Dembay café back in Mendefera which sometimes showed Premier League football. Priorities became clear, though, in the middle of a tense Manchester United v Liverpool game, when Josef turned over to Eri-TV for the renowned serial – a sort of *Eri-Eastenders*.

Fortunately this international game was on a Saturday afternoon so I took my seat with the other volunteers at kick-off. Before long it became clear that there was some disturbance on the other side of the stadium. The entrance gates had been forced by a crowd who'd been locked outside and they were pushing their way to the pitch. Immediately the police batons started raining down on heads – it reminded me of the 'rats' incident in Mai Nefhi High School when the students were beaten – and soon the gates were banged shut and order restored. Play never stopped for a second.

The match was dire mainly because the pitch was rutted and bone dry. The ball was all over the place and neither side could complain about the goalless draw. In contrast to the slightly edgy feeling generated by the broken gate episode the atmosphere was lightened by a giraffe, a camel and a hippo. A few supporters had dressed up as animals for the occasion and spent the second half dancing along the touchline. You have to be prepared for anything in Eritrea.

My email account had been opened for the first time in Eritrea and my knowledge had not advanced much since then. I could create and send an email and open one and that was about it. Staring at the screen in the internet café in Mendefera I noticed an email from my daughter with a picture of a paper clip next to it – never had one of those before. A couple of clicks later I was sat watching the egg-timer on the screen. The internet is slow in Eritrea and famously virus-ridden. After five minutes I was ready to abort whatever process I'd started when a beautiful baby appeared on the screen – it was my first grand-daughter. Thousands of miles away in what was no doubt a cold, wet English November Poppy had taken her first breath. Looking through the window at the palm trees on a hot, dusty Sunday afternoon in Mendefera it felt like Poppy was a million miles away. A donkey brayed outside the window and the smell of berbera wafted in from someone's stove. Decided I was going home for Christmas.

Hamish asked how I'd got VSO to agree to my leave but it wasn't negotiable and I never actually gave anybody the opportunity to say no by asking for permission. I suppose after well over a year I had become secure in what I was doing and with the people I was working with. Anyway, no one seemed to bother and one Programme Manager even asked me to bring back some clothes from friends in London when I returned.

Thankfully the process to get the ticket went smoothly. This, like the travel permit episode, can take weeks and worse, during those weeks, you don't know if it's going to be months. It's the way things work in Eritrea whether its waiting for the lights to come back on after a power cut, hanging around for paperwork or, according to Eritrean soldiers, waiting for your discharge from military service – you just don't know when it will end. This robs you of the ability to encourage yourself, experience some sense of progress. Not knowing the end date you can't even gee yourself up with thoughts such as 'well that's half of it done.'

All fell into place nicely with this exit visa though and off I went to see Kidane for my flight ticket. Kidane's office was similar to the one at Himbol where I changed my pounds into nakfa, peaceful, organised, business-like and most importantly – empty. There was an agent who sold tickets near Stella Pension but it was bedlam inside with folks pushing, shoving and screaming. No – not for me. I needed to feel some kind of confidence that the ticket I bought would do what it said, when it said it and take me to where I wanted to go. Kidane gave me that confidence.

Donard was also having a break over Christmas and coincidentally we had booked on the same flight. Then again perhaps not so much of a coincidence as there are not many flights from Asmara. Christina and her boyfriend offered to take us to the airport which was appreciated. I was amazed that Christina was still in the country. Some volunteers come to Eritrea and seem to fit, they thrive, it works for them and it is no surprise when they stay on, sometimes for years, making their lives here. Other volunteers arrive and immediately make arrangements to get on the first plane out again. It seemed that Christina, who had come the year before me, was closer to the 'get me out' end of this scale. Had listened to her Eri-stories a couple of times and she was not happy. Difficult first year in Dbarwa followed by a difficult second year in Asmara. Thought she would be looking to leave but here she was in her third year now living with an Eritrean man in a house next to the American Embassy. Good on yer Christina!

In the (almost deserted) departure lounge Donard told me he was off to Madrid for Christmas where he was going to meet up with his daughter. He had stayed on in Asmara during the previous summer so this was his first break since we'd arrived in September 2005. We separated in Cairo and I got on the plane to Heathrow.

Good to see the family again and, of course, say hello to my new grand-daughter – my reason for being there. Saw a few friends and got up to speed with what had been happening but found I was less interested and felt more detached – comfortably so. Living and working overseas was starting to feel more natural than living and working in England.

England was grey and cloudy over Christmas – never once saw the sun. Not once. After two weeks I was looking forward to getting back on the plane and headed for the local bus station. Bit of a send-off this time – the previous departures I'd left on my own. Not only were all the children and grandchildren there but friends who had been in touch while I was in Eritrea and supported the work by sending the parcels of equipment to the PRC. Twelve goodbye hugs in total. The passengers already on the bus must have watched the farewell session through the windows as a few commented 'Nice send-off' as I walked down the bus to my seat. 'Yes and I'm only going to Mansfield for the day,' was my attempt at humour.

As the plane climbed over the Channel I saw the sun for the first time in what seemed like ages and I knew I would see it every day for the next six months. Everything felt positive and forward-looking. I was living and working in a foreign country, not just playing at it but putting the spadework in to be part of a community, to take up arms against the challenge. This wasn't tourism or a celebrity photo-opportunity – it was real. Okay any difference I was making was miniscule but there is something to be said for going in the direction you believe is the right one even if the steps you are taking are little ones.

At midnight in Cairo airport it didn't feel very positive or forward-looking at all. The plane was delayed, I was on my fifth cup of coffee and had read the newspaper cover to cover several times. Eventually I boarded and it wasn't long before I realised that the delay was not a curse but an absolute blessing. Just as we hit the north of Eritrea the sun came up. This was a rare sight for anyone as planes usually took off and landed at night time in Eritrea – 'don't want people taking photographs of our country from above.' The downward blip that had hit my good spirits in Cairo airport vanished as mile after mile of unbelievably spectacular mountain scenery passed below me. In the middle of the day near the Equator there is little shadow and therefore no relief. The country looks stark and bleached. At this time of the morning the shadows cast by the mountains of the Sahel stretched as far as the eye could see and made for a wonderful sight. Glancing around the almost empty plane everyone else was asleep – this view was all mine and the pilot's I hoped. High on Eritrea there was an unexpected finale. The plane banked slightly and I was looking straight down on what could only have been Mai Nefhi Dam. My dam – the dam I had looked over and walked around while waiting for Elsa to cook the pasta in Mai Nefhi Hotel. The guitar solo on 'Crazy' by Aerosmith was just hitting the high notes on my earphones and provided an appropriate over-the-top soundtrack to what I was taking in below. Anyway, enough of the magic – I hadn't been asleep all night and needed a bed.

At five in the morning Bristol Pension was shut of course so I walked across an empty Harnet Avenue to Stella Pension which I knew with its reputation for prostitutes would be open. Sure enough I got a room and collapsed on the bed. Up at ten o'clock I paid the bloke on the door and carried my bags back across the road to Bristol Pension. 'Morning Mama – Happy New Year.'

January 2007 – Big Spender

Belay and I visited a couple whose child had recently died. A faded poster on the wall of their poverty-stricken hudmo struck me – the words made more tangible in this setting.

Life is a . . .

Challenge	Meet it
Tragedy	Face it
Sorrow	Overcome it
Journey	Complete it
Adventure	Dare it
Struggle	Accept it
Duty	Perform it
Opportunity	Use it
Dream	Realise it

Mystery	Unfold it
Promise	Fulfil it
Game	Play it
Blessing	Taste it
Song	Sing it
Beauty	Worship it
Desire	Satisfy it
Bore	Laugh at it
Nursery	Grow in it
Love	Give it

Kaska told me this was written by Mother Teresa.

Shewa and me were walking to Adi Mongonti to observe some lessons. On the way we stopped at a kindergarten she knew and she left me high and dry. Shewa went inside to talk to the Director while I waited outside. I turned to see thirty little wide-eyed four-year-old faces staring at me. Looking round, the door was shut – I was on my own. Okay.

At this point I blessed Yordanos my little companion who sang back in my house in Mendefera. 'Right, we're going to sing a song to help you practise English,' and off we went with the rhymes Yordanos had sung to me many times at breakfast as we ate biscuits and sipped tchai.

'Dubana has red shoes . . .'

Tried to make it live by getting them to point to shoes, hair, teeth and so on as the song progressed.

Went well, I'm getting the hang of this – next song coming up.

'Hade is one, kelete is two . . .'

Used fingers to illustrate the counting. I was on a roll.

Still no sign of Shewa so I continued on the English teaching theme beckoning a boy to the front and using his head, arm, toes and so on as examples. 'What is this?' pointing at his nose. 'This is a nose,' came back a little chorus of squeaky voices. I had just about exhausted body parts when, thankfully, Shewa came out and we set off up the track waving to the kids. Hardest ten minutes teaching I've done in my life. Tended to give kindergartens a wide berth after that. Give me the big, ugly ones to teach any day.

The novelty of the crazy bus journeys had long since worn off. Getting poked with sticks, elbowed, crushed against bus windows had limited entertainment value – time can play the role of irritant as well as healer.

It wasn't just me. A number of volunteers had given up the weekend struggle to get into Asmara and had decided to confine themselves to their villages seven days a week and get more involved with the communities. My bus journey was bad enough. Seemingly endless waiting in queues for buses that might or might not turn up, bruising hour after hour journeys with little air – 'shut the windows the nefas (breeze) causes sickness' – stroppy soldiers and so on. Janet – down the road another ten miles in Durco – had an hour's walk and had to get through both Eritrean and UN checkpoints just to get to the bus stop for a ride to Mendefera where my challenge started. Understandably, Janet became a villager – 'forget Asmara.'

For my part the attraction with Asmara was more acute. Travelling to the city had that expectation, a feeling of getting to where things were happening. The get-togethers with VSO staff and volunteers gave some perspective and offered variation. Added to this the connections with England were tangible – the letters, internet cafés and telephone. Without question, for me anyway, the Asmara weekend was a must.

The travelling solution I came up with was not without some pain. If I packed my bag on Friday evening and set the alarm for 4.45 the next morning I could get ready and be at the Mendefera bus station for 5.45 and in time for the first bus to Asmara which would have some empty seats. The walk from my home to the buses had its moments. The first time I put this plan into operation I had to stop after ten yards – for a split second I thought we were under attack. The sky was alive with shooting stars streaming across the sky against the backdrop of a million constellations. I gazed for a full five minutes wondering if I was the only spectator in the world who was being treated to this show. Felt honoured, uplifted, tiredness gone – for a little while anyway.

The streets were usually empty and quiet. An occasional old man and/or dog hurried along somewhere in the distance but there was never any feeling of intimidation or even concern. In fact the opposite was true. Okay there was an obvious downside to getting up this early but the unmistakable feeling of being ahead of the game was very real and Mendefera seemed peaceful and calm. The not-so-full bus usually pulled out at 6.15ish and I got off at the bottom of Harnet Avenue in the city before eight o'clock. By now the sun was up and Asmara was bustling. First stop – Alga, Mama and Bristol Pension. Stop two –tchai and a dry bun at Vittorio or Elsa's cafe. Third stop – internet café and then on to the VSO office. From there it usually depended on who was around, what was happening. Sometimes a walk, a meal, the Hash . . .

The second part of my travel solution simply reversed the Saturday morning journey. Up at five on Sunday morning I was down at the bus stop by six. Had a chance encounter with Phil one of these mornings. As I came out of the pension with my bag on my back Phil was on his way to

Stella after an all-night drinking session. I'd just got up – he was just off to bed. Must be an age thing.

Back in Mendefera for eight o'clock made for some long Sundays. Did a bit of work punctuated by a nap or two to recover from the early rising and maybe a chat with Mussie down at Dembay. It wasn't an ideal travel solution but it was the best I could come up with and it worked for a while.

God bless Alan and Nesta Ferguson. There was a piece of paper lying on a table in the VSO office in Asmara with the heading, 'These are organisations and people who have helped volunteers in the past.' Sat down and scribbled out some of the names, addresses and phone numbers. Back in my office in Mendefera the following week I set aside a day to write some letters to these 'helpers' explaining who I was and what I was trying to do in Eritrea with the teacher-training programme. Finished with 'if you can help in any way please get in touch.' The names I had taken down were all in the UK – I could have sent emails to some of them but considered that a letter with an Eritrean stamp would add some authenticity to my request.

I forgot about the correspondence until one Saturday morning in Asmara a few weeks later I picked up a letter from Alan and Nesta Ferguson – 'please accept this cheque for £4, 000.' What? Are there really people on this earth who do that kind of thing? Obviously yes – there it was cheque enclosed. Now, how am I going to turn this cheque into something I can spend in Eritrea? Due to my suspicions about the banking system I hadn't opened an account in the country and was cautious – this was a lot of money in Eritrea (calculated it would take over twenty years for a conscript teacher to earn this amount) and wanted to make sure it was spent as the donors wished. The £4,000 was not going to be lost in any dubious activity and end up buying guns and bullets or in some politician's Swiss bank account.

Spoke to Yohannes the VSO Director first who pointed me towards Miriam, the Finance Manager. Left the cheque with her – she assured me the cash would be available within a couple of weeks. Sure enough she gave me the nod and off I went to the bank next to Barte Meskerem Square. What happened next was a little worrying. Piled high on the counter was over a hundred and twenty thousand nakfa. Signed for it and stuffed it in my bag as quickly as possible. Didn't appreciate the glances I was getting and kept an eye open walking up Harnet Avenue. Remembered Kasi's tip about using peripheral vision to keep a check on who was behind.

Anyway, no mugging and when I got back to my house in Mendefera I crammed the notes into the drawer in my table. Didn't feel at all comfortable. Here I was being given the responsibility to use this money for the benefit of education in Eritrea and I hadn't even got a locking drawer and the door on my house only needed a good shove and you were in.

Decided two things – the money needed spending quickly and I needed to tell at least three people about the windfall. I'd only known the folks I was working with in Mendefera for a few months and although they had been great during my time here I didn't know enough about them to know who was trustworthy. (A couple of years after I left Eritrea I discovered that I was right to have been so careful when funds which were earmarked for educational purposes were used to help people escape the country.) As it turned out all went well. I told Belay and the three inspectors – Girma, Shewa and Solomon – and this gave me a little reassurance. Reckoned that the odds on them all being crooks were pretty long. Belay thought all his celebration days had come at once. There were a couple of television/electronic equipment shops in Mendefera and for Eritrean shops they were surprisingly well-stocked. I also checked out the shops in Asmara and we bought loads of stuff for the PRC. Starting with a television and satellite dish we followed up over the next few weeks with a video cassette recorder, radio, computer and printer – you name it we got it. I was particularly pleased with the satellite dish. Sitting on the roof of the PRC which was on top of the highest ground in Mendefera it was visible for miles. I thought this might send out a number of positive messages to the folks in the town – education is important and deserves to be well-funded, if they have satellite dishes in the West why can't we? And so on. Proved to be a good talking point in Dembay café.

Tuning in the television for the first time was memorable. There had been bad weather in London and the first picture up on BBC World was the Houses of Parliament with a covering of snow. Bit weird that one. Outside it was in the eighties, dusty plains as far as the eye could see and there hadn't been a drop of rain for months.

The final spend was a biggie. We struggled with paper handouts and worksheets for the training sessions. There was one photocopier in Mendefera but that was in the Zoba Ministry of Education and it seemed you had to bleed to get them to let you use it. Belay asked if we had enough money left to equip the PRC with a photocopier. Thought a lot about this. I'd seen unused photocopiers in other PRCs and had asked what the problem was. It seemed that there were three main difficulties and I generalised these for myself believing that these reasons summarised the problems of donating anything. Firstly – no spare parts. In the case of photocopiers it seemed criminal that the machine was rendered useless because the bulb had gone. Second – consumable materials. No paper or ink once it ran out. Third there was an acute lack of expertise and tools to fix things when they broke down. With all this in mind I took the chance. Shopped around a bit in Asmara and got agreement not just on the copier price but also to a service contract and paper and ink supplies. Not sure if the agreement was worth the paper it was written on but I was encouraged by the dealer actually bringing the photocopier down himself, installing it and giving Belay and me a training session. Nice bloke.

The money was gone but we'd spent it as intended on stocking the PRC and we were now in demand. Talk about raising the profile of the place. People from all kinds of offices came in to use the photocopier. Belay lorded it – he had the code and nobody printed anything without his agreement. The situation moved into classic territory when the other photocopier in Mendefera – the one in the Ministry – broke down. The boot was on the other foot and quite a few regretted turning Belay away in the past.

Never did get any further response from the donors despite sending several letters and emails expressing our gratitude. Like I said – God bless Alan and Nesta Ferguson whoever you are.

For some reason only known to herself Claire had decided to start Dave's end of semester party by reading aloud from a full-on sex novel. Don't think anybody blushed but there was some shuffling of feet and embarrassed glances. After a couple of no-holds-barred pages Claire looked around with a sweet innocent smile on her face. After a couple of seconds awkward silence Anne broke the ice. 'You should get Donard to serialise that on *Radio Bana.*'

Dave was a teacher-trainer based in Asmara. He had been offered an apartment in Sembel but didn't feel comfortable with the idea of living in luxury while his students and volunteer colleagues had basic accommodation. Also, if you're going to live and work in the Third World there is an understandable desire to be a part of the community so here Dave was in his little box in Mai Temenai, a small suburb on the outskirts of the city. Dave had a claim to fame – he had entered, and done pretty well, in the Tour de Eritrea. Bike racing is serious in Eritrea and the peloton is a regular sight around the country. The best cyclists are paid (a little) and train daily. Predictably, as with the national football team, this is sometimes seen as a way of escaping from the country which is why Eritrea does not compete significantly on the international stage – they might do well but they might not come back.

Had recently done the Mendefera to Asmara run (and back) myself on the bike. The winding road up Monguda was gut-wrenching and my gasps alerted the baboons which didn't make for a relaxing climb. Fortunately they just sat and watched as the crazy Englishman slogged his way up the incline at two mph. Wouldn't be entering the Tour de Eritrea this year.

Claire had now moved on from sex book reading to teaching the local kids Irish dancing and they were picking it up. Set the tone for the evening and, as always, it was good for everyone to meet up and share stories from the villages. Catherine, Morven and Eddie had picked up on the wad of parcel receipts in my pigeon hole in the VSO office and we had a chat about the article I had sent to the *Derbyshire Times*. During the following week they all shot off a few words asking for stuff to their local newspapers back in Britain and within a month they too were receiving books, pens and paper. Catherine had a real haul but then the *Manchester Evening News* has a wider circulation than the *Derbyshire Times* and she probably wrote a better article than me.

A little girl who lived next door to Dave did the Tigrinya dancing with a bottle on your head act. This is an eye-catching stunt, the first time I saw it in Mendefera I checked the girl's hair and the bottom of the bottle to see if it was fixed with anything but, no, it was just a question of balance. After a while the girl put a bottle on top of the first bottle and danced even more vigorously. Now that's just showing off.

February 2007 – Soldiers and a Motorbike

This day was all about me misjudging the time – again. Nigdet had been the usual socialising, eating, drinking round. Not being much of a drinker I'd decided to give myself a break in the event early afternoon. I'd discovered the need to pace myself.

During the morning I'd met Belay in Dembay and he took me to visit a friend of his. I'd never see so much mes – the floor was covered with the long-necked bottles that were filled with the sweet, golden honey drink. Naturally the house was full of men and I was offered a bottle. Nice morning eating, drinking and talking. Men drifted in and out in the usual Nigdet pub-crawl (house-crawl) fashion. The recurring sounds of happy welcomes and cheerful goodbyes was a pleasant backdrop to the scene.

At noon I made my excuses and walked home. The three bottles of mes were strong but I held it together and managed a reasonably straight line (I think). After a nap and a potter around the house I made my way out again, this time to Tibor. I'd been invited by the Director of Frei Kalsi Primary School to his home which was next to the school. I particularly wanted to take up this invitation and see Kibrom and his family. We had sat drinking tchai at break-time on many occasions. He had been a soldier and had his stories to tell. I was a keen listener. His favourites often centred around music and he talked of songs that were written with hidden meanings exhorting Eritreans to keep the faith – 'the candle must not go out.' As a prisoner-of-war he could sing these to his comrades under the nose of his captors without them realising he was actually demanding a call to arms at the same time as lifting the spirits. Kibrom strummed his kora and sang the songs for me as we sat on Tibor with our glasses of tchai and bits of bread. I would clap softly or slap on my thigh in time to the beat which Kibrom seemed to appreciate. Fleeting but very special times. I think that he realised I was at the very limit of my musical ability.

The previous week Kibrom, along with many other Directors around the country, had been ordered to leave their schools – and homes and families – and report to Mai Nefhi College where they would take up new positions teaching. Like most assignments in Eritrea there was no end-date given for the work. Kibrom would work at the college until he was no longer required whereupon he would be placed as the Ministry of Education saw fit. He would not necessarily return to Frei Kalsi – or even Mendefera. He couldn't answer my questions about how or when he would see his family, of course, and I felt bad for asking – should have known better by now. After the eighteen months I'd been in the country I knew that the only answer he could give was 'when the government says I can' and my questions only served as an irritant.

Despite being the Director of a school Kibrom's house was small, dark and poorly furnished. The sofa, though, was comfortable and Kibrom and his wife were welcoming if at first a little surprised. I'd had this reaction before. I never properly worked out if they were just being polite inviting me without really wanting me to turn up or they were honoured by my presence. Can't believe it was the latter. Soon I was laden with injera, meat, vegetables and the usual tin cup of sewa. Kibrom talked about Eritrea and the school in his deep voice while his wife busied around the house. She spoke no English but her smile and generosity said enough. I hoped that my smile said enough in return and that she was in no doubt that the honour to be invited into her home was totally mine. The time passed quickly and without noticing it had got dark.

Just as in England when the pubs turn out it pays to be aware that being in certain areas at certain times is not clever. After saying my goodbyes I stumbled out into the blackness walking carefully across the open ground to the track that went past the soldiers' camp. I'd decided against the other route as it was much steeper with some sheer drops down to the bus station. I pressed on a little wary as I knew the soldiers would have been drinking sewa all day, this being Nigdet.

Fisswana appeared in front of me out of the darkness. He was not tall – almost six inches shorter than me – but solidly built. Looked like he would be a good man digging the trenches on the border and no doubt he'd done his share. His AK 47 was across his chest as it usually was when I saw him during the day. I also used to see a smile on his face during the day. Now there was no smile, this was a soldier's face. He blocked my path. 'Smoke,' he demanded. I'd got my smiley friendly face on – this is only Fisswana isn't it? Pal of mine isn't he? We'd been discussing the football results only a day or two ago hadn't we? 'Smoke,' came the growl again, this time deeper, menacing. 'I don't smoke mate,' I replied patting my pockets to show there was nothing in them. Again 'Smoke.' And again, accompanied by more pocket-patting – 'I ain't got nowt Fisswana. No cigarettes.' Strange how you resort to your mother-dialect in times of stress. After a few more rounds of this demand-denial tennis match he turned the gun in my face and in a voice quieter than before, 'Give me.' Again my stock reply was repeated with a smile. Don't know where that came from, maybe the effects of the sewa. It definitely wasn't prompted by Fisswana – he wasn't kidding. After a couple more 'Give me' snarls the confrontation was all over and he walked into the night.

It didn't hit me till I got home when I was overtaken by undiluted anger. One of those 'I leave my family, my country to come to bloody Eritrea to help and that's the reward I get' moments. Went to sleep with the cold vision of the small black hole at the end of a gun barrel right before me.

I was determined not to let this go – no way. Next day I deliberately detoured straight through the middle of the soldiers' camp with thoughts of 'come on then Fisswana –

if you want to face me do it in the daylight.' There was no sign of him. The few soldiers who were around must have wondered what I was doing. Continued with this path to Tibor trying to work out the feelings of injustice, the twisted feelings of anger. Fisswana appeared after a few days and stood in front of me. He gently took hold of the collar of my shirt between his thumb and forefinger. He wanted it. 'Give me.' I'd heard that before. 'No chance – you're getting nothing off me,' I replied. The remnants of the Nigdet night's anger were obvious in my voice and my expression. He backed off, this time with him smiling.

A real transport solution materialised in February 2007 in the form of my beautiful Honda 125. I'd brought my UK driving licence with me when I'd come back from England. This seemed to be enough to satisfy the Ministry of Transport and after five weeks, which was a pretty sharp turnaround for Eritrea (or England come to think of it), they gave me an Eri-licence. Yohannes told me where to go for motorbike training on the spare ground behind the Lion Hotel just next to the tank graveyard.

The trainees were out in force that morning. About a dozen old Fiats and Toyotas were circling and occasionally taking a detour to weave in and out of some traffic cones. All were driving very slowly. This was a welcome feature of Asmarino driving. Although there is little lane discipline, red traffic lights are an optional stop and goats or donkeys can wander into the road at any moment; the pace is such that there is usually plenty of time to avoid a shunt.

Abel greeted me and showed me the bike – an orange Honda CD 125 in what looked like reasonable condition. My experience as a motorbike rider amounted to a total of ten minutes over thirty years before when I'd swapped my Lambretta scooter for a go on my mate's Yamaha. How hard can it be? Abel covered the basics – throttle, twist grip, brakes and I was off circling the training ground with the Fiats and Toyotas. One thought was uppermost – although you don't know what you're doing, don't make it obvious by falling off. I experimented a bit with the gears which were my main concern on the technical side and after a few laps Abel said 'All yours – you've passed.'

Not entirely sure that this was a great achievement. I got the impression that if you had the strength to stop the motorbike falling on top of you that was good enough. This was actually the reason Deng (under five feet and around fifty kilos) had failed and decided to stick to the buses. When Abel had said 'All yours' that's what he really meant. He drove off in his old Toyota Corolla and there I was – man and machine alone. I rode off into the city managing a careful twenty mph – nice and steady, no rush and it was okay. Felt like Peter Fonda riding into town. That film *Easy Rider* – no, it wasn't really like that.

I'd thought a lot about how I'd use the motorbike. There had been many horror stories from other volunteers including punctures, breakdowns, misfuelling, unseatings after hitting potholes/sheep/kids, some sheer incompetence and, the most common, running out of fuel. Reckoned if I looked after this bike properly it would be a godsend. The round trip from Asmara to Mendefera and back was around seventy miles. I estimated that on a full tank I'd just about manage that. (No petrol stations in Mendefera). So, no messing about with little joyrides using up the fuel and risking punctures on rough ground. The Honda made the trip from Mendefera to Asmara and back and was then locked in my spare room. Nobody was allowed to touch it, never mind ride it. That was it and that was all I needed. The trial by Eri-bus journey was over.

No joyrides? The motorbike ride from the capital to Mendefera was actually incredible. Apart from five potholes which I memorised the road was superb. With the exception of the usual sheep, goats and donkeys the traffic was virtually non-existent. I only ever saw a couple of UN trucks going down to the border and, of course, the buses all the time I travelled that route. Sun in the sky, wind in your face, the plains opening out in front of you, East Africa to yourself – this was some experience. The villagers in Tera Emni, Dbarwa and Sheketi got to know me and waved as I flew past at a steady thirty mph. Didn't want to overdo it on my precious motorbike. Strange how kids thought they could actually shake my hand as I drove by.

And the ride from Mendefera to Asmara was just as good. After twenty miles of open road Monguda and the climb up to the Asmara plateau loomed into view. The Honda struggled up the winding road for mile after mile. Completely focused on dodging the baboons and minding the sheer drop to the right. Don't know how high it is to the top but I do know that the temperature dropped from the uncomfortable and sticky to the pleasant and fresh. Stopping at the top and looking back the view, of course, was a killer all the way to the Simien Mountains in Ethiopia. The motorbike radically changed my trips to Asmara – it was also the means by which the course of my whole life changed totally.

Rebka comes out of left field in this account and that is how she came into my life. She managed a small, dark stationery shop on the road up from Harnet Avenue to the VSO office. I had called in maybe three or four times for pens since I'd been in the country but not for months as her biros never usually worked. The motorbike had freed up time in Asmara. Instead of being in the city from 8 am Saturday to crack of dawn Sunday I could now head off to Asmara on Friday evening. If I went at five o'clock I could just get to Asmara before dark which was necessary as I didn't fancy the climb up Monguda blind. The return journey could comfortably be made on Sunday afternoons. Additional benefits included not being knackered due to the painful early wake-up call on Saturdays.

One mid-Saturday morning in February I had done the usual – read *Eri-Profile* over tchai in Elsa's, been to the internet café and called in at the VSO office. No volunteers in Asmara this weekend – nobody about. Thought about what to do with the day ahead. Decided I'd give the Hash a miss. Thought about Rebka in her stationery shop just down the road. She had seemed friendly in the past even if she did sell me dud biros. Okay – I'll do it.

After the introductory 'Selams' and 'Kemays' – 'Do you fancy coming for something to eat?' Said she was busy. 'Okay, perhaps see you next week.'

After walking a few yards down the road wondering where to go next, what to do with myself, Rebka caught up with me. She explained that she had to take Ibrahim to the airport but after that would be able to join me.

'Good. I'll pick you up at the shop at three.' Simple as that.

March 2007 – Serious Soldiers and a Proposal

The path was pitted and stony so I resorted to pushing the bike to the school in Kuduaber. Kuduaber is another one of those Tigrinya words that is difficult to master. There's a back-of-the-throat thing that needs to accompany it – bit like encocaho (Tigrinya for egg). Anyway, Kuduaber, dusty plains as far as I can see in all directions, lost.

A young lad about ten-years-old with a big smile on his face joined me on the journey.

'Is this the way to Kuduaber?' It looked like he might know.

In a surprisingly loud, deep voice with an equally surprising American accent came back the response.

'YURSSS.'

Ah, good. We walked together in silence for a bit.

'Do you live in Kuduaber?'

'YURSSS.'

Striding along the seemingly endless track, more silence. Uneasy thoughts started to occur – thought I'd better test them.

'Is your name George W Bush?'

'YURSSS.'

Never mind. Odd how people, including me, are determined to take every opportunity to show off the one word they know of a foreign language.

Eddie had agreed to team up with me on a teacher-training session at the PRC on Tibor. I did the maths-based activities, he did the English and we had a good day. The room was full of Inspectors, Directors and teachers who appreciated the material and participated freely. Belay paid Eddie two hundred nakfa which he reluctantly accepted.

A couple of things stood out for me. Eddie held a discussion on humour and how it is difficult to translate cross-culture. He kicked off with a joke.

'Went into a shop and asked the man behind the counter for a thousand cockroaches,' he said. I looked around the room at the bemused faces and thought 'Go on Eddie, go for it.'

He continued, 'The man asked why do you want a thousand cockroaches? Well the landlord said that when I gave up the tenancy to leave the place as I found it.'

Silence. Blank looks all round. Eddie had proved his point very effectively.

At break Girmay warmed to the theme. 'There's nothing wrong with charity clothes donated from America, I've had many a good suit. Only problem is – jacket in Eritrea, trousers in Kenya!'

We finished around three o'clock. It was a Friday afternoon and the deal was that I would give Eddie a lift back to Asmara on the motorbike. This was the first time I had carried a passenger on this – or any – pillion. Didn't tell Eddie. Goodbyes said we bumped our way down the path from Tibor on to the main road where we were immediately stopped by the police. He was a serious looking bloke with no English so I offered him my Eri-driving licence with accompanying bravado. 'There you go mate.'

He studied the little white card for over a minute which always seems like an hour in tense situations. Feeling a bit exposed and not sure what was going to happen next – motorbike seized? – I looked around for a bit of support. Surprised to find I was alone. Eddie had got off the pillion and was standing about twenty yards away half hidden behind a wall. I figured self-preservation had kicked in.

The policeman gave me my licence back and walked off without a word. Eddie reappeared and jumped up behind me. 'Thanks for the backup Eddie,' and we were off.

Great motorbike ride and I enjoyed having a passenger to share the journey. Pointed out the villages to Eddie, waved to the kids, bike roaring along beautifully and, of course, the afterglow of a good day at the workshop on Tibor.

Through Tera Emni and Dbarwa in usual time (no traffic, no hold ups – ever) then onto Monguda. Started the steady climb up the winding roads and after six or seven bends saw the baboons on their usual perches. Some were high above us in the rocks overlooking the road. Some were on the opposite side sitting on the tiny concrete wall which was meant to save us from the sheer drop and others were actually sitting in the road. As they spotted us they stopped their flea-picking and went on to alert. No problem – I'll just weave in and out of them and accelerate away leaving them with the smell of burning rubber as I'd done quite a few times before. Jerked back on the twist grip throttle. The noise level went up, the velocity didn't. The extra weight was telling on the little engine and it was struggling. Glancing in the mirrors I saw a baboon who had taken up the chase and its long canines were gaining. There is a *Simpsons'* episode which flashed into view – 'baboons to the left of me, baboons to the right.' Straining on the grip the Honda suddenly found a bit more and we slowly pulled away engine screaming. Adjusting the mirror I expected to see the face of a terror-stricken Eddie. He was gazing south towards the Simien Mountains appreciating the view. 'What baboons?'

Didn't give lifts to anyone on the Mendefera to Asmara leg again.

Some of these accounts are difficult to write.

Following the gun-in-face incident with Fisswana it became clear that the soldiers were more aware of me, were up for challenging me. Walking down Mendefera high street sometimes became difficult. The usual game was to block my path standing square in front of me. My attempts to laugh this off, to share the joke, were not successful as I was the target of the joke. I resorted to changing my routes to avoid confrontation which reduced the face-offs. When they did happen I walked into the road to avoid them.

I had been to the wedding of Girmay's daughter on the Sunday. It was a well-attended event – music, food, sewa, lots of people. Two soldiers approached me and we talked about the wedding – cautiously on my part. 'Yes, I'm very grateful to Girmay for inviting me.' It became clear that this was not a casual conversation, however, when I was asked pointedly 'Most white men think sewa is like dish water – what do you think?' Clearly I was being invited to go down a road I wasn't happy with. The truth is that sewa is like any home-made beer – variable. Some is filtered and palatable, some rough and sour. It wasn't too difficult to soften the leading question with the truth saying that some sewa was good stuff – like at this wedding – and that I had a recipe from a man in Segenetti (which was true) so that I could have a go at making it myself. Success for these two soldiers was not necessarily about winning or losing an argument but simply causing one and they had failed to do that. They looked deflated.

The next day walking past the wedding tent on my way back from Tibor Girmay came running out. 'Mister Kevin, Mister Kevin you have to join us!' After a celebration there is usually food and drink left over and people are invited to finish it over the next few days. Girmay led me to a corner of the almost empty tent, gave me a tin mug of sewa and sat me down with half a dozen soldiers who had clearly been drinking all day. Thanks Girmay.

I dived in immediately with football talk – usually a safe topic, soldiers always 'had a team' in the Premiership. Not successful, the soldier to my immediate left was determined to let me know what he thought of white people in England and America. His English was poor but I got the gist when he jabbed my chest with his finger and growled 'CIA' a number of times then spat on the floor. I wasn't having it. 'Hey Girmay – come over here and translate. I want to know what he's saying,' pointing to the aggressor. The other soldiers reacted immediately, shocked into action. Girmay had been an officer in the conflict and he had status, authority and connections. What's more he had personally invited me to the wedding and this post-wedding feast – I was his guest. All the soldiers' expressions changed and they became warm and friendly – smiles all round. Talking about football had suddenly become very interesting. 'What is it Mister Kevin?' Before I could answer Girmay the soldiers caught him up in football banter and the moment passed.

I really had got fed up with this and needed to find a way to change things. Over the following days I decided to face down the challenges in the street. The constant submissive approach was wearying and more than that it was not helping to reduce the challenges, if anything they were increasing. I took to deliberately crossing the street to confront groups of soldiers giving them loud greetings as I strode past or through them. After a while I was surprised to notice they were giving way to me, moving aside. My confidence increased – this was working wasn't it?

One lunchtime I was walking back home along the high street when I saw in the distance three soldiers walking towards me. All were well built, the one in the middle particularly so. By this time it was an automatic reaction – steel the shoulders, stare straight into their eyes, lengthen the stride and aim directly for the centre. This time, though, they weren't giving way, they were not going to let me through or around them. Mustn't show any weakness – not for a second – straight on. The impact put the soldier in the middle straight on his backside. I stood over him stony-faced, accusing. His friends shouted loudly in Tigrinya. The thoughts were clear and sharp in my head.

That will teach you not to barge into me.

And it will teach everyone watching not to mess me about anymore.

And you're going to appreciate that I'm here to help your country.

And I hope you're in pain.

And then I saw he was blind.

The inner shockwaves were physical. What had I become? Was this what I had come to Africa for – to be a thug? To damage? To destroy?

The blind soldier's response was the only one that could allow a reasonable closure to the immediate incident – he laughed. I knelt down and helped him up apologising as he scrambled to his feet. Amid the commotion and noise around us we shared a friendly moment that was due entirely to his grace and in spite of my violence.

Did a lot of thinking that night. It is surprising that sometimes when things come to a head the aftermath can witness improved relations and this was the case with the soldiers and me. Maybe it's a release of pressure or a drawing back from total chaos or simply a realisation of the need to work harder to communicate. More likely it drives an awareness of the need to look critically at yourself rather than others. I'd lost my way, lessons had to be learned. When things are wrong the only approach is to put them right. When things are broken they need to be fixed. When mistakes are made they need to be learned from then left behind. I stopped ignoring, stepping around or barging through soldiers. I stopped giving brief 'Kemays' before hurrying off about my business. This was the business, the priority. I began stopping and talking to soldiers in a meaningful way, the only way that genuine relations can be built.

The Alan and Nesta Ferguson money had been spent but stocking the PRC went on. Bob had kept me in touch with events in the UK and updated me weekly on what was happening in my home town. His emails were entitled 'Home Thoughts' and were always a good read. He also sent parcels containing paper, pens, rulers – all sorts of equipment that could be used in the classroom and was not readily available out here. Used to joke that he was the UK Head of Really Useful Stuff. Another friend, Sue, used to collect unusual bits and pieces to send out. Gave her free rein and I received parcels from her with Christmas tinsel, musical spinning tops, teddy bears – a random selection. Sue – UK Head of Innovation. All was valuable either as a focus for attention in the classroom, demonstrating concepts or even as prizes for teachers and students who had done well.

Many other friends also sent parcels and there was a constant stream of pens and paper from folks I had never met but who had responded to the article I had sent to the *Derbyshire Times* back in November. Used to really look forward to getting into Asmara on a Friday evening. Parked the motorbike outside Pizza Napoli and popped round the corner to the VSO office and picked up letters and the little white slips indicating a parcel was ready for collection at the Post Office. The record was fifteen and there were always more than five. Standing in the queue with my bundle of white slips I felt like a kid at Christmas. All anticipation, but picking up the boxes was not without its problems. Every box had to be opened so that import duty could be calculated. No idea what criteria was used to calculate the tax on a box of party poppers but a serious gentleman – Aklilu – went through each box item by item and gave me a bill.

Kind folks at my church in England once sent hundreds of exercise books. I looked on delighted as Aklilu broke open the box then noticed that he was signalling to the soldier on guard. The soldier came over and flicked through one of the books. 'No,' he said. It took me half an hour to persuade him and his mate that bringing into the country a couple of hundred writing books would not destroy the balance of Eritrea's economy, nor would it put all the stationery shops in Asmara out of business. In the end they agreed but the soldier had a quiet word with Aklilu who stung me with ten times the normal amount of duty I usually paid.

Anyway, across the road I'd go laden with a mail sack full of boxes and take my seat at Pizza Napoli. 'Large Hawaiian please Timnet and a bottle of Mai Gas (fizzy water).' Timnet passed my order to the boys in the kitchen and she'd join me to go through the parcels, have a slice of pizza and listen to the news in my letters. Nice time.

My third room (first room me, second room motorbike) back in Mendefera was now piled high with equipment and this was put to good use both in the training workshops and in schools which I visited and made donations. Some of the creative items that Sue had sent made great prizes. Sara's face comes to mind. After an impressive presentation at a workshop in the PRC I awarded her a headband complete with flashing clowns' faces bouncing on the ends of two springs. As I put the headband on for her you'd have thought she had just been crowned Queen of Eritrea. Needless to say this distribution of equipment drew attention and the word spread and attendance grew.

I found many motivated and able teachers in Eritrea, an amazing and unexpected discovery given that very few of them had chosen the profession. Nobody takes up a career of choice in this country, nobody picks where they will live, nobody travels without permits and yet, given this state of captivity, many have the basic desire to do a good job and benefit others.

Felt quite sorry for Belay. Caleb had been appointed the new Minister of Education for Zoba Debub. He had recently returned from studying in America which was unusual in itself, not the studying in America but the returning to Eritrea having been allowed out. Usually the traffic is one way. Initially Belay was pleased about Caleb coming to Mendefera for all the right reasons. 'He'll bring new ideas and maybe there's a chance of extra funding to support what we're doing.' What Caleb did was shift Belay to the Emna Haile PRC about ten miles down the road. After all the years of manoeuvring himself into a nice, steady job just around the corner from where he lived with his family, after all the equipment we'd bought to stock the PRC he was told he had to go and work somewhere else – and no appeal procedure. The erratic bus service to and from Emna Haile was well known. It had been the reason Janet in Durko (next to Emna Haile) had become an infrequent visitor to Asmara staying most weekends in the village. It was a fact that Belay would have an arduous daily commute and more often than not would have to stay overnight in Emna Haile.

Ydogu took Belay's place – nice bloke, getting on a bit. He told me his name meant 'Lord please leave him.' His four older brothers had died before they were five-years-old and his mother wanted some Divine protection for this one. Must have worked as he'd made it to sixty. Within a few days of arriving in Mendefera Ydogu was called to the Court House in Asmara. A friend's son had escaped across the border and all the family and the family's acquaintances had to go for interrogation to see what they knew. The interrogation and possible persecution of the family is uppermost in the thoughts of those planning to get out. That this doesn't stop hundreds going for it every month gives an indication of the state they are in.

I used to look forward to picking up my salary from Haile at the General Office in Adi Guadad these days. This hadn't always been the case. For the first year I had to find somewhere in Asmara called Bar Tiblets where hundreds of teachers, Eritrean and Indian, were milling around all having the same problem as me – where's my money? Official looking blokes in suits and ties carrying little briefcases used to show their faces and were immediately mobbed. It was a ritual played out on the last Saturday every month and it wasn't fun. On good pay days it would take three hours before the beleaguered clerk found my name somewhere in the beautifully handwritten lists. On bad days he wouldn't find my name at all and I then had wearying journeys around various government offices filled with people who didn't have time to speak to me. All for forty quid. It's the principle though, isn't it?

Seeing Haile was a pleasure. A comfortable, empty office with a glass of tchai waiting for me when I arrived on the motorbike. Still only forty quid a month but that paid for all my food, accommodation and petrol. Generally called in for the money on Fridays on my way to Asmara for the weekend so the salary added to the upbeat Friday feeling.

By now the distinction between old and new volunteers had long since gone and it was clear that some of this year's intake knew more than me about the country which actually wasn't that much of an achievement. Going into the VSO office at the end of the week was always something to look forward to. Letters from England in my pigeon hole, a welcome from VSO staff and volunteers and always a story from the villages being aired. Sometimes the younger volunteers seemed to go a bit odd in their placements and without much in the way of guidance they undertook eyebrow-raising adventures. One girl had decided to walk to Asmara from her village in the middle of the night. It was thirty miles away but no matter she had a torch. Oh well, that's alright then. Apparently after stumbling around in the dark for a couple of hours she happened upon a checkpoint and a band of soldiers. God knows what they must have thought she was doing. Anyway they made her comfortable and washed her hair. Washed her hair – you couldn't make it up.

In the city I used to pop in and see Donard, Eddie, Hannah and John who had set up home together near Castello's restaurant. They seemed very comfortable in their compound with a room each and a shared kitchen. These four really had become city-dwellers and enjoyed all the benefits of the lifestyle. Sharing the cooking they had plenty of food and a good supply of Ariki (bit like Ouzo) available from the corner shop. There was football on the telly in the city bars and, of course, the travelling wasn't an issue. Oh, and they had a maid. Didn't reckon much to this when I first realised what they'd done. It smacked of colonialism, master-servant relations and old-fashioned British dominance giving a few pennies to the natives for them to do the dirty work. I gave a lot of thought to my knee-jerk reaction and reversed my thinking completely. In fact, not having a maid is one of the biggest regrets I have about the time I spent in Eritrea. During the first week I was in Mendefera I had found a bit of paper pushed under my steel door. Scrawled on it was some message about working for me and that someone would be calling round. A couple banged on the door that evening and asked if I could employ the wife to do my cooking, cleaning and washing. I brushed them off with the truth – I didn't cook, I didn't have anything to clean and I washed one shirt a day and that was it so I had no need for paid help. Consider this a big mistake. Not only would they have had the benefit of a few nakfa a week I would have had access to a local support network that would have been invaluable in getting up to speed quickly. I was reasonably well integrated in the Mendefera community by now but reckoned that with the sort of close relationship which would have developed through this arrangement I could have learned much more about the people and, therefore, have been able to contribute more. The cooking and cleaning were not of importance, the money changing hands was not of importance – the relation-building was the thing and I had been too blinkered to see that when the opportunity arose.

Rebka and me had just been to the zoo on Bet Gergish. It was early on a Friday evening and we had the weekend ahead.

Since we had been to the Lion Hotel that first Saturday afternoon in February we had been together every weekend – well most of every weekend. Friday evening after getting to Asmara on the motorbike, picking up the parcels from the Post Office and calling in at VSO office I'd walk the couple of hundred yards down the road past the giant palm tree and pop my head round the door in Rebka's shop. She was usually sitting in a dark corner at the old computer which was used to create wedding invitations, school certificates or anything else that needed printing. This was the main income of the shop as the stationery shelves often looked a bit sparse. Mary – her assistant – and a few kids were usually around and quite often there were others who'd just called in for a chat. Being in the city centre just up from the main thoroughfare the shop was well placed and something of a hangout for the locals. After closing time the evening was ours as was Saturday evening and all day Sunday.

We had some nice meals in some of the better restaurants in the city. I particularly remember the Rooftop Garden which has a curious menu being half Indian and half Chinese. Rebka was the only Habesha in the place – this was not somewhere that was on the social round of Eritreans earning a few pence a day. UN folks, embassy employees, international school teachers and – for the first time – me and Rebka made up the clientele and we had a good time. Being six floors up on the roof the backdrop was the night sky which took some beating as it was always clear and starlit.

It was not intentional that our get-togethers were unknown by the other volunteers to begin with, our developing friendship was never intended to be secret, we just didn't bump into anyone – that is until that Friday evening after the zoo. Grown men and women hiding! Educated grown men and women hiding! There we were holding hands walking down the track from the zoo (one ostrich and two giant tortoises) when I noticed Charlie hiding behind a rock. Grinning from ear to ear he came out from his hidey-hole followed by a crowd of more than fifteen volunteers. They had spotted us in the distance – 'let's hide and see what they get up to.' Don't know what they thought Rebka and me were going to do on the slopes of Bet Gergish but their spying was rumbled and the game was up. Introduced Rebka to all of them and had a chat before roaring away on the motorbike with Rebka on the pillion realising that we were going to be the main topic of VSO gossip for a day or two at least.

After the zoo encounter we were accepted as a couple in VSO and Rebka's shop did better business than usual with volunteers and VSO staff calling in regularly to introduce themselves as one of 'Kevin's friends.' All very nice and pleasant.

Rebka's home was in Gezemanda, a small district of Asmara about ten minutes' walk from her shop. It was one room with a curtain down the middle behind which was her bed. A blue barrel outside the back door held the water and that was about it. There was quite a bit of furniture crammed into the tiny room – wine bar, television, sofa and chairs. She had lived here for about a year and paid rent to the man next door. She was making the arrangement work and seemed to be ticking over.

Walking up to Gezemanda on Sunday mornings to see Rebka was a blessed time. Past the flower-decked gardens of the nice houses around VSO office, turn left at Sematat High School and up through some steep, narrow alleyways I came out on the main Gezemanda road into the sunshine – I was eighteen- years-old again going to call on my girlfriend.

Rebka used to do a coffee ceremony and burn the traditional incense – the mixture of smells was pure Habesha. During the first Sunday morning in Rebka's home she entrusted me with the information that had shaped her life and it was a shock – Rebka was Ethiopian not Eritrean. This needed some explaining for me to get my head round. Rebka was a yellow card carrier – all with Ethiopian ancestry have to do this so the soldiers know what they are dealing with. Rebka's parents – both dead now – were from Axum in the north of Ethiopia. They had married when her mother was thirteen which was, and still is, not that unusual. They had eleven children, four of whom had died in their early years which, again, is not that unusual. Rebka's father was a successful businessman travelling between Addis Ababa and Asmara and had accumulated land, property and wealth through his deals over the years. The family had grown up in a large house and gone to the best schools in the city. The conflict and the demise of the parents had changed all that. Property was taken by the government in many cases to house high-ranking soldiers and the family was caught on opposite sides of the border when the fighting started. Rebka, who had been visiting her sick mother, was on the Eritrean side when war broke out again in 1998. Naturally, she was careful who she told about her nationality and I was clearly trusted even at this early stage not to divulge the information to anyone.

As well as Rebka's family being dispersed she had also suffered in that one of her brothers had been taken by the military. He had disappeared and had not been seen for over five years. The nightmare stories of thousands being locked up in buried shipping containers without trial were very real to her.

A further twist in the story of Rebka's family became clear when we visited her sister and family one Sunday afternoon. They had a nice house in the city not far from the Lion Hotel. I recognised that this was not a usual situation when after being welcomed in I saw a picture of Rebka's brother-in-law shaking hands with Prince Charles on the wall. Now this was really getting complicated. I learned that Rebka's 'sister' was Eritrean and had been adopted by her parents. Not only was she Eritrean she was a hero of the Eritrean people – an ex-fighter for Isaias. (A couple of weeks after we met Rebka sat me down to watch one of the programmes on *Eri-TV* about the conflict which are on all the time. There was Rebka's sister being interviewed about her role in the war, all very graphic, all very Eritrean). Sat in Rebka's sister's home that afternoon and thought I'd be careful what I said. Best talk about the work I was involved in down in Mendefera and my family back in England. Don't mention the war. Well it was a pleasant if confusing afternoon and I was starting to get a picture of Rebka's tortured and convoluted background in a fairly short space of time. Oh, and Prince Charles was presenting an award to Rebka's brother-in-law for work he had done developing the mgogo (basic cooker) not because of how many Ethiopians he'd killed.

Didn't bother me in the slightest that Rebka was Ethiopian – I didn't even know there were Ethiopians in Asmara before she told me.

I discovered from Rebka that there were, in fact, thousands of Ethiopians in Asmara all carrying the damning yellow cards, all trying to get by in a state which treated its own citizens with suspicion never mind the 'enemy.' Rebka told me that most Ethiopians lived in a slum area down past St Mary's Cathedral. I asked her to take me which astounded her. Abashowal wasn't a place she visited herself and she couldn't understand why anyone would choose to go there. In this respect she learned a bit about me. I wasn't in Eritrea for fun as a tourist, I was there to work and just because the job description said teacher-trainer that wasn't the full remit. After a while badgering her we went to the 'bad area.'

Abashowal is grim, the dwellings (you wouldn't call them houses) were single rooms made from stone and corrugated iron. The first thing that hits is how close together these shacks are built. The rough tracks between them are so narrow it is easily possible to touch the two homes opposite each other. The place stinks of sewage and the grimy faces peered at the white man as Rebka and me clambered around. Casting glances inside the dark rooms it was clear they were crowded – don't know how they slept, don't know how they lived and breathed. Serious stuff. Rebka was not comfortable and was eager to leave. Talking about what we had seen afterwards it was clear that she was not going to return and advised me against going back and 'never go there after dark.' Seemed good advice but it begs the question, 'if I am not going back to a place that needs somebody to go back to as much as any place on this earth then who will?'

'HP sauce – where did you get that?'

Dave Wright had invited me to his place one Sunday afternoon. He lived a few miles north of Asmara which was not a problem on the Honda. After asking a couple of folks to direct me to 'Dave the white man's house' I was soon banging on his compound gate. Inviting me in I could see the table was laid and he was ready for me. We were having shepherd's pie and there was a choice of HP sauce or English mustard to go with it. Again, it's the setting that makes a spread like this catch the breath. Then again, why should I be surprised when a down to earth Bradford-born seventy-year-old sticks to his Yorkshire principles and diet no matter where in the world he finds himself.

After his time in the Merchant Navy Dave had turned up in Eritrea in the mid-Nineties as a VSO volunteer. After his initial two-year placement he'd stayed on in the country and made it his home. He was married to an Eritrean woman and they had a six-year-old boy who was riding a bike outside as we ate. Over dinner I learned that Dave didn't work for VSO anymore but kept close ties with the office in Asmara and still had a pigeon hole there for his mail. In return he helped VSO out giving lifts to volunteers and staff when he was heading off up North to Nakfa in his battered Toyota Land Cruiser.

With the help of friends back in Yorkshire and The Rotary Club of Bradford Blaize Dave had set up a registered charity – The Tigre Trust – and over the years had brought doctors from all over the world to Eritrea to perform operations on the poorest children in the country. Dave's work has led to children seeing who would otherwise be blind, walking who would otherwise be lame and in some cases being alive when they would otherwise be dead. Apparently there are doctors in the world who are happy to offer their services free of charge for a short while and Dave had built up a network of specialists in many countries.

He had strong links with the nomads in the north of the country and in some cases even brought their children back to Asmara to live with him while they had treatment. Yorkshire can be proud of its son.

Dave had travelled to all corners of Eritrea and had become a bit of an Eri-scholar. I certainly never met anyone – including Eritreans – who had a fraction of his knowledge about the geography, history and customs. Actually, on knowing more about Eritrea than most Eritreans, that isn't too great a claim due to their restricted movement within the country and, in most cases, lack of basic schooling. However, the knowledge Dave had accumulated was impressive and he was always willing to demonstrate this which didn't always go down well with some of the younger volunteers. 'Bloody know-all.' Truth was though he did know it all and, more than that, it wasn't book knowledge. Dave was not a tourist travelling the country sightseeing. He had become well-known by all the tribes and his work was much appreciated. As such, he was trusted and was welcomed to spend evenings drinking coffee and talking in even the remotest regions.

Naturally, to be able to travel like he did, Dave 'knew' people in the government. His permits were usually, but not always, granted in minutes and often, in areas where he was really well-known, he didn't bother with the documents at all. Told me that he had a regular coffee with one particular Minister. The only message Dave wanted from him was 'keep your head down, keep doing what you're doing and you'll be okay' and that was all the authority to work in Eritrea he had ever been granted.

After the meal Dave had visitors – three pastors. Judging by their robes these men were of some standing in the Orthodox Church and, again, the evidence was plain that Dave had made all the right connections. The pastors sat and finished off the shepherd's pie while Dave showed me some of the photos of sick children he'd taken over the years. These were of the 'before' and 'after' variety. Some of the 'before' photographs were horrific showing extreme disfigurement – the 'after' pictures showing happy faces following a successful operation were joyous. 'We used to say that now we need another operation to get the smile off the face of the mother,' was Dave's comment about a particular family.

Before I left, Dave couldn't resist showing off a bit more of his knowledge.

'Why were girls in the Kunama tribe always given away to be married by their uncles not their fathers?'

'Go on Dave – I know you're going to tell me.'

Apparently, as part of an extremely generous Kunama culture, men were so honoured to receive certain visitors that they offered their wives for the night. Consequently, daughters never knew if their father was really their father whereas they knew for certain that their mother's brother was a blood relative.

'And did you know that you can tell women from a certain area because they urinate standing up.'

'Enough Dave, enough.' I rode back on the bike with a smile on my face and looked forward to visiting Dave again.

Always reckoned that I – and some other volunteers – could claim that they chipped in a bit in Eritrea while others seemed to be on their holidays. Dave belonged in another category entirely. This one was populated by people whose heart belonged to this country and who had committed their lives to the place.

Zeta was another in this group – she used to kiss the runway tarmac when she got off the plane at Asmara airport. Zeta was sixty-something and in a previous life used to work for the UN. Now she was a freelance visiting Eritrea two or three times a year to raise awareness about sexually transmitted diseases. What a great way to spend your retirement – beats that bowling green and bingo any day. Always thought Zeta was a brave lady. People have said that I was brave going out to live and work in the Third World but in my case it's not true. I was with an organisation and supported as such given weeks of training before ever getting on the plane and received the benefits of the VSO structure while in the country. This wasn't the case with Zeta who was completely alone and psychologically is a different state entirely.

It seemed that you can only embark on her kind of mission if your belief in what you are doing is total. 'This is what's going to happen and nobody's going to stop me.' How else do you carry on when the bumpy times come along and there's nobody to lean on?

Zeta, Sami (a teacher at St George's High School in Mendefera) and me had dinner one evening in Dembay. Zeta had bumped into Sami in Asmara and she was keen to get into his school to give some talks on STDs. Sami was going to introduce Zeta to the school director to get permission. I'm sure she got it. In response to my question about how you start up doing what she was doing the example of St George's seemed to be the answer.

1. Fly to a strange country.
2. Talk to as many people as possible.
3. Find some who are able and willing to help.
4. Do it.
5. Keep on doing it and build up the network as you go.

Easy really.

Of course, most of the time people say 'Clear off weirdo,' but so what? Young people were getting the benefit of her teaching and that was all that mattered to Zeta. That she was embarrassing a government that was doing little in this area was seen as a spin-off prize – not a reason to stop.

There was a kidnapping in March 2007. Read about it on the BBC website one Thursday evening in the internet café in Mendefera. Five British folks from the British Embassy in Addis Ababa had gone on a joyride to the Danakil region in the north of Ethiopia. You can see the border with Eritrea from there – I can think of better places to go for a joyride. Didn't turn out to be a smart move. Their vehicles had been found full of bullet holes and a grenade had been lobbed in the passenger door of one. This area is Afar country and, as Meles Zenawi (Ethiopian leader) said, 'the tourists were in the wrong place at the wrong time.' After nearly two weeks missing the sightseers had turned up on the Eritrean side of the border where they were being held at a military camp. From there they had been flown out of the country and reunited with their – no doubt – relieved families.

I wondered if this was anything for me to get bothered about. After all, I was British and not too far from the border. Looking out of the window I could see a few goats trotting by. A couple of kids were kicking a burst ball around and a group of women were stood on the corner of the street having a natter. Nah – looks alright, no worries. However, it occurred that the kidnapping might have made the news in England and, possibly, my family could have caught something on the television. Thought I'd make some kind of contact to let them know everything was fine.

The Indian teachers back in Mai Nefhi used to say that the government stopped all emails that contained certain words – usually, but not always, place names. Words like Ethiopia, Addis Ababa, border, bomb would trigger some safety net system and the email would be diverted. There were also stories from a number of volunteers about telephone calls being cut off. Catherine's mother had made some comment about 'the terrible situation in Somalia' and that was the last Catherine heard from her mother that day. None of this had happened to me but thought it wise to be careful. In the end I sent an email to a friend with the familiar day-to-day stuff in it but then inserted 'all is well' very pointedly in the text a couple of times and asked him to pass it on. Did the trick.

April 2007 – Folks

Women's wrongs sometimes became very stark. Rachel could speak Tigrinya better than me, everybody could speak Tigrinya better than me. This gave her insight that revealed a situation I had been unaware of when she came to visit me in Mendefera for a few days. She had some free time – due to various reasons quite a few of the volunteers had free time over the course of their placement. In her case the people she had been working with in Hagas, she called them The Brothers, had been closed down by the government and she was using the time before she picked up another assignment to see a bit of the country. It's also the case that working as a teacher-trainer or adviser has nothing like the intense timetable as teaching in a school. I speak from the experience of my first year.

I say Rachel came to visit, we actually both caught the bus to Mendefera together one Saturday lunchtime from Asmara. I remember the walk to the bus station clearly as for two or three minutes of the walk we were screamed at continuously by a hysterical woman. Hadn't got a clue what she was so upset about. 'Perhaps we should stop and talk to her,' said Rachel. 'No – keep walking.' I really didn't want to get involved.

After warning Rachel about the usual crush on the bus we, predictably, got on a very comfortable governmental bus with spare seats all round. No idea why today this should be as empty as it was but appreciated it rather than agonised over it. In Mendefera we went to market – I knew where it was but was not a frequent visitor. Rachel had kindly offered to do some cooking, a first in my Mendefera home, so she wanted to buy vegetables – lots of vegetables.

That evening Rachel set to making a sort of stew which smelled great. Just as it was about ready to serve Rahwa came round from next door. 'Come Teacher Kevin, come.' I went. Habtom and Eden sat me down to eat. Didn't know what to do. Didn't want to offend them so started eating and they gave me a lot. All the time I was thinking

'What am I going to tell Rachel?' After an hour I thought 'I ought to do something' so I asked Rahwa to go and get Rachel. She came in with a face like thunder. I could feel the icy stare she was giving me as I concentrated on finishing my injera. After a while we said goodnight and went back home. Rachel had a go at me along the lines of 'I'm here slaving over a hot stove to make your dinner and you just walk off and start eating next door – well now I've cooked it you're going to eat it!' After about ten minutes of this rant the absurdity dawned and Rachel, thankfully, turned to laughter. 'I sound like an old northern fishwife.' Sorry Rach – my fault.

Next day we went to visit Fikadoo, the cleaner from Frei Kalsi School. Her husband spoke no English and rambled on pretty loudly in the background as Rachel and I talked to Fikadoo. After a while Fikadoo suggested we go and visit Solomon in the next village. Sounded a good idea. As she went to prepare herself I was surprised when Rachel said softly that she was not happy in this house. Apparently Fikadoos husband's ramblings had consisted of torrents of verbal abuse directed at his wife along with the occasional threat of physical violence. During my past visits I had witnessed heated exchanges in this house and some worried looks from Fikadoo but had not picked up on the seriousness of the situation.

Solomon lived in the next village – small, around twenty little houses. We walked the three miles along rough, dusty paths. Very open landscape under a very big sky.

Solomon welcomed us at the door and we went in. We were greeted by his sister and her husband. His wife sat on the floor in a corner stirring the pot, she looked up only fleetingly – said nothing.

The food was served and we ate well. Solomon was keen to tell the story of his marriage. His big joke was how much his, then, thirteen-year-old wife had cried when he had asked her father for permission to marry her. He was in his twenties at the time and his discussion with her father had been brief – at no point was his bride-to-be asked for her opinion. Now, after ten years of marriage, she looked crushed – completely wasted. She was painfully skinny, it is hard to believe how thin a wrist can be and her face was deeply lined. Her appearance was that of a woman in her sixties. Her silence throughout Solomon's story – our entire stay – was deafening.

Solomon's wife was not an isolated example of the kind of life women endured in villages. In Asmara, however, many women had seized the opportunity to express themselves following Independence. Women held three ministerial positions and I attended seminars and Education Department meetings where women led debates and addressed large audiences. Even here in the capital, though, the majority of women managed the home while men went out to work.

Leaving Bristol Pension one day I noticed a distressed woman in a nearby house cutting pieces of meat from a freshly killed goat and throwing them in the dust around her door. The following weekend I told Alga what I had seen – Alga knew the woman and was a witness to the events which unfolded later that day. The husband had cut the goat's throat that morning and then headed for the bar to meet his friends. His wife then set about preparing the meat for him and his mates who had planned to return at lunchtime. During the morning a friend of the woman had called to tell her about her husband's adventures the previous evening with another woman at a discotheque in Expo. Hence, meat in the dust. Alga was clearly on the side of the woman as she went on to cover the story of the stabbing of the husband later that day.

Never been much of a drinker – perhaps this is why even a little beer has unfortunate effects.

Janet and John invited a number of volunteers, including me, to their home one Saturday evening. Also invited was Nick, the British Ambassador. Plenty to eat and drink – nice atmosphere. It was getting towards the end of the two years so volunteers were relaxed. We knew a bit about Eritrea, the pressures that had led to others dropping out had been negotiated – we were going to finish our term. Wish I'd had chance to get to know Nick better. T'other end of the social spectrum from me – wealthy background, public school education, etc.

As the evening progressed it became clear that Janet and John were serious conversation-types wanting everyone to get deep and meaningful rather than daft and childish. After several failed attempts to drive us down the 'what do you think can be done about Eritrea?' route the assembled gathering started to pick up the theme. Our hosts were pleased – they were thinkers, talkers, debaters. Somehow the discussion turned to colonialism and, with one Asmara Beer inside me, I made a remark along the lines of Europe raping Africa and stealing its resources. Silence. Nick broke the silence. 'I wouldn't necessarily agree with that.'

'Oh yeah? What about gold, diamonds, copper and slaves for starters?'

Silence. Janet and John looked uneasy, others looked at the floor.

Nick, 'But we have to look forward – move on.'

Me, maintaining the belligerent tone. 'Ah yes, but that's a different matter. We can only move on honestly if we acknowledge the past honestly, identify mistakes made and learn from them together.'

Janet, 'Another cake Kevin?' Nice one Janet. We wanted a polite, agreeable natter not something that might turn into a confrontational slanging match. Divert him before this gets too serious. Janet played her part as the good host and the rest of the evening was pleasant.

Reflected on the evening walking back to Bristol Pension. Wasn't happy – with myself – that I had been misunderstood. Tim had commented in the kitchen that 'You don't seem to think like the rest of us about this government.' I took this to mean that he'd interpreted my standpoint as somehow being pro-Isaias, pro-Eritrean policies. Not so. The Eritrean Government has much to answer for – the simple point made was that they, we, can only move forward constructively if people made the effort to understand the historical reasons for suspicion and lack of trust. Europe's colonial expansion is a pretty good reason for suspicion and lack of trust.

It had also struck me that not one volunteer present took up and supported what I thought was a self-evident viewpoint. Quite a few did, though, over the next few weeks in Asmara's cafes and the VSO office. In the next round of development grants issued by the ambassador I reckoned my chances were slim. I was right.

Ydogu was one for old sayings of the 'too many cooks spoil the broth' variety. These, of course, were East African versions. His favourite – which was regularly trotted out when we were considering whether or not to put on a training workshop in some middle-of-nowhere place – was, 'If you put your hand in the river you may catch a fish – if not well at least you've washed your hand.' Good positive message – stop messing about thinking of reasons not to do stuff and get on with it. Even if it doesn't work out as you planned there will be some benefit. Doing nothing is often the killer.

Another one of Ydogu's was actually played out as we were in the middle of a workshop in the PRC. I'd stepped in to stop a few fights when I was in Mai Nefhi High School. They didn't tend to be too serious but to my mind fighting in any form was not acceptable in the school. Recalled almost deciding to give up my role as resident peacemaker one day when I waded into a big crowd of students near the canteen at Mai Nefhi only to find not two brawling kids but a snarling baboon. For some reason Tesfai had brought his pet down from Mai Nefhi Hotel and the students were entertaining themselves driving it crazy by pelting it with little stones. Told Tesfai to clear off with the creature and then backed off pretty sharpish.

Found it curious that I was the only one who broke up the scuffles as other teachers hardly paid any attention. Also, bizarrely I thought, I got puzzled looks from the students involved in the confrontation and those watching and cheering on. Ydogu provided a clue with his old saying, 'If two men are fighting never stop them.' His argument, and the basis for the old 'wisdom', was that if you break it up the issues will fester and lead to bigger problems and more violence in the future. Better to get it sorted in a short, sharp exchange of punches. How's that for a foreign policy?

Anyway – the workshop was ticking along fine when suddenly we heard a crowd screaming and shouting outside. It was Frei Kalsi's break time and a girl and boy had decided to get stuck in for some reason. Dashing outside the crowd of baying students must have numbered over thirty and there were two teachers looking on with arms folded. The girl, about thirteen-years-old, seemed to be on top but she had blood running from her nose. Managed to separate the scrappers and started shouting at them. 'No fighting near my PRC! You should be ashamed!' I had a really good rant and got the looks I had come to expect in Mai Nefhi – total bewilderment from both students and teachers. In fact, I turned into the sideshow – 'what's the crazy white man think he's up to?'

Ydogu was spending a lot of time in court as he seemed to know quite a few folks who were getting over the border. As such I was holding more training sessions on my own. Set off on the bus to Adi Quala one Thursday, Charlie had organised the venue in his place for me to hold a training session on the Saturday morning. I wanted to give myself a couple of days there to set up the room, observe a few classes in Charlie's school and to see a bit of the town.

Didn't have the fuel to use the motorbike so took the bus and was glad I did as I was able to see some of the country on the way down. Passed the two checkpoints at Emna Haile within sight of each other – one Eritrean, one UN. Guess they were keeping an eye on each other as much as bus passengers. The fields we passed seemed in good shape in that crops seemed to be thriving and the cows looked well fed. Noticed more people walking without shoes than I'd seen in Mendefera though. Saw a number of spectacular mountains before the country started to open into a flat plain.

Charlie met me off the bus and after a tchai at his local café we headed off for his place just off the main street. Adi Quala is only a few miles from the border with Ethiopia and therefore is a frontline town about half the size of Mendefera. Unsurprisingly some of the buildings were bullet-holed, surprisingly – for me anyway – there were several spent mortars lying in the gutters. Not seen that before. Nobody else paid any attention.

Charlie had been in Adi Quala since 2005 when we'd flown out together and as such he was now established here in the community. He had done a TEFL course prior to flying out and had spent all his time in Eritrea teaching English in the Adi Quala Middle School. The rooms in his house were draped in mosquito nets. I had never used them myself as mosquitoes were not a problem in Mendefera or Asmara. Charlie explained that the insects were not a problem here either but scorpions and snakes were and the nets offered some protection should anything squeeze through the big gap under his door in the night.

That evening we went to the bar and met up with some UN soldiers he had got to know. It was here I finalised my full set of continents. While in Eritrea I had met people from around the globe but had yet to meet anyone from South America – the Uruguayan UN soldier enabled me to tick that box. The majority of the soldiers were from Pakistan and we spent an hour or so discussing the tension in Kashmir with them as well as the problems they were having doing a proper job observing the Eritrean and Ethiopian forces massed on the border.

The next day was spent in Charlie's school with him teaching and me observing a few classes. Popped in the PRC where I was holding the workshop the next day and was pleased to see it was built on exactly the same lines as the Mendefera PRC. Big room, plenty of space.

Over dinner that evening Charlie showed me his landmine map. 'I shouldn't really have this' and we talked about the town and his time there. It was impossible to get away from the fact that we were on the border and the tension was more keenly felt here than in, say, Asmara. If Ethiopia attacked Adi Quala would be in the firing line. The mixed-up history of the two countries and the mixed-up genes of the people is even more apparent, and strange, when you learn that Meles Zenawi's family (Ethiopian leader) had roots in Adi Quala.

VSO had drawn up an evacuation plan in case of attack. This had been implemented when the 1998-2000 conflict had started and volunteers were airlifted out of the country. Being in Adi Quala I reckoned that Charlie was number one for rescue, Janet number two and I was probably number three. Mel (who had been in Asab) and

Deng (Adi Keyh) had already been relocated to Asmara when it seemed that the likelihood of an attack was increasing. For the time being, at least, all the signs indicated that Charlie was a fixture here for his last couple of months.

Rebka's English was quite good which was an essential attribute given the standard of my Tigrinya. She had built on her school English lessons by watching lots of American films. As such her spoken English had a number of Bruce Willis influences. 'Kevin, what is godamshit?' and 'When would you use sonofabitch?' were just a couple of the questions that threw me. Oprah Winfrey and Dr Phil were other Rebka favourites – the satellite dish was working well. Watched an Oprah programme with Rebka one evening which showed the American supporting girls' education in the townships of South Africa. A little odd how Rebka was praising the charitable work in poor countries without overtly making the connection that people in the West would probably put Eritrea up there as one of the top seeds in the poverty stakes (if they knew it existed). Rebka was not and never had been a villager and had never been confronted by the poverty of the people who lived there. Asmara and, briefly, Addis Ababa had been her home cities and she had done little travelling around the countryside. The bigger towns – Keren and Massawa – had been visited but she had never called in at a village either in Eritrea or Ethiopia. It dawned that even with my limited experience I might even knew more about the poverty people had to deal with here than she did.

Went on a Hash with Rebka one Saturday afternoon. The Hash was not what it was in the Carlo and Brian days. Christina – ex-volunteer - had taken over as Hash leader. She was really throwing herself into Eritrea but was restricted in that she didn't have a car of any description never mind a Land Rover like Brian's that comfortably seated a crowd of people. Still, there were some unique people on the Hash. Christina's friends from the American Embassy provided the beer and the Israeli Ambassador provided the one-liners. Some folks can just do that. The Hash that Rebka came on had only two small vehicles but the fourteen folks assembled squeezed in somehow. We only went a few miles north of the city to the 'other' dam that supplied Asmara. Nice walk – although Rebka like all Habesha people don't really get the idea of walking for its own sake – and the dam looked pretty full with crops growing on the nearby plains where the irrigation system was doing its job. The hundreds of mud bricks standing in rows drying in the sun was a new one for me and we opened up the back of the cars for a beer and sandwich next to them.

After the Hash we went to visit Helen who lived near the VSO office. Helen was Rebka's best friend, she was half Ethiopian and had married an Eritrean. Even half-Ethiopians have to carry the yellow card and she and Rebka had become close over the years partly because of the shared challenge they faced due to their nationality. We ate and talked and I realised that this was something approaching true integration. Within a few weeks Rebka and me were known and accepted in the Eritrean community, the VSO community and the Hash community – groups that were comprised of people from at least a dozen different countries from all over the world. This probably doubled after we were invited to the International School's Quiz Night – yes the ex-pats have quiz nights even in Eritrea. Our team – the Eritrean Spoon Badgers (long story) – lost but it was a good night and Rebka was taking it all in her stride.

Four weeks after we had been to the Lion Hotel on that first Saturday I asked her to marry me. The bigger shock was Rebka saying 'yes.' Now we had a bit of thinking to do so we did it. One Sunday we got together in Rebka's home and worked it out. Rebka had to get out of Eritrea – the disappearance of her younger brother showed that there was a constant threat to her freedom and she could quite easily be next. Marrying an Englishman would provide no protection whatsoever in this country but there was a solution and this was a critical step in the plan. Every three months Red Cross buses leave Asmara packed with Ethiopians who were caught on the wrong side of the border when war broke out. The buses head off south – coincidentally – down the Mendefera road to the Ethiopian border where the passengers are handed over by the armed Eritrean guards to the armed Ethiopian guards. Rebka was going to take her chance and try for a seat.

First step in the plan, though, was to sell all Rebka's furniture which would raise a few thousand nakfa. The money would be used firstly to pay for the wedding in Asmara and secondly for the rent on an apartment in Sembel for four months until Rebka got on the bus. That would be the end of her money and it was a smart move as she would not be allowed to take any currency out with her. She knew that an intimate strip search would be performed before she got near the bus so smuggling was out of the question. After getting over the border she would be held in a camp for at least a week as the Ethiopians are as wary as the Eritreans about who comes into their country. Fortunately the camp was near Axum in the north of Ethiopia, the origin of Rebka's family, and she had many relatives living there who would visit her in the camp and bring food. This bus journey was not going to be a joyride nor was the time in camp going to be a picnic – survival was the first objective.

For my part, after I'd finished my work in Mendefera and after we'd married in Asmara, I was going to head off back to England and buy a house. We knew that I would have to demonstrate to the British Government that I was able to accommodate and support Rebka in order to get the necessary visa for her to be allowed into the UK. Once I'd bought the house and heard that Rebka had safely negotiated the border crossing, survived the camp and managed to meet up with her brothers in Addis Ababa then I would catch a plane to Ethiopia and we'd take on the 'get Rebka a British entry visa' challenge together. Oh, and we'd legally marry there as well – the Asmara wedding was only the celebration. Lots to do and a lot of energy and determination required to make it all happen which was okay because we had more than enough of both.

The wedding preparations were all Rebka's as I was in Mendefera Monday to Friday up to my ears in training. Friday evenings were a riot of wedding arrangements and Rebka updating me on what cake she'd ordered, the invitations she'd delivered and the dresses she'd chosen for her and the bridesmaids. And Sembel – we went to look at apartment 301 in block 301 in Sembel.

Ambassadors, UN delegates and politicians live in Sembel which is a complex of apartments near the Intercontinental Hotel on the road to the airport. The United Nations Mission in Ethiopia and Eritrea was housed there – this was Asmara's Belgravia. The agent met us at the foot of the stairs. No lifts, not even in Sembel, as the power supply is too erratic. Walking through the door of the apartment I was overwhelmed not by the relative luxury compared to my houses in Abarda and Mendefera but by the immediacy I was struck by the thought 'I could make my life, we could make our lives here.' This idea had never occurred at any time during the previous year and a half. In the villages I always knew that I was there to do a job on a fixed-term placement. I was enduring the conditions because I believed in the work I was doing and the basic living was just a part of that. This was different – nothing out of the ordinary compared to homes in England – but this had enough about it to trigger considerations of settling.

Of course, it was never going to happen. Rebka's status in Eritrea was too precarious but it was great to speculate for a while. The front door opened into a large dual-purpose lounge and dining room. It was fully furnished with three large sofas, a mahogany table and chairs and large-screen TV. The marble floor had a couple of exotic rugs and the pictures and ornaments were stylish. There was nothing here of traditional Eritrea. Off the main room was a purpose-built kitchen with taps and water. Taps and water. Yes, taps and water. The kitchen window looked out over the car park (where my beautiful orange but scruffy motorbike stood next to a Mercedes) and beyond that was open ground to the main airport road. I could really see myself living here.

The two bedrooms were large, the beds in them were large and the windows looking out over the Sembel area were large. There was a bathroom with taps and water. Yes, more taps and more water. The donkey with the water-filled, maize-cob-stoppered skin on its back seemed far away. Yes, I could live here. We'll take it.

Commander Beka was 5′ 6″ tall, 5′ 6″ wide and had to turn sideways to get through the doorway of my office on Tibor. Bracing myself a bit more than usual we shared a shoulder-banging handshake. It wasn't just his build that made me prepare for the social niceties. Soldiers seem to regard the handshake as a test of strength and to an onlooker it looks more like a collision than a friendly greeting.

Bruising over with, we walked to the canteen to get tchai. I'd never met him before but the reactions of Freweini and Milli, the tchai girls, indicated that when he walked in the room people jumped. Guessed he'd heard about my confrontations with his men and he'd decided to see who this awkward Englishman was sitting in the PRC.

Sitting on stones looking south over the plain towards the border I heard stories of how he and a small band of men had been surrounded by Ethiopians 'just over there behind those rocks' so they had fought their way out and killed every one of them. Pointing to the high ground behind the church he went on to tell how he had stumbled upon an Ethiopian soldier raping a girl so he killed him. Apparently the burnt out tank I passed every day was his doing also – 'dropped a hand grenade in the turret and killed them all.' There was a theme developing here.

Nothing was said about my little skirmishes with the soldiers. Beka just seemed like he was enjoying himself having found somebody new who hadn't heard about his exploits in the conflict. I recalled that I'd once bumped into Hagos at Mai Nefhi Hotel – Donard had told me the Ethiopians called him 'the tapeworm' during the fighting because they couldn't shift him and his troops once they'd dug in. 'Do you know my friend Hagos the hero of Mendefera?' ('Friend' was stretching it a bit but we had shared a beer once.)

'You know Hagos?'

'Oh yeah, yeah – we drink in Mai Nefhi Hotel.'

Beka was now in the presence of someone who (in his eyes anyway) had touched greatness. Obviously Hagos had killed even more Ethiopians than Beka and over the course of the next hour I think I heard stories about every one of them. Military folks – don't you just love 'em. We said cheerio and with a friendly wave Beka made his way back to the barracks on the other side of Tibor. Clearly, through Hagos, I was now Beka's mate and I felt secure in the knowledge that if a band of Ethiopian soldiers were ever to attack me Beka would be right there by my side fighting them off.

Over tchai in Portico's café Catherine was talking about the successes and failures of integrating with the people in her village. She didn't mean the soldiers or work colleagues but the Eri-neighbours, the folks next door. It was a Saturday morning in Asmara and about half a dozen volunteers had travelled in, usual stuff – pick up the post, catch up with folks and try to manoeuvre through the bureaucratic system on the road to getting your hands on the necessary exit visa. Some were leaving the country in May, some June but whenever it was you didn't leave document-gathering till the last moment.

Picking up Catherine's theme we all threw in a few villager stories. The fact that we were all still in the country well into our second year was evidence that we'd done okay in our placements so the 'failure' stories tended to be light-hearted rather than placement-ending tragedies. The volunteers with the real horror stories had got on planes a long time ago – often without sharing their experience with anybody. Kaska set the level for the discussion. She had been hit between the shoulder blades with a lemon, yes a lemon, thrown by a kid as she rode past on her bike through Adi Guadad. John and Janet topped that recalling a volley of stones hurled at them. I chipped in with the argument I'd had with Tesfai and Mehari about the misunderstanding over the fluorescent light bulb back in Abarda. Others had run-ins over locked-up dogs barking all night – 'it makes them tough' – cheeky kids and stuff going missing but these were comfortably outweighed by the villagers' invitations to share food, coffee and, more importantly, their homes and their time.

Michelle probably took the integration honours with her story. Michelle is a Londoner with Jamaican roots. She had clearly made an impression in her village reckoning that she had an advantage by looking like an Eritrean – the villagers believed there must be East African ancestry somewhere in the past. She had been asked to be a godmother twice, first to Milcah and then to Ariana – she chose both names. She was particularly excited as she had no children herself. She also recalled going to Asmara to buy the traditional zuria to wear to the christening, having her hair plaited Eri-style and playing her part in the Tigrinya church services without really knowing what was going on. She had even been at the hospital for Ariana's birth calming the husband down as he paced up and down outside the delivery room. Men are kept outside in Eritrea. Following the birth and immediate transfer home Michelle had been alarmed that the new mother, Leteab, was then expected to get on with preparing the coffee ceremony. No time for sitting down.

May 2007 – Wedding Day

I had not intended to upset anybody but my story did upset. Joe and Barbara had invited me to the American Ambassador's house that Saturday evening. On the Hash Barbara told me the Ambassador was throwing a party and I was welcome to join them as their guest. By now I think they accepted that I would be turning up in the same clothes that I was striding along the dusty paths in and they were fine with that. Checked shirt, jeans and solid walking boots had almost become my uniform.

I always looked out for Joe and Barbara, was interested to hear about their family and home back in California, the life they had chosen travelling in many countries and how they reconciled the two. Naturally their work had taken them to many parts of the world – not necessarily the pretty bits but the edgy places where stuff was happening. Iraq was to be Joe's next posting.

Lots of elegant ladies at the party – beautiful dresses, sparkling necklaces and ear-rings, classy make-up. Men favoured open-necked shirts and casual trousers. I must have stood out a bit still sweaty and with the usual dust covering from the Hash but nobody commented and the evening was very pleasant.

'Have you had a good week in Mendefera Kevin?' I had joined a little group of people I had seen occasionally on the Hash and was sipping my white wine when the spotlight was turned on me. I responded with an account of an accident that had happened near to my home. For every hundred stony roads in Eritrea there is a smooth tarmac road that is a pleasure to drive on. These decent roads often go straight through rural villages and nobody has bothered to teach children much about road safety. A few days earlier a bus had hit a boy playing on the tarmac.

'Oh – I hope he wasn't injured,' said Sarah.

'He was killed,' I told the gathering.

After the initial shock the topic of conversation was changed and people moved away. I needed to give some thought to how I talked about what I saw and did in Eritrea.

Rebka was now the proud occupant of an apartment in Sembel and, at weekends, so was I. Since taking over the tenancy I didn't need to stay with Alga and Mama in Bristol Pension but I did want to introduce Rebka to my former landladies so we dropped in one Sunday afternoon. After breaking the news of our wedding Alga's ululating could be heard down the street. This happy noise was often heard during celebrations or when long lost friends met up again. I was pleased they were pleased but knew we would not have got this response from an ex-fighter if she had known that Rebka was Ethiopian not Eritrean. Mama took Rebka to one side and engaged her in serious matters, a real intense session while I talked to Alga about her Eri-Tourist Board meetings, the pension and her family in Italy.

Rebka was laughing as we walked down the street to City Park after saying our goodbyes. 'Go on then, what was Mama saying?' Apparently she had been telling Rebka not to marry me under any circumstances, 'Don't trust him –

he's married, I've seen the photographs of his children.'
Nice one Mama.

All thanks to Rebka the wedding preparations seemed to
be going well. It was an odd feeling not being involved in
the arrangements – felt like I was just something that was
going to be installed as part of the proceedings. I guess
Eddie – best man – may have felt something similar. One
evening Eddie and me followed Rebka down to a tailor's
shop somewhere near the market. Tiny place inside,
Rebka had been joined by Helen and a couple of other
friends. Eddie and me tried on a few jackets and were
tugged about a bit by the tailor and that was the limit of
our contribution. The rest of the fitting consisted of lots of
high-pitched Tigrinya discussion between the girls and the
tailor and, although Eddie's knowledge of the language
was pretty good, neither of us really got the gist of what
was going on. 'Don't mind what colour the suit is but I'd
like it to fit,' whispered Eddie. Thought to myself 'don't
get your hopes up.'

I was sort of involved in choosing the venue in that Rebka
showed me around Savannah Hotel before she booked it.
The place looked fine to me, next to a disused Alfa factory
just behind the Swedish Embassy. Afterwards we went
back to Sembel for my Sunday afternoon Tigrinya dance
lesson. On the day I would be expected to shake my
shoulders and jog along to the Tigrinya beat so Rebka was
keen that I wouldn't make her look a fool. So, on went the
Helen Meles CD and off we went with Rebka adjusting my

shoulders to the rhythm, Tigrinya dancing is all about the shoulders. I managed to get to the level of 'you'll do for a foreigner' which was good enough for me. After the dance lesson Rebka would put on her friend's wedding video she'd borrowed to show me the ropes. There isn't much to do for the bride and groom at their actual wedding ceremony other than sit like a king and queen on the stage surveying the guests as they ate and danced. Our dancing, as the celebrated couple, would finish off the night as we joined everyone else on the floor. Reckoned I could manage what was required although looking like a king would be a stretch.

I had another tutor back in Mendefera. Sami was a teacher at St George's High School in the town and lived only five minutes' walk from me. VSO gave all volunteers forty nakfa a week to set up and pay for Tigrinya language lessons. This was a lot of money for a conscript teacher so Sami was happy to visit me every Wednesday evening. Wasn't too bothered with the language – it was too late in the day for me to develop any real proficiency – but I was keen to learn about the customs, history and geography of Eritrea and Sami was a good teacher. Naturally, as the wedding was on the horizon, I was eager to share his knowledge on the Eritrean matrimonial procedures so with his and Rebka's instruction I felt reasonably comfortable as the big day approached.

On Sunday May 13th 2007 I was standing in Eddie and Hannah's home in Asmara in a navy blue suit that was a little too big. Eddie was standing there in a dark green suit that was much too big. Well, that's not entirely true, it was only our jackets that would have fitted the Hulk – the waistcoats and trousers weren't bad and we reckoned that the jackets could be ditched once the ceremony was underway and we'd be alright.

The cars arrived and we were off on the road to Sembel to pick up Rebka and the bridesmaids. There was time for a bit of reflection on the short journey. I was nearly at the end of my time in Eritrea. The teaching was almost finished, I had bought my flight ticket back to England, a challenging time stretched out before us with Rebka leaving Eritrea and here we were getting married. The cars slowly made their way along Asmara roads and past buildings that were by now very familiar to me – Nyala Hotel, The Gallery, Nakfa House, the white Lufthansa offices, Alpha supermarket and, most evocative, the Lion Hotel where I had slept on my first night in Eritrea nearly two years ago.

At Sembel we got out at Block 301 and mooched about a bit. The bride wasn't ready yet so we had to wait. Lots of kids gathered and made a welcome audience on a bright day that was special and needed to be shared. Joked with Helen's sons who were the page boys, talked to Tsegay and Woldu about their cars. Sengal and Eddie busied around making sure that everything was in place. On some signal I was not aware of we made our way up the stairs to apartment 301 and waited again. Then the door opened.

Inside Rebka was seated on the sofa with a veil over her head. Beautiful white dress, beautiful brown face – caught my breath. To recall the beauty of times past is wonderful but to be aware of senses locked into the beauty of the present moment is a special if fleeting joy. This was really happening and Rebka was going to be my wife. Semera led the procession down the stairs casting white flower petals around from a basket for us to walk on and we went outside into the gardens at the side of the apartment block. Over the next hour we were posed and re-posed and a photographer took pictures of everyone from every angle in every group permutation possible. By now I was on automatic, very relaxed and happy to be manoeuvred where I needed to go. Rebka had thought of everything and Sengal was doing the business in his organising role – all was under control and calm and there was a sense that what was happening was meant to happen.

At the Savannah Hotel we prepared for the big entrance. Rebka's older family ladies were throwing freshly cut grass around the porch and the traditional band of four musicians – three on tubular pipes and one leaping around with a drum – were tuning up. All expectation – this was going to be a big, noisy entrance.

Inside was packed with guests who were all clapping. Semera was still throwing petals all over the place, the pipers had launched into their hypnotic rhythm and the drummer was springing up and down erratically as he banged the drum with his hands as hard as he could. The air was filled with the smell of incense and this was accompanied at intervals by the smell of injera, spicy berbera and chiro which were being cooked in the kitchens. Seated on the stage Rebka and me gazed around the room – quite a sight. Tables seated with, mostly, white-faced folks on the left (my volunteer friends) and to the right tables seated with brown-faced folks (Rebka's family and friends). Barbara had a brainwave which served us well a couple of weeks earlier when the volunteers were all in Asmara for a VSO meeting. Barbara and her family and quite a few others didn't get to the city very often as the demands of the arduous bus journey and teaching commitments meant that the challenge was too great to take on regularly and certainly not every weekend. I had taken the opportunity to invite them all to the wedding and this had set people thinking – most had work in the villages on the following Monday and would not be back in time to teach if they came to the ceremony on a Sunday. However, Yohannes had earlier asked us to set a date for an end of year volunteer meeting and Barbara linked the two together – 'we all go to Kevin's wedding on the Sunday and have the meeting in Asmara on the following Monday – sorted.'

That afternoon in the Savannah Hotel we all ate and drank and listened to the traditional music played by the

Eritrean band. As we moved into the evening a group of young musicians took to the stage, the volume went up and the modern stuff was aired. Everyone was up dancing. Sitting on the stage watching events unfold it was memorable to see how the previously separately-seated brown and white faced folks merged as the music played. During a break in proceedings Rebka and me took to the floor for a slow dance to 'When a Man Loves a Woman' and the volunteers who had drunk a bit by now went alarmingly wild. Only time in my life my dancing has ever had that effect. The Asmarinos were a little more reserved – the light kiss I had given Rebka at the end of the dance was 'not the done thing' at all.

Ten cakes. Ten wedding cakes – there was enough to go round and more besides. The cake cutting was accompanied by triumphal deafening music and this was followed by Rebka and me joining the dancing. Some day.

Strange how sometimes life works. Occasionally the bits fall into place and a kind of natural train of events start to flow that have no connection to any effort that anybody is putting in to make things happen. Poppy's birth led to me going back to England at Christmas. While there I had picked up my UK driving licence which saw me right for an Eritrean driving licence. The motorbike released time in the capital which meant that Rebka and myself could spend days together, get close and, inevitably, marry.

Isaias – military dictator of Eritrea – was directly involved in the next turn of fate. True, he was an unwitting ally but his role was crucial. Following a marriage in Eritrea the bride and groom stay in their home for two weeks where they are visited daily by family and friends who bring gifts and food – usually cake. The traditional coffee ceremony is enacted throughout the day and the married couple are welcomed into the community as man and wife. The work ethic got in the way of this and my concern for the tradition was not perhaps as it should have been. Didn't reckon much to sitting around drinking coffee and eating cake for two weeks and I had workshops to deliver in Mendefera. I wanted to finish the assignment properly – my two years was nearly over and I had no intention of leaving loose ends and not saying goodbye.

Monday morning and off I went on the motorbike. I was not Mr Popular with Rebka or her family as she would have to welcome guests alone in the apartment until I returned the following weekend. Arriving at the checkpoint just past Adi Guadad I stopped the motorbike and got off. While the soldiers checked my papers we usually had a chat about football and I had got to know a couple of them quite well – Arsenal supporters of course. This time was different – it was obvious from their expressions that they were soldiers first and friends with Teacher Kevin second. Zemichael who had been talking to me like a blood brother only the previous Friday on the way into the city was now thrusting the travel permit back at me and angrily demanding the 'right' papers. I didn't know what he was talking about. After a couple of minutes an officer looked out of the soldier's shack to see what was going on and clicked his fingers at me motioning to come. 'Independence Week coming – need special papers to travel.'

That was it then – I was stuck in Asmara for two weeks on the authority of Isaias. Well thank you very much – I can go and do my traditional duties like a good Eritrean husband and have a couple of weeks in the city. Rode back to Asmara, called in at the VSO office and phoned Belay to explain what had happened at the checkpoint knowing that there was nothing he or I could do to get me to Mendefera. He said that the workshops could be rearranged easily enough so everything worked out well. Strange turn of events.

Could have lied to Rebka along the lines of 'had second thoughts and am going to sacrifice the workshops for your sake' but I didn't. However, like me she was pleased about the situation and we looked forward to two weeks together. Being Ethiopian Rebka was fully aware of the heightened tension and, therefore, heightened security over the Independence Day period. Since 1993 Eritrea has spent a week each year celebrating their independence following the thirty years of armed struggle. The streets are decorated with lights and there are fireworks and lots of colour everywhere. Motorised floats from all parts of the country festooned with Eritrean flags lead processions through Asmara every evening and there is much singing and dancing. Offices close down and the work stops while the national festivities are underway. This can be frustrating for foreigners trying to get permits or flight tickets but that's the way it is. The number of soldiers on the streets increases tenfold and their attitude to foreigners changes. Twice the contents of my rucksack were scattered on the pavement by zealous young soldiers looking for my non-existent bomb.

Rebka – and her Ethiopian friends – were extra careful during this time hiding at home for most of the days. A yellow card found on anyone near the processions in the city centre would probably have meant imprisonment for at least the duration of the festival. There was also the matter of her being married to a white man – now that was a magnet for any soldier at this time so, bizarrely, being seen walking hand in hand with me down Harnet Avenue was not possible.

In the end the situation wasn't too restrictive for us. Because of the tradition people were visiting us in Sembel so we weren't out and about on the streets too much. When we did go out we were sensible and, using the motorbike, we had visors which hid our faces.

In truth, and this applied for all the remaining weeks in Eritrea, living was not in the slightest overshadowed by any restrictive situation on the streets. In fact, for me anyway, living became lighter. I wore the cloak of experience and knew the country and people a little bit. I had worked through the challenges in the school and was confident that the teacher-training had achieved its objectives. Relations with people I had met in Eritrea, both nationals and foreigners, were something I would treasure all my life, I was married to Rebka and we had a plan. Now looked good, the future looked great.

Independence Day itself was an odd one. There was wall-to-wall coverage on *Eri-TV* of the festival centred on Barti Meskerem Square. The five MiGs flew deafeningly low over our heads in Sembel and a couple of seconds later they flew across the television screen. This crazy dual viewing of the air show went on for a while so we turned over to Oprah.

On other days, as well as visits from Rebka's friends, we had callers from the VSO gang. One afternoon we had an all singing and dancing session when twenty volunteers turned up on the doorstep. Good job we had a big lounge. Helen brought round an enormous jubana (coffee pot) and the coffee ceremony was up and running. The wedding video had now been developed and delivered so we put it on – lots of people looking for themselves on the TV screen and laughing at each other's dancing.

After the 'sit-in' I made my way back to Mendefera to finish off the work and told Rebka I'd be back on Friday afternoon. By this time Rebka had applied for her place on the Red Cross bus so would spend the week badgering them and sorting out things in Asmara in readiness for her departure. She had been born in the city and apart from a couple of years in Addis Ababa had lived her whole life there. She was actually in a very weak position. Many of her close friends who had known Rebka for years had no idea she was Ethiopian – the secret had been closely guarded – and they reacted badly to this 'enemy' in their midst. Others took advantage of the situation by refusing to pay back money Rebka had loaned them. They knew that there was no way Rebka would take them to court – her nationality meant she could never win. The other aspect of this was she had married a white Englishman and they are all millionaires aren't they – 'we know this because we see the pictures on the internet of Buckingham Palace and Rolls-Royces so why do you want back the few thousand nakfa we owe you?' After Rebka was granted a seat on the Red Cross bus the situation, if anything, got more delicate. Once Rebka had her booking there was no way she wanted any trouble with the authorities which might lead to her passport out of Eritrea being taken back.

The few weekends we had left in Asmara were very different for Rebka in that she saw less and less of the Eritreans she had grown up and lived with all her life and saw more ex-pats in company with me. We went to the British Ambassador's party along with most of the other volunteers who were also celebrating the end of their time in the country. This was a lively affair which went on until the early hours. The ambassador and three of his mates were dressed in *Sergeant Pepper* Beatles outfits. Pink, yellow, green – the full works. Every half an hour somebody put on a Beatles track and up they were playing their part singing along at the top of their voices. Not sure what Rebka made of it – 'mad English' I suppose.

This had been our second invite from Nick the ambassador. In April the Queen had a birthday in Eritrea and she might be pleased to know we all celebrated it at the embassy in Asmara. I was keen for Rebka to wear traditional habesha dress and she went in a beautiful zuria. As is often the case with these events a real mix is apparent. Rebka in her finery, Eritrean Ministers, lots of suits, a dozen or so scruffy VSO volunteers and to top it all a Scotsman playing bagpipes. There was lots of food and drink of course and a speech from Nick. VSO volunteers got a mention. Apparently we were the ones who were doing the real work 'out in the field.' Very nice. Next came a reference to relations with the Eritrean Government 'who we never agree with about anything.' Oops. Wish I had my camera to take a picture of the expressions on the faces of the seated Eritrean Ministers at that moment – brilliant.

June 2007 – A New Adventure

Two o'clock in the morning on the night before my last
workshop and there I was chasing invisible cockerels. I'd

been woken in the middle of the night by a pathetically weak cock-a-doodle-doo. Tried to ignore it but no, it wasn't going to stop. Sounded close so I had a look round outside. Eventually I noticed that, jammed between the steel bars at my window and the glass, was a sickly looking bird still attempting to crow. Needed an early start, Kuduaber is a long way, the noisy cockerel had to go. Pulling it through the bars it was quickly launched over the wall into next door's compound where I hoped it would be safe from the howling dog pack which raced around Adiga Berai all night.

Back in bed the night naggers started. Only the previous week I'd read on the internet about the global bird flu epidemic and here I was picking up sick cockerels with my bare hands. Got up and washed my hands then got back into bed. What if the kids next door picked it up tomorrow morning? What if the whole of Mendefera was struck down? Went outside to see if I could find the scrawny bird – this had become a farce. No chance in the dark, forget it, it'll be okay.

Janet and I were going to meet up in Kuduaber where she would take the English and I would do a few maths sessions. I'd been to Durco the previous week to see Janet and plan the workshop. She made tchai and introduced me to her neighbours – good to meet them. Like most of the volunteers Janet had lived and worked in several countries before Eritrea. Her list was more impressive than most as her Dad was an international investment banker travelling the world so she and her family had been on the move from an early age living in various locations including Nairobi and Hong Kong.

The Dahlak Islands adventure sounded great. Janet and a few other volunteers had spent a few days at Easter on one of the Dahlaks in the middle of the Red Sea. Over tchai I listened to her stories of swimming in phosphorescence, catching fish among the unspoilt coral and sleeping under the stars – made a mental note to go myself one day.

We walked to Emna Haile together and had another tchai in a little canteen at the junction with the main road. A few boys were rolling a big smooth stone around near the bus stop. This was the famous Black Stone of Emna Haile. Apparently nobody could lift it off the ground. Don't know what its composition was but it comfortably resisted my attempts. It's surprising how accessible national treasures like this are in Eritrea. Climb the Big Tree in Segenetti? Of course – carve your name on its branches if you like. Roll around the famous Black Stone? Go on, have a go. During my time in Eritrea the only month I wasn't there was August when the Exhibition of Eritrea takes place at Expo in Asmara. Officials from all the Zobas bring items representing their part of the country – the Black Stone was displayed the previous summer as a prize exhibit and here it was being manhandled at the side of a dusty bus stop. Presumably after its starring role in Asmara a few blokes had hauled it back on to a Land Cruiser, ferried it back to Emna Haile and lobbed it back where it had come from.

The workshop went well. I was exhausted from the night's cockerel-chasing antics but rolled the sleeves up and went for it – mostly on automatic having delivered the workshop many times by now. Lots of good feedback, a great way to finish the programme.

My last few days in Mendefera were spent in and around the Resources Centre. The third room in my home was cleared of all the equipment that remained – there was a lot – and taken to Ydogu who set about logging every item. I'd seen this meticulous approach the year before in Mai Nefhi where the staff had compiled a handwritten list of every book (including authors) sent by Royal Mail. Here, Ydogu was listing Christmas crackers, coloured building bricks, teddy bears and all sorts of trinkets even though he had no idea what they were. He didn't appreciate me pulling a party popper behind his ear but reluctantly was persuaded to have a go himself. Not easy to describe the fun element to someone who had spent his life trying to avoid loud bangs in war-zones.

Caleb – Minister of Education for Zoba Debub – called for me to meet with him in his office. Unusually for someone at this level he was young. His English was perfect and the accent gave away that he had spent time in the United States. After a brief discussion about how the workshops had gone he offered me a job constructing and rolling out training programmes across the south of the country. By now my head was turned in another direction and although I was flattered and grateful for the offer it was never seriously considered. Definitely one of those crossroads moments you look back on and wonder 'what if I'd said yes?'

Caleb had organised a leaving-do for me on my last evening and all the people I had worked with and come to know were there. Plenty to eat and drink and a few speeches at the end – even a short one from me expressing a lot of thanks particularly to my 'brothers' Belay and Ydogu. Caleb presented me with a wooden carving of a camel bearing a nice inscription. Need to pack that carefully.

The next morning Fish came with the truck and we loaded up. Two hundred kids (well it seemed like that) helped with the lugging and my home was soon empty except for the table I had bought in Asmara nearly two years before. Stained with candle wax it held a memory or two having spent most evenings working on it. Lots of bits and pieces were left including pen knives, antiseptic cream and coins in the little drawer for whoever came next. Hoped the new owner would find it as useful as I did. Carefully negotiated the motorbike through the waving children and headed off to Asmara with Fish in pursuit. Bye-bye Mendefera.

The motorbike had, sadly, been handed back to Yakiem at the VSO office but I still had the push bike for one more day. This was useful as I still had a couple of documents to collect before I flew off and didn't fancy the walk. Headed off to the police station to pick up a bit of paper stating that I had not committed any criminal offences while in Eritrea. Apparently this was needed to support job applications for teaching vacancies in other countries. Then, on the bike to the Ministry of Transport to hand in my Eri-driving licence. Didn't make it as far as the Ministry as a multitude got in the way.

I'd been fortunate to attend many festivals and commemorations in Eritrea. As well as the local family celebrations such as weddings and baptisms I'd been to the Ceremony of the Holy Cross which takes place in Barti Meskerem Square in September. Lots of rhythmic drum banging and swaying to the beat and a big bonfire to cap it all off. A few days after (our) Christmas Abraham's sacrifice is celebrated and thousands of goats and sheep are killed. I remembered the sight of bloody animal skins – and the accompanying stench – piled high at the side of the streets as I rode into Asmara that particular Friday evening. Martyrs' Day followed the Independence Day celebrations and was a bit like our Remembrance Sunday – very solemn, very respectful.

But Gordaif on that day in June – now that was a celebration to remember. Guess it was all tied into my de-mob mentality and post-wedding euphoria but it is difficult to imagine a more uplifting sight. Stretching as far as the eye could see were Eritreans in their finery playing music and dancing. The best part, though, was actually being included in this occasion. This wasn't done in an artificial 'let's get the foreigner up dancing like a fool' way but in a genuine 'Hi Teacher Kevin, good to see you' kind of way. Some of the people had come from Mai Nefhi, some I knew from offices in Asmara and some I had just got to know talking to them in the shops and streets. The procession went by and every now and then one or two of these friends would stop and we'd have a few minutes to catch up before they dashed off to re-join their group. Big smiles all round.

A man came out of the shop behind me and we got talking. He told me the gathering was a coming-together of the many Orthodox churches in the area. I suppose there must have been a particular biblical link somewhere but Tewelde, my new friend, didn't know what it was. He invited me into his shop where we went in the back and I met his wife. Injera was served followed by tchai. Felt good to be part of this – do I really want to leave Eritrea?

Sitting alone outside the locked gates of Asmara airport where the lights were out and no one was at home was very peaceful. It was about half past one in the morning and on the cool side with a light breeze blowing. The sky was starry and I could see a long line of orange street lights stretching back the way I had come to Sembel and beyond that to the city centre. The Egypt Air flight wasn't due to take off for well over three hours but I had wanted to be early partly because I didn't want to miss it and partly because I didn't want to go to sleep and then disturb Rebka setting alarms for the middle of the night. Some friends, Helen and Sengal, had been round to the apartment that evening and we had eaten and talked for a while until my taxi came.

Looking at the street lights with time to ponder it occurred that my wife was asleep just beyond the last light and I was about to get on a plane and fly thousands of miles away. Sitting on a stone in the dark my thoughts wandered and I could see the faces of students at Mai Nefhi quite clearly in front of me. There was also the library in the school stocked with rows and rows of books sent by decent folks back in England. Belay and Ydogu figured prominently in the reminiscing as did the times when I had cycled, a now unlit, Mendefera road about five hundred yards from where I was sitting. At those times walking across the tarmac to a departing flight for England had seemed so distant it was beyond the imagination. Yet here I was, about to do just that.

Other stuff that had happened in just the last few days also came to mind unprompted. Eritrea never lets up on its revelations right to the end. Rebka and me had called in at her shop around eleven o'clock one night and it was raining. She had wanted to pick up some photocopying to deliver early the next day to a customer so we had taken a detour on the way back to the apartment. Next to the shop was where Semera, the little girl who had cast the petals at our wedding, lived with her mother. Semera was sitting on the steps in the light rain. Rebka talked to her in Tigrinya for a while before giving her the jacket she was wearing. We said goodnight and left Semera on the steps. Back in Sembel Rebka explained that Semera's mother was a prostitute and Semera had to wait outside while she earned her keep. This was not a one-off, Rebka had seen this and other examples of abuse many times since she had begun working at the shop and had taken Semera under her wing.

A group of lads used to kick a burst plastic ball around in the road outside the shop. Usually there were around a dozen of them aged between five and thirteen. They were always ragged – city street kids. Rebka knew the father of the oldest boy who worked in an office around the corner and she had his phone number. I asked her to call him to tell his son to come to the shop with his friends to pick up some footballs, shirts and newspaper pictures of footballers that had been sent to me. Rebka made contact but didn't give the father the full picture. Getting hold of the wrong end of the stick he thought Rebka was asking him to send his son round for a date. He reproached her with – 'Don't you know he's only thirteen-years-old?' Misunderstanding eventually resolved, the lads came round on my last Saturday morning in Eritrea. Everyone got something and it made for a nice photograph. Off the team went in their (oversized) Arsenal, Charlton Athletic and Manchester City shirts – proudest kids in the city, the envy of every lad they bumped into.

The Israeli Ambassador also came to mind. Just this week we had seen him with his son playing near the swings at Sembel, only swings I ever saw in the country. Father and son out together, nice scene, all perfectly normal except for the armed guards shadowing their every move. Didn't look right at all – growing up like this?

For no reason at all the privileged few appeared in my thoughts as well. Just before my first Christmas in Eritrea Barbara, the German Ambassador's wife, asked us all back to her place as she'd prepared a few things to eat. So, instead of opening up the car boots we set off to her house. I stood for a while in awe at the spread which seemed to go on as far as you could see. Pate, smoked salmon, Black Forest gateaux and on and on and on. For months I'd been living on pasta every night at the Mai Nefhi Hotel, breakfast had been biscuits and tchai. The neighbours had been living on injera and lentils if they were lucky and here – in Eritrea – was a banquet. While we ate Carlo kept us all occupied with tales of drunken Irish UN soldiers, fights with the locals and a number of over the top experiences during the time he had been incarcerated. The ambassador appeared with five – FIVE – bottles of single malt whisky and for some reason Carlo challenged all comers to a 'put your foot behind your head' contest. No takers so he did it anyway.

'Kemay.' The random, disparate, ridiculous and violently contrasting scenes in my head were interrupted by a couple of Eritrean men walking towards me out of the darkness. They worked at the airport and after the customary Eri-handshake they asked me what I had been up to in their country. I told them about the training workshops in and around Mendefera. They interrupted my list of villages I'd been to with 'Kuduaber? We were born in Kuduaber!' Yet another example of this small, lightly populated country showing it really is a village itself where everyone seems to have a close connection with everyone else. After a while the two men said the guard shouldn't be too long before he would open the gates. Sure enough, after half an hour, an old chap came and fiddled with the padlock and the small crowd that had assembled made their way in.

The undisciplined, idle thoughts that had occupied me outside the gate took a more questioning turn as I waited in the tiny room that passed for a departure lounge. Wondered if I'd changed much after a couple of years in Eritrea. Didn't think so. Figured that if I'd been in my twenties instead of my forties and a bit more impressionable there'd have been more likelihood of adopting a new outlook, a new perspective given the experience of my time here. There had been some realignment of what mattered though. For all the challenges I'd had in the classroom at Mai Nefhi and when confronted by the soldiers in Mendefera they were not worth a mention to people like Mulu, Fiori and Semera. Given my awareness of lives such as these the ups and downs of my days could only now be recognised very obviously as no more than that.

I passed on a few comments to volunteers coming out to work in Eritrea for the first time. Yes, don't forget your sleeping bag, pen knife and antiseptic cream but more important than all the practical bits and pieces keep in mind the absolute necessity to build the relations before tackling the job, build the relations while tackling the job and keep building the relations after the job is done.

Really appreciated getting close to a real insight into the country and the villages. Important to recognise I was 'close to' without really being totally 'part of.' Elsa, the young student standing in her row during the singing of the anthem at Mai Nefhi High School, hit the nail on the head when she saw an aircraft in the sky caught my eye, pointed up and mouthed the words 'bye-bye Teacher Kevin.' I have a friend in England who has been in a wheelchair many years following a motorbike accident when we were teenagers. By sitting in his wheelchair I can get an idea of what it must be like to be a paraplegic but not really because I know that at any moment I choose I can stand up and walk away – he can't. Similarly, although I managed to serve out my time living and working closely with people in the villages, there is a truth underpinning everything done and that is 'I can fly away at any time' – the people in the village can't. A world of difference.

How should Eritrea change? Now addressing that one with any seriousness after a couple of years in the country would be beyond arrogance. Listening to people from developed countries forcefully stating what should and should not happen in places like Eritrea it always seem to come from the standpoint that we have got it sorted and we know best. But have we got it sorted? What about drug and alcohol abuse, child pornography on the internet, pollution, levels of youth unemployment, terrorism, war? Are we really in such a sound position to dictate to others?

Two observations cannot be understated though and these strike every foreigner who visits Eritrea and, more importantly, are known by every Eritrean I met during my time in the country. First, Eritrea is all about undeveloped potential. The ports on the Red Sea are so favourably placed they could become strategic gateways in and out of East Africa. Instead they are used by a few old fishing boats and unwanted, but needed, aid rots on the quayside. Import and export is not what Eritrea is about at this time. When you first research the data on this the immediate thought that strikes you is 'there must be some mistake with the figures' – but there isn't.

The climate and geography of Eritrea is of the kind that countries trying to encourage tourism can only dream of yet Massawa is a wasteland visited by a few privileged

Eritreans and one or two white faces who are allowed there for the *Eri-TV* cameras. 'Look we have a thriving tourist industry.' Unbroken sunshine for month after month cries out to be tapped and used as energy and there isn't a working solar panel in sight.

The most important waste by far, though, is a young population that has such a craving for freedom and knowledge that hundreds risk being shot and killed escaping across the border every month. They are living proof that freedom is as essential as oxygen to live in any meaningful sense. By definition, the courage and resourcefulness needed to undertake such a mission cannot be questioned. Why are these qualities not being used to develop the country? Why is the only attribute being seriously developed is the ability to pull a trigger? Further, having personally witnessed the work of many teachers and students in Eritrea I can vouch for their intelligence, their potential – and the one university has closed down.

The second observation relates directly to the first – nothing will change in Eritrea while Isaias is in power. Actually that's not true, the stranglehold will get tighter as it did during the brief time I was there. Ever more checkpoints and permits, agencies kicked out of the country and church after church closed down. Photo Walter sits across from City Park near the President's Palace, there are lots of photographers in Asmara. Stepping inside you are confronted by a four foot square black and white photograph of the view looking down Harnet Avenue. Somebody has written on the bottom 'Asmara 1965'. Walking out of the shop and up the incline to the top of Harnet Avenue you are struck by the fact that the scene looks exactly the same as in the picture. Buildings, cars, fashion unchanged, a static sight.

Barbara from the American Embassy would shoot from the hip when we talked about Isaias and looked for every opportunity to put this one to him. 'Everyday people risk their lives trying to enter my country while everyday people risk their lives trying to leave your country. When this changes I'll listen to your criticism of the West.' Indisputable – but no basis for constructive dialogue or a progressive relationship. Surely it is necessary to be born in a country that has been colonised to really understand the reasons for suspicion.

Did I just support a military dictatorship in Eritrea? At face value the only answer is 'yes.' I and all the other VSO volunteers were on the payroll of the Ministry of Education. We delivered their curriculum, worked within the policies handed down to the schools and collected our twelve hundred nakfa every month. There is another viewpoint though and it could be seen working at different levels. Individuals unquestionably received an education. Students received the benefit of diligent teachers such as Janet and Charlie who showed the utmost commitment to their work. The classroom is where the small but vital seeds are planted without which the people with the brains can never overcome the people with the bullets.

At a family level relations benefit and progress when acquired knowledge leads to constructive and informed questioning. The thousands of informal discussions that took place in homes, staffrooms and even bars not dictating to people but raising awareness feeds into the consciousness of the community. Why do we practise FGM? Why do girls have to marry at thirteen? Why do we all become soldiers? Why can't we live where we choose? Why can't we make real the dream to become lawyers, doctors, pilots? Many young people actively seek out volunteers, foreigners generally, not just for financial support like Mussie but simply to talk and engage, to challenge themselves with the kind of external stimulus of which the government is fearful. Ministers know, of course, that the momentum of dialogue at a local level can grow to the point where it is felt at national level, anathema in a country where the only directives are top-down.

Even more important than the dialogue generated is the simple, physical presence of a woman or man standing at the front of a class full of students who can choose to live, work and travel where they want. That must prompt the question in every Eri-student – 'why can't I?'

My own contribution on all these fronts is virtually invisible but however insignificant I want to be part of that and my steps need to be in that direction. Small as they are I am pleased to make a few basic claims. All my grade 9 classes progressed to grade 10 the following year – not always the case in many schools. The library at Mai Nefhi stands as testimony to the goodwill of people in England who sacrificed time and effort to put those books on a plane and send them to me. The feedback from teacher-training indicated that the young people attending appreciated the sharing of knowledge and there were plenty of examples of good practice being deployed in the classroom after the workshops. The PRC equipment was a bonus. I would be surprised if the photocopier was still operational but the concepts it allowed us to distribute widely may still feature in lessons in Eritrean villages today. Talk is cheap – there's such a thing as do and I am grateful for having the opportunity to have done a bit.

Rebka and I did what we said we'd do. Back in England I bought a house just across the road from Chesterfield Football Club. It took just over six weeks from viewing to signing. During that time an email came through from Rebka – 'I'm over the border.' That was a moment. She'd had a difficult few weeks in Eritrea following my flight back to England. Strip searches, abuse from former friends who'd only just become aware of her nationality after knowing her for many years, threats concerning money and so on. Helen and her family had waved her off at the bus station, the bus pulled out of Asmara and headed straight down the road to Mendefera and beyond to the border. I pictured her looking through the bus windows at the shops and cafes on Mendefera High Street. Maybe she could see Tibor where I worked.

Once over the border the tense handover was followed by many Ethiopians kissing the ground before being brought back down to earth under armed guard in the camp. This didn't last for much more than a week though and the wait was eased for Rebka by visits from relatives not seen for many years who came and gave her food. At the end of the week, when the Ethiopian soldiers were finally convinced they had not just welcomed bomb-laden terrorists into the country, the inmates were given a thousand Ethiopian Birr each and set free. Rebka promptly used the cash to buy a flight ticket and caught the plane to Addis Ababa. Reading this on email I also promptly bought a flight ticket and caught the plane to Addis Ababa to be reunited.

We were made to wait a couple of months for Rebka's visa by the British Embassy in Addis Ababa. 'You need to bring evidence that your marriage is not a fake – bring lots of wedding photos of you standing with WHITE people.' Yes that's what the jobsworth said, I'm not kidding. Fortunately we could do better than that as we had the video and yes, many of the faces on it were white.

Rebka is now getting used to a new, strange country where you can see your breath on cold mornings. This was a first – 'Kevin get me to hospital quick, my insides are on fire and there's smoke coming out of my mouth.' People also clear up dog mess with little trowels and put it in plastic bags after their pets have made a deposit on the pavement in this country. That one made the jaw drop. 'What IS that woman doing?'

No account of present-day Eritrea should end on a happy note though and this one won't. Eritrea and every individual in it is locked down. The best you can say is that the country is not in chaos and is not suffering from the turmoil to be found in some other countries at this time. I know that I could walk down Harnet Avenue today and all would be calm. The old girl will still be selling her Eri-Profiles, students will be going to school to copy from the board and old folks will be sitting outside cafes in glorious sunshine sipping coffee. But this is not a travelogue.

This book will undoubtedly be banned in Eritrea and I will never be granted an entry visa again. Nothing in the scheme of things but important to me and a small indicator of the stranglehold that grips the country.

Two years after our wedding Selam, one of Rebka's bridesmaids, was shot and killed trying to escape across the border along with many others.

The Asmara VSO office was closed down. Several of its Eritrean former employees now email me from various countries in Africa, Europe and America having escaped.

The pastor at our wedding disappeared shortly after Rebka left the country along with many others. Wouldn't renounce their faith.

Millette, another of our bridesmaids, died after contracting AIDS – along with many others. Not much treatment available in Eritrea and denial from the government that the condition even exists in the country.

Rebka's brother has now been missing over ten years – along with thousands of others.

Hundreds of Eritreans trying to cross the Sinai Desert to escape indefinite imprisonment or conscription have been killed, dismembered and their organs sold.

In Calais squalid camps teem with Eritreans who nightly try to jump on the back of lorries bound for England.

Since we left Eritrea thousands of Eritrean bodies have been washed up on Italian beaches. Families catching rusty old boats that haven't a hope of making it to Europe.

The happy ending for Eritrea will come but it will be a while yet.

And ... Rebka and I now have a daughter – I enjoyed breaking that news to my other children all now in their thirties – and it's the greatest pleasure watching her play with my grandchildren. We tried to relocate permanently to Addis Ababa in 2013. Big lesson learned – it's one thing living and working in a developing country alone, quite another with a child. How do I continue the work I started in Eritrea? How do I give my daughter the best start in life in a secure environment?

Well, with one foot in the UK and one foot in East Africa there's a rare opportunity here. Build a home for my daughter in England and set her on the path to a decent education while simultaneously doing a spot of fund raising. Over in Addis Ababa in partnership with my wife's family set up a children's home and grow this with any income I can generate in the UK. It occurred that I might be able to raise a bit by writing a book about my time in Eritrea – hence 'Inside Eritrea – A Volunteer in East Africa'

Appreciating that as a writer I make a good maths teacher, I've had a go. I've been flattered by the comments of friends not related to the quality of the text – which is questionable – but the fact that nobody believes that the accounts are from memory. Never kept a diary in my life, the grey matter must still be intact.

Although the book is presented in chronological order it wasn't written that way. Stuff was scribbled down as it came to mind and filed in the month it happened – and it shows! Appreciate that this makes for a disjointed read (apologies to the reader) but am pleased that this approach means that you just don't know what's going to be on the next page. I didn't.

The personal pronoun has also been dropped throughout. This was a conscious decision to keep the focus on Eritrea and Eritreans – not me. Obviously a bit of a challenge as the incidents are through Teacher Kevin's eyes, but that was the aim. Again, I appreciate that this doesn't make for a flowing text.

So, not predictable and not about me – what then? Paradoxically, the more dying Eritreans we see on television the less the impact to the point where bodies being dragged out of the Mediterranean are not even seen as human. Many times I've heard comments along the lines of 'nothing on the box tonight except a programme about warring/starving/drowning Africans and I'm fed up with all that.' The aim of this book has been primarily to show a little of the daily lives of people living under a repressive, brutal regime and make that lifeless body being hauled out of the sea real – that was Rahwa, I taught her at Mai Nefhi High School. She was a good student.

The following was printed in my local paper and gives an overview of what the children's home is about – maybe you can help.

Saltergate Children's Home – Ethiopia

In November 2006 the *Derbyshire Times* kindly printed an article covering the work I was doing in Eritrea, East Africa. After 48 years I had left Chesterfield and was teaching maths in a rural High School before moving into teacher training. *Derbyshire Times* readers responded magnificently to my appeal by sending enough books to open a library – a real achievement which benefits children to this day. On behalf of the students of Mai Nefhi High School – many thanks.

I am now involved in some work in Ethiopia. Addis Ababa is a big city with about four million people and is very different to the African villages I have lived and worked in. There has been some development over the past few years, some progress, but there are still many people at the back of the queue. All kinds of websites can give you the unacceptable health and education figures.

Particularly outrageous are the child mortality levels here which are still among the highest in the world. Getting to five years old is quite an achievement in this country. Usual reasons – no access to clean water and sanitation facilities are the main cause of preventable sickness and premature death.

Official estimates indicate that there are around 100,000 children sleeping rough on the streets of Addis Ababa every night - Abel, Filimon and Daniel are three of them. These lads are shoeshine boys and like many other children they have left their families in the village to earn some cash working in the city. Early morning, mid-day and evenings they are hard at it cleaning and polishing. During slack times they sell peanuts – anything to earn a bit to send back to their mothers. This is gritty survival, any talk from me about them getting a bit of schooling prompts some bemused looks – 'our brothers and sisters need to eat tomorrow Teacher Kevin.'

Abel talks proudly of 'supporting my mother.' He is not a beggar or a thief – he wants to work and be independent. At night the lads climb into the corrugated iron shelter they have built on top of four stilts as packs of hyenas scavenge around the city when it goes dark. These are the kind of challenges children have to face in Ethiopia.

And then there is the really serious stuff. Desiet holds a long grey rag to her nose as she taps on car windows begging with an outstretched hand. The rag has been used to wipe up spilled petrol on filling station forecourts as the fumes mask the pain of hunger. There are thousands of children on the streets of this city all clutching their stinking petrol-soaked rags. Does it get any worse?

One of the things I have set up here in the city is a small children's home – you need to start somewhere. It is a tiny place but it provides a base, food and shelter for a few kids. Tsege is getting on a bit but she manages the day to day running of the place and makes sure the children behave themselves. Abel, Filimon and Daniel might be too proud to ask for hand-outs but I'm not. Simple request – our children are short of educational equipment. If you can send a few pens and paper in the post that would be great and I will put them to good use. Alternatively, you may wish to donate. Currently I can feed, clothe and educate a child for roughly £30 a month so anything you can chip in would be great.

Kevin Morley/ Tsege Gebremariam

Saltergate Children's Home #1

PO Box 31916

Addis Ababa

Ethiopia

Made in the USA
Columbia, SC
20 June 2017